Global Terrorism

Recent Titles in the
CONTEMPORARY WORLD ISSUES
Series

Books in the **Contemporary World Issues** series address vital issues in today's society such as genetic engineering, pollution, and biodiversity. Written by professional writers, scholars, and nonacademic experts, these books are authoritative, clearly written, up-to-date, and objective. They provide a good starting point for research by high school and college students, scholars, and general readers as well as by legislators, businesspeople, activists, and others.

Each book, carefully organized and easy to use, contains an overview of the subject, a detailed chronology, biographical sketches, facts and data, and/or documents and other primary source material, a forum of authoritative perspective essays, annotated lists of print and nonprint resources, and an index.

Readers of books in the Contemporary World Issues series will find the information they need in order to have a better understanding of the social, political, environmental, and economic issues facing the world today.

CONTEMPORARY WORLD ISSUES

Global Terrorism

A REFERENCE HANDBOOK

Steven J. Childs

BLOOMSBURY ACADEMIC
NEW YORK · LONDON · OXFORD · NEW DELHI · SYDNEY

BLOOMSBURY ACADEMIC
Bloomsbury Publishing Inc
1385 Broadway, New York, NY 10018, USA
50 Bedford Square, London, WC1B 3DP, UK
29 Earlsfort Terrace, Dublin 2, Ireland

BLOOMSBURY, BLOOMSBURY ACADEMIC and the Diana
logo are trademarks of Bloomsbury Publishing Plc

First published in the United States of America 2023

Library of Congress Cataloging in Publication
Control Number: 2023010683

ISBN: HB: 978-1-4408-7825-1
       ePDF: 978-1-4408-7826-8
       eBook: 979-8-216-17164-5

Series: Contemporary World Issues

Typeset by Westchester Publishing Services, LLC
Printed and bound in the United States of America

To find out more about our authors and books
visit www.bloomsbury.com and sign up for our newsletters.

Contents

Preface

The topic of terrorism has taken on added importance in recent years. Examples of terrorism date back to antiquity, and many other instances abounded during the postindustrial era into the Cold War. The reality of the impact regarding domestic terrorism for Americans hit home in 1995 after the bombing in Oklahoma City. The turn of the millennium saw a new scale of terrorism with devastating effects, with monumental effects on foreign and domestic policy after the attacks on September 11, 2001. Although terrorism in the United States is very much thought of as being a phenomenon with origins overseas, the debates and issues related to it affect all manner of life situations such as whether, how, and where we travel as well as political and legal issues regarding where to appropriately draw the line between security and civil liberty. The extremism of an increasingly polarized political system at home coupled with increasing disorder abroad indicates that the prospect for extremists adopting terrorism will likely increase in the coming decades, and that they will perhaps do so with increasing ferocity.

The study of this important topic encompasses many dimensions and as such is truly transdisciplinary in its approach, despite being uniformly about politics given the aims sought by terrorists. This book is intended as a gateway resource for the study of terrorism and its many facets. As such this book is arranged into seven chapters. Chapter 1 provides background information for context. It offers a definition of terrorism as a diagnostic to assesses what is counted and what is discounted. It next reviews major waves of terrorism based on underlying ideologies that track with major political, sociological, and philosophical developments following industrialization.

Chapter 2 considers the main problems that terrorist actors present given their attacks. These pertain to challenges facing the government in preventing terrorism in the first place as well as the challenges and controversies facing the state's response. The chapter next considers policy approaches available to governments with an evaluation of the relative merits and demerits of these approaches.

Chapter 3 offers different perspectives related to the effectiveness of terrorism, the relative danger of competing ideological motivations, and debates regarding geographical theaters of prominence. Chapter 4 features profiles of landmark terrorist organizations, terrorist leaders and operatives, statesmen, and counterterrorist bodies.

Chapter 5 presents aggregate data related to the number of people impacted by various terrorist attacks, along with statistics about the degree of success such groups enjoy and the cause of death for rebel leaders. It also outlines primary sources from key thinkers who supplied ideological influence about the major waves of terrorism seen since the modern era; these are anarchism, nationalism, leftism, rightism, and religious orientations.

Chapter 6 provides the reader with a portal to additional works and resources regarding the various aspects related to terrorism. The book concludes with a chronology of key attacks and a glossary of important terms.

Acknowledgments

Any project is truly a team effort, and I have been fortunate to have had such a wonderful team to partner with. I thank my colleague Christina Villegas for connecting me with ABC-CLIO; the introductions ended up yielding the opportunity to write this book. I would like to offer a very special "thank you" to my project editor at ABC-CLIO/Bloomsbury, Kevin Hillstrom, who showed me tremendous patience and grace throughout the project. I appreciate having been given the chance to write for the Contemporary World Issues series and want to thank the entire ABC-CLIO/Bloomsbury team for their assistance in producing the final product. I also express my gratitude to California State University, San Bernardino for its support of my research in the May 2021 semester. My essay contributors Benjamin Acosta, Max Abrahms, Kevork Kazanjian, Simeone Miller, Anibal Serrano, Timothy Milosch, Kevin Petit, and Candace Cook deserve praise for their forbearing. I treasure their friendship in addition to their scholarship, and I am excited to see their through-provoking work appear in this volume. My sincere thanks to my good friend Benjamin Acosta and his colleagues Reyko Huang and Daniel Silverman for their comprehensive work on datasets that help advance our study of this important topic. Excerpts from their data is featured in this book. Along these lines I also thank the National Consortium for the Study of Terrorism and Responses to Terrorism at the University of Maryland for allowing me to feature aggregated data from their Global Terrorism Database.

Most of all I acknowledge the love, patience, and support of my amazing wife Lauren. Projects such as these are a marathon and not a sprint, and she endured the race with me every step of the way. Babe, I love you more than words could ever say and am blessed to have you as my best friend. To my children Ethan and Elizabeth: Your daily giggles and smiles bring me more joy than I could have ever possibly imagined, and it is my privilege to be your daddy. As dark of a subject matter as terrorism can be, I thank you three for being a daily reminder of the beauty in the world that God created.

Steven J. Childs
March 26, 2022

Global Terrorism

1 Background and History

Terrorism as a Concept

Terrorism is one of the most important topics in contemporary times. A Gallup poll of Americans in March 2019 found that 60% of respondents were fairly or greatly worried about the possibility of terrorist attacks against the country (Gallup 2020). A June 2017 poll by the same organization found that 46% were less willing to travel overseas due to the fear of terrorism.

Despite collective fears about terrorism, as a term it is among the most misunderstood and abused in discourse today. Popular and political figures regularly use the word as a form of name-calling against their opponents as well as to mobilize supporters. The term is hardly used to portray a person or group in a positive light, and the concept would also seem to have wide-ranging use. But even when more accurately employed, does the term refer to foreign cases, domestic ones, or both? What

---

One of the essential criteria in defining terrorism compared to other forms of violence is that the violence is used for political purposes. Here a pro-republican mural depicts a petrol bomber during the 1969 Battle of the Bogside at the onset of the Troubles. Note the patch with the map of Ireland on the bomber's jacket emphasizing the territory of Northern Ireland. Republicans seek to unify this territory with the rest of the Republic of Ireland whereas loyalists wish to remain in union with the government of the United Kingdom. The political clashes are even evident in the name of the city where the event took place, with loyalists referring to it as "Londonderry" and Irish republicans calling it "Derry." (Andrea G. Ricordi/Dreamstime)

specifically makes a terrorist? Can loosely organized groups or unorganized individuals be considered terrorists? What about the leaders of governments? Without further elaboration, one gets the sense that the common use of the word proves more confusing than clarifying.

The use and abuse of the term is not surprising given the present deep political polarization in the United States. Nonetheless, for the concept of terrorism to have any analytical utility requires a disciplined definition. Despite its frequent use in rhetoric, the word does have an objective analytical meaning. Just as a doctor needs an unbiased criterion based on evidence to diagnose an ailment based on symptoms and tests, terrorism as an issue needs to be clearly defined to be understood. Moreover, a definition is required before it is possible to address effective policy responses for dealing with it. Stated simply, terrorism is *the threat of or use of violence by a non-state actor against civilians in order to advance a political agenda* (Ganor 2002, 294–295). This definition features three elements that address the "who," "what," and "why" of terrorism.

The Perpetrators and Victims of Terrorism

In terrorism studies, the actors who "terrorize" are individuals or organizations that do not have direct control of the state or its apparatus. That is to say, a *non*-state actor is "who" perpetrates the violence. German sociologist Max Weber provides a widely accepted definition of the state as a government within a specific territory that "can lay claim to a monopoly of legitimate physical force in the execution of its orders" (Weber 2019, 136). In the Weberian sense, anyone who uses violence outside the framework of a state or unsanctioned by the state is illegitimate in doing so. A simpler way to think of this is that a non-state actor is unofficial when it comes to governance. They can certainly have an organized hierarchy with specific bureaucratic functions the same way that states do, but they are not *the* state. Non-state actors frequently maintain an organizational capacity composed of those who collectively share the same goals, but they can also be single individuals acting alone or inspired by others. The actors may also maintain alliances with the governments of other countries, but the principal actions are carried out by the non-state actor.

Historically states have used violence for political purposes against civilians, and many continue to do so. The Rwandan genocide, the Holocaust in Nazi-occupied Europe, and the Armenian genocide are all clear and tragic examples of government-directed violence on a mass scale. However, to maintain analytical precision, this violence constitutes crimes against humanity and is not classified as terrorism because the perpetrators were governments.

Although the perpetrators of terrorism are non-state actors, it is civilians who are attacked. This demonstrates the dramatic power imbalance, or asymmetry, in the capabilities between the non-state actors and the government whose legal duty is to defend its citizens as part of its mandate. In this manner terrorism is "a weapon of the weak."

This does not mean, however, that the effects of terrorism are benign or non-lethal. Many terrorists have demonstrated the destructive means of mass murder, despite the overall power imbalance between the non-state actor and the state's security forces.

Terrorists specifically attack *civilian* targets; these victims are individuals who are not in the security services of their state. Civilians do not have membership in the military or police forces. There are cases where civilians can use force legitimately, such as in self-defense; however, these rarer types of cases are sanctioned by the governments who retain the authority and legitimacy to make such a determination. As non-state actors, terrorists have no such authority or legitimacy.

The Means of Terrorism

Second, the definition addresses "what" terrorism is by emphasizing its most identifiable feature: the use of *violence* or intimidation through threatened violence. It is this element that is most responsible for mislabeling actions as being terrorist in nature when they may not be. There are many instances of violence, but not all forms of violence constitute terrorism. The definition offered previously is important because it excludes a great many instances of violence that are sometimes described as acts of terrorism. Individual actions such as assault, murder, and rape, as well as collective actions such as mob violence, mass murder, and genocide, are all horrible and tragic forms of violence. However, these examples do not constitute terrorism just because they are violent; the element of violence is important but not sufficient.

Specifically, terrorists tend to practice tradecraft that includes kidnaping, hijacking, assassination, bombing, and shooting, but these are not the exclusive forms of violence that are used. Insurgency is the most similar type of violence to terrorism in that it is waged by non-state groups who use violence for political reasons, and the tradecraft of insurgents also frequently entails bombings and shootings. However, the targets of insurgents are the security forces of the government, be they military or police. Insurgents hardly "fight fair" in a conventional sense on the battlefield, given that they prefer dispersed hit-and-run style attacks, but their conflict is waged against an armed opposition. Terrorists attack the unarmed who have no expectation of being put in harm's way in the course of their daily lives.

The means of violence is critical to understanding terrorism, but why do terrorists use violence against civilians? First, it serves to demand attention to the cause. Although many times terrorists are organized, they are weaker than the state and lack political support to advance their platform. The journalistic aphorism that "If it bleeds, it leads" emphasizes how audiences are drawn to coverage of violence, especially when it is committed on a large scale. No matter how much individuals may abhor and detest violence, acts of terrorism receive plentiful coverage, and many find themselves glued to their television sets or mobile devices after an attack. Stated simply, "Terrorism is theater" and the violent acts of terrorists bring the stage to the society (Jenkins 1974, 4).

Terrorism can also be understood as a sort of political bullying, but one where the actor bullying is physically weaker than the actor who is being bullied. Alternatively, it can be thought of as the ultimate rogue action in that terrorists do not play by the socially accepted rules surrounding their platform. By attacking civilian targets, those in society who do not expect to face the hazards of a career in the security services feel acutely vulnerable. This is even though the actual probability of any one individual being harmed or killed in a terrorist action is statistically low. Data suggests that the risk of dying from a terrorist attack in the United States is lower than that of dying in a bathtub (Mueller and Stewart 2018, 2). This comparison does not control for important factors tied to the actual *relative* risk, such as accident versus intentionality, age, location, and lifestyle. Someone who is younger and travels frequently to urban areas in foreign countries wracked by violence is clearly in a higher risk pool than someone who is older, lives in a rural area, and remains at home for much of the time. Nonetheless, terrorism is far from being a leading killer in much of the developed world compared to automobile accidents, health-related illness, and crime.

The psychological effects of the randomness of terrorist attacks can be disconcerting and damaging. Between 1994 and 1996, for example, Israeli buses carrying civilians were bombed nine times by Palestinian suicide attackers, with eight of these attacks by the group Harakat al-Muqawama al-Islamiya (also known as Hamas, "Islamic Resistance Movement"). Many Israeli citizens became fearful of using their regular form of public transportation to shop or go to work, given the possibility that a suicide bomber might be on board. The aim of Hamas in this instance was not only to give power and momentum to its political platform of eliminating Israel to create an Islamic Palestinian state but also to coerce Israeli citizens to pressure their government toward a more accommodationist policy.

In many instances, however, using violence as a tool of coercion can prompt a backlash that worsens their position. In 1996 Israeli voters elected hawkish candidate Benjamin Netanyahu as prime minister, who supported hardline military and governmental policies regarding Palestinian issues. Public fear about the bus attacks was frequently cited as a factor in his victory.

On other occasions, however, intimidation through coercion works. Al Qaeda's 2004 bombing of the Atocha Train Station in Madrid, Spain was carried out three days before the country's general election, and the incoming Spanish government changed the country's policy to withdraw its troops from the international coalition in Iraq. Thus the violence used by terrorists garners attention for the cause but also seeks to intimidate the population in hopes of changing policy. The key determinant of what makes an action terrorism is the motivation for the violence, which is covered in the third element of the definition.

The Aims of Terrorism

The final element of terrorism pertains to "why" it is used. Simply stated, terrorism is a form of *political* violence. The reason why non-state actors engage in violence is to fulfill a political aim or objective based on their ideology and beliefs. Given that politics is a reflection of beliefs, experiences, identity, and values, political aims can be broadly classified as leftwing, rightwing, religious, or ethnonationalist.

To help understand this political element, consider the work of the Napoleonic-era Prussian strategist Carl von Clausewitz. His book *Vom Krieg* ["On War"] is widely read in war colleges and serves as a foundational text in the field of strategic studies, a diverse field that studies conflict by considering strategy, operations, and tactics. One of Clausewitz's most famously cited idioms is that "[W]ar is not merely an act of policy but a true political instrument, a continuation of political intercourse, carried on with other means" (Clausewitz 1989, 87).

For Clausewitz, the purpose of war is not to use violent measures for their own sake but rather to use violent means as an instrument to pursue political ends. In this field of strategic studies with its heavy military and security influence, it is politics that ultimately reigns supreme. Politics is about determining who governs, how they do so, and ultimately how scarce resources are distributed in a society. Consequently, terrorists see violence as a tool to achieve specific and identifiable political goals. Individuals and organizations, not just the state, have such political aims.

Those specific and identifiable political goals are not necessarily realistic, however. The Japanese group Aum Shinrikyo ("the teaching of the universe's truth") was established as a cult by Shoko Asahara, fusing elements from Buddhism, Hinduism, and the notion of the apocalypse from the book of Revelation. The group's specific beliefs required hastening the end of the world, which would be marked by a nuclear conflict. Following the war, Asahara and Aum expected to take over Japan and then the rest of the world. In 1995 Aum members deployed sarin nerve gas in a coordinated attack on the Tokyo metro system at rush hour. The attack, ostensibly to provoke a nuclear conflict involving Japan, killed 12 and wounded over 6,000 (Fletcher 2012). The likelihood of the sarin attack actually leading to this outcome of nuclear war is dubious, but the political aims were clear. The political aims desired by a group alone say nothing about the rationality of pursuing those ends.

That said, it is important to acknowledge that there are a plethora of actions non-state actors can also take in pursuit of their political aims, and a great many of them are nonviolent. Examples include boycotts, peaceful rallies and other protest activities, and various forms of peaceful civil disobedience. Many examples abound where groups use nonviolent actions to highlight worthy causes related to equality and civil rights. Mahatma Gandhi famously adopted nonviolent resistance to spearhead the independence movement for the country of India, and the American civil rights movement led by Dr. Martin Luther King Junior in the 1960s also used peaceful marches to advance their campaign for racial equality.

In practice most terrorists seek to create an alternate political order, not just destroy an existing one. In some instances their aims are less ambitious. For example, they may desire a change regarding a specific policy in a society rather than reordering the entire society's political system. This means that in most cases terrorists are oriented against the status quo—existing conditions—although there are rare instances where non-state actors use violence against civilians or political figures to *preserve* the political status quo rather than upend it. A historical example of the latter would be the terrorist organization Ku Klux Klan (KKK) when it used violence to reinforce the racist laws of the Jim Crow–era American South, preventing African Americans from exercising their political rights. A more contemporary example of counter-revolutionaries would be certain loyalist groups in Northern Ireland who seek to maintain the territory as part of the United Kingdom rather than see it join the Republic of Ireland. In both the cases of the KKK and certain loyalist militias, violence was used by non-state groups to maintain the existing political order.

The political goals discussed so far are considered "outcome" goals by scholars in that they define the reason for the group's existence and its use of violence. These tend to be more long-term in nature as the group challenges the more powerful state. A secondary form called "process" goals are instrumental and short-term in nature. These goals are designed to ensure the survivability of the group (Abrahms 2012, 367). A terrorist group may engage in bank robberies, narcotic sales, and human trafficking, all examples of criminal behavior that yield financial gain. However, if the group's ideology was motivated by political outcome goals, this behavior could constitute process goals of raising funds to arm, equip, and carry out terrorist attacks in pursuit of the outcome goals.

Examples of Terrorism

Specific cases of violence and those who perpetrate them can be evaluated in a generally dispassionate sense to see if they fit with the pillars of the above definition of terrorism. The attacks of September 11, 2001 are the most well-known example of terrorism in contemporary times because they were so starkly dramatic and because they resulted in the deaths of nearly 3,000 people in a single day. Harnessing the preceding definition helps clarify why these attacks were terrorism. First, they were committed by an organization founded by Osama bin Laden called al Qaeda ["the Base/foundation"], and al Qaeda is not a state or a government. The core of the group was able to set up shop and plan the attacks while in Afghanistan under the protection of the Taliban government there, but it was al Qaeda that directly engaged in the violence, not the Taliban.

Moreover, the victims of the attack were predominantly civilians. Hijacked planes were flown into the twin towers of the World Trade Center in downtown Manhattan and the Pentagon in Arlington, Virginia. A fourth hijacked plane targeted the Capitol building in Washington, D.C., before passengers fought back against the hijackers, forcing the airliner to crash into a field in rural Pennsylvania. All targets were highly visible, had considerable symbolic value, and were overwhelmingly civilian in nature. Even the Pentagon, which is the headquarters of the U.S. Department of Defense, features a majority of civilian workers; approximately 59% of Defense Department personnel working in the county where the Pentagon is located were civilian employees at the time of the attack (U.S. Department of Defense 2001, 49). This is reflected in the Pentagon casualty figures, where more civilians than military personnel were killed (Stone 2002).

Next, hijacking civilian airliners and turning them into guided missiles was unconventional compared to mainstream terrorist tradecraft, but it was violence nonetheless. Although al Qaeda undertakes nonviolent actions such as propaganda to complement its attacks, violent attacks such as those on September 11th are the primary focus of the group's behavior. This was also true of al Qaeda attacks before 9/11, such as in the 1998 bombings of American embassies in Africa, as well as post-9/11 attacks like the 2002 Bali bombings in Indonesia, the 2004 Madrid train bombings, and the 2005 bombings in London.

In looking to al Qaeda's beliefs, it is apparent that the group is motivated by a religiously based ideology of Salafi-Jihadism, and al Qaeda's end goals from this ideology are politically motivated. The group seeks to recreate the Islamic caliphate in the Middle East, an Islamic theocracy governed by a single ruler first founded after Muhammad's conquest of the Arabian Peninsula in 630. It grew to the height of its influence and power during the Abbasid Caliphate around the year 800. Abbasid rule was geographically centered in Baghdad and extended from North Africa in the west to Central Asia in the east.

The idea of the caliphate is essentially that of an Islamic empire whose leader, the caliph, is a political ruler over a society based around Islamic law (*sharia*). Moreover, members of al Qaeda believe that the caliphate should expand beyond historical holdings in the Middle East to control the rest of the world. Whether the goals of those who practice terrorism, such as al Qaeda, are considered realistic is not an element of terrorism's definition. The power imbalance between the non-state actors and the government is a regular feature, and what matters in a definitional sense is that the non-state actors use violence against civilians to advance a defined political aim.

Another organization notorious for its support of terrorism is Iran's Quds ("Jerusalem") Force, which the U.S. State Department identified as a "foreign terrorist organization" (FTO) in 2019; it marked the first time that a part of a foreign government had been designated as such (U.S. Department of State 2019). Quds Force is one of the most active covert action organizations in the world, with a history of direct bombings and assassinations and sponsorship of other violence that has global reach. The group has been highly active in Lebanon by supporting Hezbollah in carrying out its many attacks, has armed Shi'a paramilitaries and militias in Syria and Iraq, and has sponsored bombing attacks against U.S. troops in Iraq.

Outside the Middle East, Iran's Quds Force used a suicide car bombing attack in Buenos Aires, Argentina that targeted a Jewish community center in 1994, killing 85 and injuring over 300. Additional attacks against Jewish targets took place later that month in Panama and London. In 2011 the group was purportedly involved in a foiled assassination plot to kill the Saudi foreign minister in a Washington, D.C., restaurant.

But is the organization a *terrorist* group? Quds Force uses violence against both military personnel (such as U.S. troops in Iraq) and civilians (such as in Buenos Aires; Jewish people who are seen as representatives of the state of Israel are particular targets). The group also takes these actions with a political motivation to advance the interests of the Islamic Republic of Iran.

However, based on the established definition of a terrorist organization, Quds Force does not qualify. The definition asserts that terrorists are non-state actors, be they organizations or individuals. Quds Force is an arm of the Islamic Republic of Iran's Revolutionary Guard Corps and as such is part of a state. That Quds Force uses violence for political purpose is without question, but it is not a non-state actor.

In the days that followed the murder of African American George Floyd at the hands of police officers in Minneapolis, Minnesota, some Antifa affiliated demonstrators engaged in rioting, looting, and the defacing of monuments in Washington, D.C. Then-president Trump tweeted on May 31, 2020 that he would "designate Antifa as a terrorist organization" (Trump Twitter Archive V2, May 31, 2020a). A mere ten days later, he called individuals who had occupied the Capitol Hill neighborhood of Seattle "Domestic Terrorists" (Trump Twitter Archive V2, June 10, 2020b). Both Antifa members and Seattle's autonomous zone activists were non-state actors respectively comprised of groups and individuals. Additionally, their motivation for acting was for political reasons. Although not centrally led as an organization, the many chapters of Antifa derive the name from the term "anti-fascist," and as a far leftwing political movement opposes perceived far-right extremism in government and society. Those who occupied the Capitol Hill Autonomous Zone/Occupied Protest (CHAZ/ CHOP) in Seattle in June 2020 were comprised of many groups and individuals yet were leaderless. Nonetheless, the participants did outline political goals, including reducing the Seattle Police Department's budget by 50%, redirecting the funds to community programs for black communities, and calling on amnesty for protesters (Frohne, Chin, and Dompor 2020).

It is the third element of the definition pertaining to violence that is noteworthy. By and large the activities of protestors in the CHAZ/CHOP were peaceful, with isolated although deadly instances of violence. Amid the absence of police, in mid-June, an African American teen was shot and killed in the zone (Green 2020), and toward the end of the occupation two African American teens in a vehicle were shot at a checkpoint, with one teen dying from the injuries. The second case ultimately led to police reentering the zone upon orders of the mayor (Gutman and Brownstone 2020).

With respect to the definition of terrorism, there was no evidence that the homicides were politically motivated in support of the aims of the occupiers. Activities by self-described members of Antifa, however, could be considered terrorism when members engage in violence against civilian targets such as when they physically assaulted audience members who came to hear controversial figure Milo Yiannopoulous speak at Berkeley, California on February 1, 2017 (Jones 2020). In August 2020 a self-described member shot and killed a rightwing protester in the streets of Portland, Oregon. Elements of Portland's Antifa chapter engaged in sustained violence against the city's federal courthouse in July and August 2020 as well.

A simple checklist is apparent in reviewing the definition of this complex subject. Terrorism occurs when:

- Non-state actors engage in violence
- The violence is directed against civilians
- The non-state actors do so for political purposes

The definition is detached from the beliefs and emotions that surround the politics of these cases. This framework does not address the "justness" of the issues that motivate terrorism in a subjective sense, as indicated by the phrase that "one person's terrorist is another person's freedom fighter." That statement implies that terrorism is an entirely subjective concept that depends specifically on one's own views. Rather, in a clinical sense the definition assesses the perpetrators, victims, actions, and politics, all necessary preconditions to tackling the issue (Ganor 2002, 300). As such, the definition does not wade into justifications or criticisms of politics, but rather emphasizes the qualities of terrorism.

Moreover, it is important to understand that terrorism is political violence based on targeting civilians. Terrorism can be also used by actors who engage in political violence against government security forces, or even the political process in a society. A group such as Lebanese Hezbollah may simultaneously act as a political party standing in elections, a terrorist actor that bombs its Sunni political opponents (notably the involvement of its operatives in the 2005 assassination of former prime minister Rafik Hariri), and an insurgent group that launches attacks against the security forces of neighboring country Israel.

In the case of Hezbollah, the umbrella term of "militant group" is an apt description; otherwise scholars and analysts tend to describe a group based on its primary activity.

Terrorism at Home and Abroad

Having addressed the "who," "what," and "why" of terrorism, the final elements to consider are "where" terrorists strike. There are two broad categories of terrorism based on where terrorism occurs—domestic and foreign terrorism.

Domestic terrorism is carried out by groups or individuals of a specific country against civilians within that same country. For example, the deadliest case of domestic terrorism in the United States was the 1995 attack against the Murrah Federal Building in Oklahoma City that killed 168 and wounded almost 700. This attack by two far-right antigovernment radicals, Timothy McVeigh and Terry Nichols, was an attack *by* Americans *against* fellow Americans in America.

In multiethnic countries, terrorist groups can belong to one race or ethnicity and target those from another. So long as both were citizens of the same country and the violence was internal to the state, this would still fall under the category of domestic terrorism. In the United States, for example, members of the white supremacist Ku Klux Klan (KKK) organization have carried out numerous terrorist attacks against nonwhites since the group's nineteenth-century founding. Elsewhere, in the island country of Sri Lanka, the Liberation Tigers of Tamil Elam (LTTE) were comprised of ethnic Tamils who targeted both rival Tamil parties and ethnic Sinhalese. Despite the groups forming along these ethnic lines, the overwhelming majority of the LTTE's violent attacks were domestic, or within the boundaries of the country. Compared to foreign terrorism, domestic terrorism is more likely to feature individuals or very small groups in addition to larger organizations. Groups that conduct terrorist activities beyond the borders of their native country tend to be better organized, with more bureaucratic functions due to the increased complexity of planning and carrying out attacks across international borders.

Foreign terrorism, also referred to as international or transnational terrorism, is when a terrorist group crosses a country boundary in order to attack its civilian target. For example, the majority of the terrorist acts carried out by LTTE occurred in its native Sri Lanka, making them acts of domestic terror. But the group also carried out an infamous act of foreign terrorism with a 1991 suicide bombing in India that assassinated India's Prime Minister, Rajiv Gandhi, in retribution for India's earlier deployment of peacekeeping forces in Sri Lanka against LTTE militants (Roberts 2010, 26). The September 11 attack in 2001 is also a notable example of foreign terrorism, with the attackers coming from Arab countries, but having planned the attacks in Afghanistan before finally attacking the targets in the United States. The terrorist organization al Qaeda further demonstrates how foreign terrorism need not feature the terrorists coming to a country to launch attacks. The group's 1998 bombings of the American embassies in Dar-a Salaam and Tanzania are examples of American targets struck in foreign countries.

State-Sponsored Terrorism

An additional category of terrorism today is "state-sponsored" terrorism. This is the term used for cases in which a terrorist organization receives logistical and material support (money, weapons, etc.) from a state government. States may opt to support terrorist groups if they share a common adversary but wish to minimize their own profile or exposure. When considering the limited military budgets of most nation states, terrorism can be a cost-effective means of tying an opposing state down. Frequently, state-sponsorship occurs where a terrorist group operates from an area bordering the supplying state, with both the group and the state opposing the central government.

The government of Pakistan, for example, has long supported Islamist insurgencies and terror groups, the most prominent being Lashkar-e-Taiba (LeT; "Army of the Righteous") against India. The two countries fought a number of wars since they each gained their independence in 1947, much of it over the contested territory of Jammu and Kashmir. In supporting LeT, Pakistan has a direct action means of increasing the costs of India's presence. Officially banned by the Pakistani government, LeT receives regular support from the government's covert action arm, the Inter-Services Intelligence (ISI). LeT operates training camps in Pakistan that are attended by members of the country's military, whose militants engage in militant and terrorist actions in the disputed territory, along with terror strikes against India. Such is the extent of cooperation that LeT's 2008 terror attack in the Indian city of Mumbai was planned using intelligence gathered from ISI agents in the city and was directed in real time with the aid of ISI officers (Kilcullen 2013, 53, 55). Ten attackers killed 157 and wounded over 300 in the city using small arms and explosives.

Victims of state-sponsored terrorism, however, can also be found outside the country in question. The former government of Libya, headed by Muhammar Gaddafi, infamously used terrorism as a state policy against the United States and United Kingdom following military clashes in the Mediterranean. In 1986 Qaddafi had Libyan agents bomb a West Berlin disco frequented by American military personnel, killing two soldiers and a Turkish civilian and wounding over 200. President Reagan retaliated by ordering airstrikes against Libyan military targets in Operation El Dorado Canyon. Notably, many of the warplanes that participated in that operation were based in the United Kingdom.

The strikes were broadly successful; however, in 1988 Libyan intelligence agents planted a bomb on board Pan-American airline flight 103. The bomb detonated in mid-flight when the plane was over Lockerbie, Scotland. To date it is the deadliest act of terror ever in the United Kingdom, killing 270 victims, with most being Americans returning from travels in Europe. Moreover, Libyan agents renewed a strong relationship with the Provisional Irish Republican Army, shipping weapons such as Semtex plastic explosives to aid the group in its attacks against United Kingdom civilians (British Broadcasting Corporation 2011).

The earlier example of Iran's Quds Force is also illustrative of state-sponsorship. As a covert arm of the Islamic Republic of Iran, it is a state-based organization. Nevertheless, much of Quds Force's historical actions involve supporting terrorist and militant groups to carry out attacks against civilians in the Middle East and beyond. Imad Mugniyeh was officially the chief of staff for Lebanese Hezbollah but received orders directly from

Qassem Soleimani of Quds Force (Goldberg 2002). Mugniyeh was long sought by the United States until his assassination in 2008, charged with orchestrating the 1983 suicide bombing of the U.S. embassy in Beirut (63 killed), the 1984 assassination of academic Malcolm Kerr in Beirut, the kidnaping of numerous American citizens in Lebanon throughout the 1980s, and the 1992 Bueno Aires attack on a Jewish center.

State sponsorship can also take important forms of indirect assistance. For example, the Taliban government in Afghanistan helped al Qaeda to plan the September 11th attacks by hosting Al Qaeda camps in its territory. The Taliban did not provide any other material support to al Qaeda; in fact, the reverse was the case: al Qaeda supplied the Taliban with weapons and fighters over the course of Afghanistan's civil war in the 1990s. Al Qaeda also aided the Taliban regime by assassinating its key rival, insurgent leader Ahmad Shah Massoud, just days before the September 11 attacks. But the Al Qaeda training camps were vital to the terrorist organization's growth and capacity for carnage.

A History of Terrorism

Terrorism from Ancient Times to the French Revolution

The Sicarii

Political violence is traced to the earliest historical records, but the best-known example of terrorism in the ancient world is the *Sicarii* ("dagger-wielders") of Roman Palestine, who emerged in the 50s and carried on through the Great Revolt in 66 (Horsley 1979, 444–445). Deriving its name from the dagger members used in their attacks, the group was opposed to the Roman occupation of the Jewish homeland. These assassins would conceal their daggers beneath their cloaks, enter populated areas to kill Roman-sympathizing Jewish aristocrats, then melt away back into the crowd.

These murders sought to coerce the governing Jewish officials into ending their allegiance to Rome. Compared to the

Herodian monarchy and their Roman overseers, the Sicarii were non-state actors. They also targeted civilians, and they did so for political purposes in attempts to overthrow the Roman occupation. Despite their efforts the Sicarii did not succeed in achieving liberation from Rome.

In the year 66, however, many Jews rose against Roman rule in what became the Great Revolt. During this general uprising, Sicarii killed the Roman guards at Herod's mountain fortress of Masada ("Fortress"). According to the historian Josephus, after the Roman destruction of the holiest site for Jews, their temple, the remaining Sicarii fled to the Masada fortress. After two years of Roman siege, the remaining Sicarii reportedly committed mass suicide to avoid eventual capture.

The Hashashiyan

An example of political violence from the medieval era is the *hashashiyan* ("hashish users") from which the English word "assassin" is derived. This 12th century Nizari sect of Ismaili Muslims inhabited the western region of the Alborz Mountains of present-day Iran and the Syrian coastal mountain range. The Nizari did not have the capacity to build large standing armies, given the mountainous terrain and limited populations. Instead, the hashashiyan—like the Sicarii—were partial to using daggers against the political leaders of foreign powers seeking to conquer the Nizari and their holdings.

The violence carried out by the hashashiyan was largely defensive and narrowly targeted in its application, but it was an instrument of the state rather than that of a rebel group or other non-state actor. In targeting the specific leader of aggressor armies, the chances of the assassin surviving the attack were slim. To overcome the natural tendency for self-preservation, the Nizari Imams created a sort of heaven on earth. According to the accounts of Marco Polo, the most militarily promising youth from the mountainous region were given opium and then introduced to the Imam's pleasure garden. Here they witnessed dancing women singing and adorned in beautiful cloth, saw gilded buildings and rich silks, listened to fine music, smelled wonderful fragrances and plants, and feasted on delicious wines and foods.

Polo reported that after several days of this sumptuous treatment, the men were then taken into the presence of the Imam, who told them he had granted them access to paradise once—and could so do again. He promised a return to the pleasure garden to anyone who carried out the assassination of one of his adversaries (Polo 1929, 74–75). Consequently, these men—the hashashiyan—set out into the world as assassins who did not fear death but rather welcomed it.

In specifically targeting the leadership rather than the rank and file of approaching adversaries, the Nizari created a form of deterrence that warded off foreign invasions from the larger Seljuks and the Crusaders before finally succumbing to the Mongols in 1275. Unlike the Sicarii, these assassins were part of the state who used political violence to protect the state; whatever the morality of their actions, they do not qualify as terrorists according to many contemporary scholarly definitions.

The French Revolution

In the modern era, the genesis of terrorism was ushered in with the republicanism of the French Revolution (1789–1799). Derived from the Latin *res publica* ("of the people"), the term "republicanism" emphasizes representative governance rather than rule by an absolute monarch or dictator. In this manner, popular sovereignty was a hallowed value of revolutionaries, who held that government was only legitimate if it operated with the support and consent of the general public through representatives selected from the population. Historical examples abound, with some of the most famous being ancient Rome, Venice of the Middle Ages, and the Netherlands in the early modern era. Many of the world's early historic republics were geographically small and prominent in maritime trade.

In France, the rising republicanism gave way to radicalism after Jacobin revolutionaries overthrew the monarchy and quite literally decapitated the government, beheading Louis XVI in 1793. The Jacobins replaced the monarchy with a republic, with part of the provisional government taking the name of the Committee of Public Safety. Maximilien Robespierre took the helm of the committee after eliminating rivals. The committee subsequently instituted a period of governance self-described as *la Terreur* ("the Terror") from which we derive the term "terrorism" used today.

The committee's radical actions during this period were meant to completely reorder French society. They entailed not only a change in political order away from monarchy but attempts at a full social revolution such as renaming the months of the calendar from the Gregorian names to ones named after seasons and nature.

Additional examples of the fervor at this time included a state-sponsored religion of atheism termed the Cult of Reason to replace the Catholic Church. The revolutionary movement in France was marked by a secularism that was expressly antireligious given that the church in France was one pillar supportive of the monarchy. The atheist cult, however, was later replaced by Robespierre's state religion, which was centered on deism (belief in the existence of a supreme being on the basis of rational thought and natural observation). Looking to add religious justifications for the French revolution—but differentiate those from both atheism and Catholicism—Robespierre termed the new religion the "Cult of the Supreme Being" and used its influence to eliminate his atheist rivals within the Committee of Public Safety. For Robespierre, the committee's reign of terror was seen as an important societal good vital in preventing other elements from hijacking the revolution's gains. For the revolutionaries, everything of the old aristocratic order had to go. Robespierre stated that "Terror is nothing but justice, prompt, severe and inflexible; it is therefore an emanation of virtue" (Rapoport 1992, 1061). Thousands fell to the blade of the guillotine in violence purportedly undertaken to preserve the ideals of the revolution and stamp out all vestiges of the old regime.

By attacking both the monarchy and the church, the revolutionaries sought to diminish the key pillars of the old regime and make way for a popular-based republican regime. The key significance of the revolution was felt beyond France, with reverberations around the continent everywhere that featured monarchical rule. The notion of "power to the people" via mass civic participation was radical at the time.

In short order, however, political, ideological, and moral fault lines grew within the new regime until the revolution effectively began to eat its own, including Robespierre. He and his associates fell to the guillotine a year after assuming leadership of the committee.

It is worthwhile to note that although the Terror of the French Revolution was a clear case of political violence and is the genesis of the word "terrorism," Robespierre's actions were a form of counter-revolutionary activity by the organs of the state at its time. Because the committee was effectively the state of its day and not a non-state actor engaged in the violence, the example does not fit with the contemporary scholarly definition of terrorism. Terrorism as it is understood today is the use of violence by non-state actors against noncombatants for political aims. By contrast, the key operating principle of the terror during the French Revolution was to intimidate counter-revolutionaries.

Global Terrorism in the Modern Era

In the modern era, terrorism has undergone five significant transitions based on the broad type of aims pursued:

- Terrorism by members of the anarchist movement at the turn of the 20th century (elements of the "Old" Left)
- Terrorism by national liberation movements during decolonization
- Terrorism for Marxist revolution with the rise of the "New" Left

- Terrorism against globalization during the post–Cold War
- Terrorism that is religiously motivated in the new millennium

This does not mean that all terrorist acts in each phase belonged to only this type of violence, but rather that they were the most prevalent. The rise of any specific type of terrorism coincides with the dominant political currents and clashes of the time. Clear overlap exists between these aims in some instances, but in practice scholars identify these five transitions in line with four ideologically distinct typologies of terrorism: leftwing, ethnonationalist, rightwing, and religious (Cronin 2003, 39–42).

Terrorism for Anarchy

The first period of modern terrorism was marked by the anarchist movement in the late 1800s and early 1900s. The key motivation for anarchist terrorists in this period was the mobilization of primarily working-class people toward political revolution.

Ideologically, anarchism is an outgrowth of the broad French currents toward republicanism and with it shares the desire to eliminate the old regime of the monarchy. Deviating from anarchist wishes, the subsequent rise of French general Napoleon Bonaparte to emperor reinforced the state as an institution.

Anarchism calls for the elimination of the state and its hierarchy and replacement with a communally based and voluntarily self-organized arrangement. Simply put, anarchists view government of any sort as a supremely vertical arrangement of control and imposition, and in turn seek the destruction of the state to be replaced by a society of horizontal, people-to-people relationships.

Brands of anarchism varied from nation-state to nation-state, reflecting differences in how anarchists wanted replacement societies to operate. Although theoretically not strictly leftist in orientation, in practice anarchists of this era often maintained links and relationships with labor movements whose masses they saw as necessary to carry out revolution.

One of the major schisms within organized labor was between anarchists and socialists. Uniform in the notion that the state had to be brought down, anarchists diverged based on what should come after the state. Should the state be torn down in favor of direct trade union governance, or should the state control and redistribute economic resources as preferred by socialists? Anarchists were also split as to the method to achieve the eradication of the state. Some in the movement advocated for this through peaceful political activism, whereas others called for violence. Theorists emphasized outreach through pamphlet and union halls, but most activists advocated Kropotkin's "propaganda by the deed." This concept argued that the organs of the state were not invincible and only needed to be challenged directly to spark revolution by the masses (Merriman 2016, 63). Beyond hoping to start a revolution, the actions also demonstrated the full devotion of anarchists to the cause by risking everything in their violent actions. Additionally, even if the state and capitalism would not topple immediately, surely such violence would force the state to react with harsher measures that in turn could tip the population against it. The concept became a mainstay of the movement, reinforcing its violent calls and justifying violence against monarchs, the state, and major business figures.

In the early anarchist phase, many targets for assassination were the royals of the respective kingdoms. This movement coincided with the first true era of globalization, where rapid industrial, technological, and social changes increased the connectivity of nation-states. New technologies like the steam ship, telegraph, and use of passports for international travel effectively shrank the world, and increased immigration encouraged the spread of new ideas and intellectual currents.

By the 1890s anarchist violence was widespread in both Europe and the Americas, with attacks taking the form of assassinations and bombings. Among the most famous was the murder of Empress Elisabeth of Austria in 1898 by blade, and the shooting of American president William McKinley in 1901.

All told, the 1890s and 1901 saw anarchists kill the leaders of France, Spain, Austria, Italy, and the United States (Jensen 2014, 31). Anarchists were also truly transnationalist, since the identity was based along class lines and the new technological, economic, and political developments of the time enabled such connectivity. As David Rapoport writes, "The [Russian] Terrorist Brigade in 1905 had its headquarters in Switzerland, launched strikes from Finland (an autonomous part of the Russian empire), got arms from an Armenian terrorist group Russians helped train, and were offered funds by the Japanese to be laundered through American millionaires" (Rapoport 2004, 52).

One illustration of how widespread violence was actually encouraged by anarchists came in 1881, when the International Anarchist Congress of London formally adopted the principle of "propaganda by the deed." This principle validated violence by individuals acting on *behalf* of the masses rather than outright collective action *by* the masse (Fleming 1980). In short, the concept of "propaganda by the deed" solidified the idea that a violent vanguard would need to create the spark to generate radical political change. This was a departure from earlier militant movements that sought a mass uprising on its own accord instead of a vanguard generating an uprising action.

A number of technological developments aided anarchist militants. At first the typical anarchist terrorist attack profile featured specific targeting of individual leadership figures via blade or pistol, as was the case in the spate of assassinations in Europe and North America in the 1890s. As the movement progressed, political, business, and religious leaders and other civilians increasingly bore the brunt of anarchist attacks. Supporters of such attacks argued that civilians were legitimate targets because their cooperation propagated the corrupt system.

The invention of dynamite in 1867 enabled bombings to be undertaken in a more operationally feasible manner. Black powder had been the primary explosive for gunpowder and bombs, but dynamite was portable, stable, and had 20 times the destructive potential per unit of mass. Its invention enabled a sort of "democratization of destruction" where smaller groups of individuals could more easily carry out more lethal attacks. In the subsequent decades anarchists increasingly relied on dynamite bombings, and the target set shifted to a broader array of civilian targets in addition to the government officials and captains of industry.

The inauguration of anarchist bombings in the United States took place in 1886 at Chicago's Haymarket Square during a labor protest event. Someone in the crowd threw a bomb at police, and the resulting explosion triggered a riot and gun battle that claimed the lives of seven officers and at least four civilians.

Dynamite became a steadily more popular tool of terror for the anarchist movement. In 1908 the *New York Times* asserted that a bomb was going off in the city on a monthly basis (Mihm 2016). In Los Angeles, elements from organized labor carried out a dynamite campaign against firms that had implemented union-busting tactics. The violence culminated in the bombing of the Los Angeles Times building in 1910. The attack killed 21 and wounded many more.

The zenith of anarchist violence in the United States came in April 1919 when the country was still engaged in World War I. Followers of anarchist Luigi Galleani mailed 36 bombs to key American government and business officials, religious leaders, and journalists across the country. The Galleanists, as the followers came to be known, specifically targeted nativists who were opposed to immigration and had supported the Espionage Act of 1917 and the Sedition Act of 1918. Among other things, that legislation allowed the federal government to determine speech deemed hostile to the government or the U.S. war effort to be subject to criminal prosecution.

In subsequent weeks, the Galleanists sent larger bombs to nine individuals, including a second bomb to U.S. Attorney General Mitchell Palmer. In Fall 1919 the Justice Department worked with law enforcement around the country to launch the Palmer Raids against suspected anarchists, with thousands of mass arrests and detentions and hundreds of deportations of resident aliens. As a reprisal for the raids, in September 1920 the Galleanists detonated a wagon-based bomb on Wall Street in downtown New York's financial district. The attack killed 38 civilians and wounded many more.

The violence of the anarchist movement was meant to serve as an instrument to expose the weakness of the capitalist state system and in turn mobilize the masses to revolution. Despite the significant number of assassinations and bombings carried out by anarchists, however, their "propaganda by the deed" never inspired the mass uprising they envisioned. The state proved far more durable than anarchists anticipated, and nationalist identities proved stronger than class-based ones as evidenced by the battle lines of World War I. In that "Great War" it was nation-states that did battle with one another regardless of the class differences within them. The dominance of the nation-state as the form of organization also in part hampered the initial international efforts to counter anarchists. Many governments, adhering to the concept of sovereignty, were reluctant to pursue anarchist opponents based in foreign states who were not actively operating on their own soil.

Terrorism for National Liberation

The second transition in terrorism pertained to national liberation movements throughout the era of imperial decline and decolonization. In this phase, terrorism's primary purpose was to intimidate and provoke, and it was frequently used as part of an active guerilla movement. The period following World War I featured ethnic groups across Europe seeking self-determination and security, as Woodrow Wilson's Fourteen Points called for the peoples of the former Austro-Hungarian and Ottoman Empires to have "autonomous development." While the anarchists looked at the world in class terms, national liberation movements drew inspiration from the same heightened sense of nationalism that animated nation-states. In turn, unlike anarchists, the national-liberation struggles generally used a mix of insurgency with terrorism, striking both the security forces and civilians of the states who blocked their self-determination.

Ethnonationalist groups are members of an ethnic identity who seek independence and sovereignty. These groups around the world had campaigned for independence well before World War I. The spark that lit the powder keg of this war was a Serbian assassin seeking independence from Austro-Hungarian rule. Later in the war, Irish republicans in Dublin rebelled against the British Empire in the 1916 Easter Rising. This effort was crushed but instilled a revolutionary spirit among republicans on the island. After the war concluded Serbia did gain independence in Yugoslavia, and Irish Republicans gained a free Irish state in 1922, with complete independence in 1948.

The era in the aftermath of World War I can be seen as the first rumblings of what would become a massive anticolonialism movement in Africa, Asia, Latin America, and other parts of the world after World War II and into the early Cold War. Weakened by the toll of World War II, once powerful European nations like France and the United Kingdom maintained vast imperial holdings but lacked the capacity to retain them. As their grips loosened, leaders from native populations rose to lead popular independence movements. Not all such movements were violent; for instance, Mahatma Gandhi led the Indian National Congress to nonviolently resist British colonialism and ultimately succeeded in securing independence for India. Nonetheless, terrorism scholar Bruce Hoffmann notes two examples of terrorism used by national liberation movements, in the Middle East and in Africa north of the Sahara desert (Hoffmann 2006, 46–62).

The Creation of Israel and Political Instability in the Middle East

The genesis of the state of Israel is traced to the Zionist movement. In light of repeated antagonism and violence against

Jewish communities in Europe, Theodore Herzl's 1896 book *der Judenstaat* ("The Jewish State") launched the modern Zionist movement that was committed to creating a Jewish national homeland, preferably in the ancient lands held by the Jews. The following year the World Zionist Congress met in Switzerland and subsequently established its headquarters in Berlin.

The driving force in the birth of the Zionist movement was the failure of regimes across Europe and Russia to integrate Jews as equal citizens under law. Instead, Jews were repeatedly made the scapegoats and targets of anti-Semitic attacks and laws in country after country, despite their efforts to carry on as citizens in their home countries. In Russia and Eastern Europe, anti-Semitic riots called pogroms were a regular occurrence in cities and towns. The disjoint in treatment was epitomized by the 1894 Dreyfus Case, in which a French military officer of Jewish descent was falsely accused of treason. The actual culprit, another French officer, was exonerated while documents were forged to implicate Dreyfus. Dreyfus was convicted and given a life sentence before eventually being pardoned, but the case exposed deep anti-Semitism in Europe. Consequently, the Zionist movement that gained steam in the late 1800s and early 1900s operated under the assumption that since Jews would never be seen as equals in the countries where they resided, they needed a country they could call their own.

The World Zionist Congress considered a number of geographic locations for establishing a permanent Jewish homeland before settling on the Levant, a region of the Eastern Mediterranean that was the historic homeland of Jews and was then under the control of the Ottoman Empire. Early Jewish settlers immigrated to Palestine at this time. In 1917 amid World War I, the British government endorsed the idea of a Jewish state when Foreign Secretary Lord Balfour issued his declaration, in what would become British-controlled Palestine after the war ended and the Ottoman Empire dissolved. Per a British and French agreement made during the war, the lands of the former Ottoman Empire were to be split by those colonial powers, who would rule them as trustees for the territories, now termed "mandates." The Balfour Declaration included the proviso that the civil and religious rights of the non-Jewish population in the territory remain protected. As anti-Semitism and fascism spread across Germany and other nations in the 1930s, Jewish immigration exceeded established British quotas, and by 1936 Jews formed one-third of the mandate's total population (Anglo-American Committee of Inquiry 1947, 10).

Within British Palestine, relations between the Arab and Jewish communities boiled over. The increased Jewish immigration combined with rising Arab nationalism in the interwar period triggered a series of riots and revolts by Palestinian Arabs. British forces were caught between the conflicting parties, some of whom engaged in acts of terrorism. The Jewish militia Haganah ("The Defense") was originally formed in the 1920s and became the nucleus of Israel's Defense Forces after independence in 1948, but a radical break-away group called LeHi ("Israeli Freedom Fighters") split from Haganah in 1940.

Comprised of Jewish immigrants from East Europe and Russia, LeHi undertook operations against the British during World War II, even offering to ally with Nazi Germany and Fascist Italy in exchange for the emigration of those countries' Jews to Palestine. These proposals by LeHi were rebuffed. LeHi targeted British forces as illegal occupiers, but the group also engaged in terrorism designed to intimidate the British government. In 1944 LeHi assassinated Britain's Egyptian minister, Lord Moyne, the most senior British official in the region at the time. Three years later, the group orchestrated a failed bombing attack on the British government in London and followed this attempt with 21 mail bombs addressed to various British government officials. By May 1948, after bearing the brunt of insurgent strikes, burgeoning sectarian conflict, and terrorist attacks, Britain withdrew from its Palestine mandate. The United Nations took the lead in pursuing a peace arrangement between the Arab and Israeli sides after British forces departed, but Israel declared itself a state in May 1948.

Immediately afterward the combined forces of regional Arab countries mobilized for war against the newly declared state of Israel.

Over the course of the conflict the Arab armies were soundly defeated. During this time LeHi and other organized Jewish forces used the threat of violence against Arabs in Israel to encourage their resettlement. Over the course of the war over 700,000 Palestinians fled or were driven into refugee camps in the surrounding Arab countries of Lebanon, Syria, Jordan, and Egypt during what Palestinians called the *Nakba* ("disaster"). In efforts to consolidate the new state of Israel's holdings, in 1948 LeHi assassinated the United Nations mediator for the Arab–Israeli conflict, Folke Bernadotte. This operation was undertaken to prevent Israel's new leaders from accepting the terms of the Swedish diplomat's proposal, which LeHi opposed.

Terrorism in Algeria

Perhaps the clearest example of terrorism during the decolonization phase is the Algerian case. There, the French government bitterly resisted efforts toward independence, claiming that Algeria was part of France proper. To support their argument, France pointed out it was the only African country to be organized as formal French departments like the regions in France proper. Algerians who wanted to be free of colonial rule ridiculed this justification.

At the end of World War II, French police opened fire on Algerian Muslim demonstrators in the coastal province of Sètif. Algerian Muslims then rioted, killing 100 French. This initiated a massive bout of counter-violence by French-Algerians against Algerian Muslims that culminated with the massacre of thousands. The legacy of the Sètif massacres sparked growing Algerian nationalist sentiment after the war.

In 1954 the National Liberation Front (FLN) and its armed wing, the National Liberation Army (ALN), emerged as the leading rebel army in Algeria. France had recently lost its colonial holdings in Indochina and was determined not to lose

Algeria, which it regarded as its African jewel. The situation was complicated by the many Algerian-born descendants of French settlers in Algeria, the *pieds-noirs* ("black feet") who wished for Algeria to remain a part of France. Initially the FLN and its armed forces adopted an insurgent approach by targeting French security forces rather than noncombatants. This changed after the attack at Philippeville in 1955, when the FLN's forces invaded the city and deliberately killed over 100 combined *pieds-noirs* and Algerian Muslims that the FLN branded as collaborators. The reprisals from these murders saw French security forces and *pieds-noirs* kill hundreds of Algerian Muslims in return; the FLN's turn to terrorism had been successful at dividing the country. The legacy of Philippeville was to eradicate the prospect for harmony between *pieds-noirs* and Algerian Muslims. Moreover, the FLN targeted fellow Algerian Muslims with terrorism at a greater rate than French. Historian Alistair Horne estimates that the FLN killed over 7,000 civilians in the early years of the war, at a ratio of approximately six Muslims to every non-Muslim (Horne 1978, 358). Terrorism both provoked unpopular French reprisals and intimidated Algerian Muslims not to defect against the group or the movement.

By 1956 the FLN formally adopted terrorism in conjunction with its guerilla warfare operations. This type of strategy is succinctly described by Brazilian guerilla leader Carlos Marighela: "It is necessary to turn political crisis into armed conflict by performing violent actions that will force those in power to transform the political situation of the country into a military situation. That will alienate the masses, who, from then on, will revolt against the army and the police and blame them for this state of things" (Horne 1978, 118).

In the Battle of Algiers, the FLN shifted focus to urban operations with an eye toward provoking the French-aligned factions and the French government. In June the FLN ordered random shootings against civilians in the city, which was followed by a *pieds-noirs* revenge bombing that killed over 70 Algerian Muslims (Horne 1978, 183–184). Next, the FLN used female operatives in Western dress to target three French targets in the city with bombs. Two restaurants were destroyed, and a third target at the airport was only spared due to a fault in the bomb's arming mechanism. At year's end the FLN assassinated a leader of French-Algerian mayors in the nearby town of Boufarik, then bombed the cemetery where his body was interred. These outrages spurred revenge attacks against innocent Algerian Muslims, continuing the cycle of violence.

In 1957 the French government placed the city of Algiers under martial law to quell the general disorder of these rival terrorist campaigns. As part of its operations, French forces arrested thousands and regularly used torture and execution as part of their efforts to quell the unrest. These policies yielded military intelligence that enabled the French to target many FLN terrorists in the city; however, this information came at great political cost. By one estimate, over 30% of Algiers' male Muslim population was arrested by French forces during the period (Horne 1978, 199), which turned large swaths of the Algerian Muslims against the government. Horne summarizes the crux of the disjoint in the French and Algerian positions: "France was strong, militarily, in Algeria, but weak, politically at home; the FLN was weak, militarily at home, but strong, politically, abroad" (Horne 1978, 230).

In May 1958 the wedge between French and Algerians seemed to be growing with each passing day, and the pressures were weighing on the government in Paris. The degrading situation in Algiers brought down the government of the Fourth French Republic, with a military coup calling for Charles de Gaulle to come out of retirement to establish a new constitution for France. These senior officers feared that the French government would not sufficiently work to retain Algeria as part of France and saw de Gaulle's leadership as necessary to reinvigorate the military efforts and preserve the union. Considering the developments in Paris, the FLN's response was more terrorism. Fearful that de Gaulle would make inroads with moderate Muslims, the FLN implemented a widespread program of terrorism to intimidate Algerian Muslims. This was undertaken ahead of the referendum for de Gaulle's Fifth Republic constitution (Horne 1978, 317). Three years after de Gaulle's return to French politics, he broke with elements of the French political right by holding a referendum on Algerian self-determination. Consequently, former French military officers and militant *pieds-noirs* formed the Secret Armed Organization (OAS). Fearing the French government's intention to grant Algeria independence, the OAS as a counter-revolutionary group waged a terror campaign against de Gaulle's government. It failed to assassinate de Gaulle but did kill 2,000 people through various bombings and assassinations. The efforts were not rewarded, and continued referendums in France and Algeria ultimately enabled de Gaulle to proceed with granting Algeria independence in 1962.

Though certainly bloody, of all the major phases of modern terrorism, this variant yields the greatest chance of success for two reasons. First, the aims are the most concrete and tangible. These movements do not seek the lofty aims of total revolution against the state or society; rather, they push for autonomy or independence over specific and prescribed territories. Their aims are also consistent with taking power and governing in the existing state system, and not so much radically restructuring it. Second, the ambitions are broadly more popular in their respective society than attempts by groups like the anarchists. Nationalism historically has proven to be a powerful form of identity, and ethnonationalist groups seeking independence of their sacred homelands find broad support in their communities, more so than groups seeking to enact policies based on more societally fringe ideologies (Cronin 2003, 40). Terrorism broadly is a weapon of the weak, but national liberation movements in practice married terrorism with insurgency, somewhat evening the balance of forces compared to that of isolated groups.

Just as militant groups can use terrorism as one tool among others, so can groups straddle the main phases. The third major phase is leftist terrorism, popularized in the latter era of the Cold War. Two major examples of groups that fused the national liberation and leftist categories are the Irish Republican Army (IRA) and the various Palestinian militant groups under the umbrella of the Palestinian Liberation Organization (PLO).

The Irish Republican Army had its root in the modern Irish struggle for independence. In the years following the failed 1916 Easter Rising, Irish forces took the mantle of the Irish Republican Army in continuing the insurgency against British rule. Negotiations by Irish leaders and the British resulted in the United Kingdom granting the Irish "free state" status that would enable domestic autonomy but not complete independence from the United Kingdom. Revolutionaries fell into two broad camps. In one, the free state was seen as progress toward the eventual goal of independence. For the other camp, continuing to recognize the British crown was a deal with the devil and traitorous to the cause of Irish independence. Ireland's narrow ratification of the Anglo-Irish Treaty in 1922 bitterly divided the revolutionaries of the IRA, and a significant number split from the state into open rebellion. This Irish Civil War ended with the anti-treaty elements losing heavily, and the diminished IRA's "irregular" shifted to the political left during the remainder of the interwar period. The IRA had never given up its aim of complete independence and continued to oppose the free state that it viewed as illegitimate.

By World War II, the marginalized IRA shifted its orientation from a leftist emphasis to militant nationalism. The nationalist turn paved the way for cooperation with Nazi Germany's military intelligence, which benefited from information provided about targets in the United Kingdom. The orientation was also pragmatic and maintained intelligence-sharing arrangements with the Soviet Union. In 1939 just days before the outbreak of the war, the IRA bombed the English city of Coventry, killing five, injuring dozens, and inaugurating a bombing campaign of sabotage against the British war effort. Altogether IRA operatives would detonate some 300 explosions against industrial and infrastructure targets in this "S-campaign." The campaign was short-lived, and intense counter-intelligence efforts by the British Special Branch police turned the tide.

Following the war, the IRA remained but did so in relative obscurity. During the early interwar period, the six northern counties of the island elected not to join the Irish free state and considered themselves to be part of the United Kingdom proper. This was due to the descendants of Ulster Scots, Scottish Protestants who had settled the region in the 1600s at the behest of the Crown. Dedicated to a fully united Ireland independent from the United Kingdom, Irish republicans refused to accept the partition of the island and in the late 1950s waged a guerilla campaign from the borders of the republic. Militarily the effort was an abject failure, with hundreds of republican militants arrested and imprisoned by both the Republic of Ireland and the United Kingdom. Politically, the move facilitated the return of leftist leadership of the IRA. In the radicalism of the 1960s, the IRA adopted a Marxist platform and corresponding class-based perspective. The aims did not change from seeking a united Ireland, but the basis of that united republic was to be a socialist worker's state. Latent tension within republican circles boiled over due to the politics of Northern Ireland the 1960s.

The 1960s saw the rise of a civil rights movement among Catholics in Northern Ireland. Aware of discrimination by and disparities with Protestants, activists organized marches for better conditions and treatment for Catholic nationalists in the territory. Protestant Loyalists intent on retaining the union with the United Kingdom countered, as did the overwhelmingly Protestant police force. The resulting clashes between the police and activists yielded ethnic riots in 1969, when entire Catholic neighborhoods in Belfast were firebombed. Following the violence, a splinter organization called the Provisional

IRA emerged to guard Catholic nationalist neighborhoods and then moved to offensive action against the United Kingdom. As dedicated Marxists the remaining Official IRA did not seek involvement in the conflict since as it was between working class communities on both sides, and declared a ceasefire in 1972.

By contrast, the Provisional IRA ignored this class-based view, adopting a sectarian perspective while still retaining the nationalist-leftist aim of seeking a united Ireland under a socialist republic. The violence in 1969 marked the start of a 30-year campaign of violence between Catholic nationalists and Protestant loyalists termed "the Troubles." The bulk of the Provisional IRA's actions were insurgent in nature, targeting British soldiers and Northern Irish police; however, this was supplemented by terrorist bombings and assassination attempts. All told, approximately 30% of the IRA's victims were civilians. Notable bombings included the 1972 Bloody Friday, where 20 bombs placed at transportation hubs were detonated in and around Belfast within a 30-minute time span. Nine were killed, with 130 injured. As the campaign carried on, the Provisional IRA shifted its approach further toward terrorist bombings of commercial targets in the hopes of economically bankrupting the British. Moreover, the group attempted assassinations of the senior levels of the British government, targeting prime ministers Margaret Thatcher in 1984 and Johnathan Major in 1991.

On the Protestant loyalist side, a constellation of paramilitary groups retaliated against IRA attacks by specifically targeting civilians as reprisals attacks for IRA violence. Chief among these groups were the Ulster Defense Association (UDA) and the Ulster Volunteer Force (UVF), their victims were civilians in roughly 80% of each group's killings, and the favored form of violence was in the form of shootings and bombings.

In the Middle East, Palestinian militants shared many traits with Irish republican nationalists, and in fact the two groups cooperated over the course of their militant campaigns. In

1964, the Arab League of nations formed the Palestinian Liberation Organization as a militant organization for Palestinians in exile. The purpose of the group was to wage an armed campaign to liberate Palestinian territory from the state of Israel, eliminating the Jewish presence from the territories in order to facilitate the right of return for Arab refugees who had fled during the 1948 war. In its early years the PLO served as an extension of the broad pan-Arab movement. This changed after the 1967 war, which ended disastrously for the combined Arab forces of Egypt, Syria, and Jordan and doubled Israel's holdings of territory to include the West Bank and Gaza. Following the significant defeat, the PLO's leadership shifted to Yasser Arafat, who oversaw the changing composition of the umbrella group. As with the IRA, the PLO ideologically took a leftist turn in the 1960s while retaining its stated aims of national liberation. Arafat led the largest of the PLO's parties, the Palestinian National Liberation Movement (Fatah), which carried out the greatest number of guerilla actions against Israel from Arab countries and Palestinian refugee camps. Fatah was joined in its militancy by the Marxist Popular Front for the Liberation of Palestine (PFLP) and the Communist Democratic Front for the Liberation of Palestine (DFLP). Both Fatah and the PFLP sought the creation of a Palestinian state. With its communist ideology, the DFLP called for a people's state made of both Arabs and Jews. All three organizations adopted terrorism with high-profile examples.

The primary motivation for Palestinian terrorism against Israeli civilians, as opposed to insurgent attacks on Israeli security forces, was to secure the release of captured militants. Fatah sponsored the Black September Organization, which launched the most visible terror attack until September 11.

Black September derived its name from the massacre of Palestinians by the Kingdom of Jordan's forces in 1970. Fearing instability, King Hussein expelled the group for using his territory to launch attacks against Israel. In 1972 during the Summer Olympic games in Munich, Germany, eight terrorist operatives took the Israeli wrestling team hostage, and the subsequent crisis played out in front of the world's cameras. Chief among Black September's demands were the release of over 200 Palestinian prisoners, as well as two Germans from the terror group Red Army Faction. The terrorists eventually negotiated for a helicopter to transport them to a waiting jet liner, but a bungled German rescue operation led the deaths of all the hostages and all but three of the terror operatives.

Both the PFLP and DFLP also engaged in actions that targeted citizens. The PFLP launched a spate of hijackings in the 1970s in attempts to elevate the Palestinian cause, pioneering the tactic and leading to the first round of basic airport security measures seen in wide use today. Among the more famous operatives of the PFLP are Venezuelan-born Illich Ramirez Sanchez, better known as "Carlos the Jackal." Carlos and other PFLP militants hijacked the meeting of the ministers of the Organization of Petroleum Exporting Countries (OPEC) cartel in 1975. The DFLP's most significant attack was the massacre at Ma'alot in 1974. Terrorists infiltrated northern Israel from their base in Lebanon, killed six Israelis, then took a school hostage. In the ensuing rescue attempt, the terrorists killed 25 hostages with automatic weapons fire, most of whom were children. Another 70 Israelis were wounded in this attack.

In both the Irish and Palestinian cases, terrorism was used in an instrumental fashion as the main political conflict was by way of insurgency and guerilla combat. The perceived gains of terrorism were to bankrupt the opposing state, as well as to secure the release of imprisoned insurgents. There was also a clear transition from the foundation of a national liberation to a national liberation couched in leftist ideology. There was a high degree of cooperation by these various groups with the shared ideology as seen in the other leftist cases.

Terrorism for Marxist Revolution

The third broad phase of modern terrorism entails those with leftist motivations. Globally the period saw the rise of the

"New Left" during the counter-culture movement's rise in the 1960s. Leftist ideology had animated a number of national-liberation struggles during the era of decolonization in the 1950s and 1960s, but in that case terrorism was mostly an aid to insurgency, and the main struggle was about gaining independence from colonial powers. In the developed world during the 1970s, however, terrorist groups conspicuously emerged in Western states during the Cold War that sought to overthrow the capitalist democracies outright. The countries affected cases in Europe, Asia, and the United States. These groups shared a great deal with the anarchist forebears in seeking the overthrow of their countries' political and economic systems, with a key difference being that they sought a communist state as a replacement instead of a non-state society.

A notable example of one group was the Red Army Faction (RAF) formed in 1970 by Andreas Baader, Ulrike Meinhof, and Gudrun Ensslin. Respectively, prior to creating the group they were a high school dropout, a journalist, and a radical leftwing activist. Members of the group were a militant outgrowth of the German student movement who thought that Nazis were prominent in West German government and society, and the RAF's aim was to generate a worker's revolution in West Germany. Over the course of its history the group received material support and training from communist East Germany (Leighton 2014, 652–657). Moreover, the group worked with many other terrorist groups in other countries. For instance, Baader and Meinhof trained with PLO and PFLP militants at camps in Jordan shortly after its founding in 1970 (Karmon 2000). Later in 1977, the PFLP aided the RAF by committing a hijacking of a German airliner in attempts at securing the release of the RAF's captured leaders.

A key concept for the RAF was the "urban guerilla." Brazilian guerilla Carlos Marighela coined the term in his 1969 publication, and RAF cofounder Ulrike Meinhof described it as the "form" of the group (Meinhof 2009, 100). The concept was an application of the rural guerilla warfare model into the cities, using safehouses and storehouses as opposed to remote camps. Strategically, the model relied on provocation in seeking to goad the state into taking repressive countermeasures against the group's violent actions. These countermeasures were expected to drive popular opinion against the state and in favor of the group. The RAF's attack tradecraft included shootings and bombings, with many targets being West German security and American armed forces stationed in Europe. The group also engaged in bank robberies, but these were ostensibly to gain funds for their operations.

All told the group failed at achieving its objectives. Strategically, its urban guerilla model turned civilians toward the state rather than against it, with West German authorities measuring their reactions to the RAF's violence. Tactically, civilians informed the authorities with tip-offs such that within two years the RAF's senior leadership was captured. The movement continued and took a turn toward hostage-taking to secure the release of the original leaders. Among the most notable acts of terror were kidnappings and assassinations of West German industrialists, politicians, judges, and bankers. In 1977 a string of these activities came to be called the "German Autumn." Fundamentally the group did not succeed despite these violent efforts, and its senior leaders committed suicide in prison in October. In 1998 the remaining members of the group officially announced its deactivation.

The RAF is the better-known German leftwing terror group from the 1970s, but the lesser-known group actually engaged in more violent attacks. The Revolutionary Cells (RZ) also adhered to the urban guerilla concept but unlike the RAF encouraged a broader base of participation in the movement, especially among the working class. The group was also outwardly anti-Semitic. The most noted RZ attack was the hijacking of Air France Flight 139 in 1976, where two RZ operatives worked in conjunction with five members of a PFLP splinter group. The flight originated in Tel Aviv, Israel, and had a majority of Israeli nationals on board. Such was the ethnic motive of the target selection that the hijackers separated Israelis from non-Israelis. The hijacked aircraft was flown to the Entebbe Airport of the African nation of Uganda; at the time the country was controlled by dictator Idi Amin. Amin supported the aims of the terrorists, and Israeli commandos mounted a daring night-time rescue operation against Ugandan forces and the RZ terrorists that was successful in rescuing most of the hostages.

The leftwing Marxist sentiment that animated the German groups was also found in Italy under the Italian *Brigate Rosse* ("Red Brigades"). Like the RAF, the Red Brigades targeted industrialists and political figures in hopes of launching a class-based revolution. The group was founded in 1970 by a husband-and-wife team of university students named Renato Curcio and Margherita Cagol. Four years later Curcio was arrested, and a year after that Margherita was killed in a shoot-out with police at a farmhouse. Following Curcio's arrest, the group grew in numbers and expanded outside its original base of operations in the north of Italy. Frequent targets of Red Brigade attacks included Italian national police and judges, as well as court-appointed lawyers for captured Red Brigade terrorists. The highest profile incident was the 1978 kidnaping and murder of Aldo Moro, a key figure in the center-right Christian Democrat political party who had pushed for the "Historic Compromise" in Italian politics. Until Moro's efforts, the Italian Communist Party had affiliations with the Soviet Union. Following the compromise, the Italian communists broke with the Soviets and entered into joint governance in parliament with the Christian Democrats.

The Red Brigades kidnaped Moro in hope of negotiating with the government; however, the government refused to do so. Consequently, the Red Brigades shot him to death. Moro was a popular figure in Italy, and the action started the downfall of the group. The following year the Brigades killed a popular union organizer, Guido Rossa, for reporting the distribution of Red Brigades literature. The group's goal of intimidation failed, and instead the murder alienated the Red Brigades from the very working class that it counted on for its revolution. The group continued to carry out violent actions in the 1980s but continued to lose influence after an internal split of members in 1981. During its run the Red Brigades were assisted materially by the PLO and Czech secret police, who furnished firearms and explosives.

The spate of leftwing terrorism during this time was not limited to Europe but extended to Japan and the United States as well. Founded in 1971, the Japanese Red Army engaged in a series of hijackings around the world. Perhaps more than any other group, it signified the international nature of the leftwing wave of terrorism. Following 1972, it was essentially kept in action due to the efforts of a PFLP offshoot. Its highest profile attack saw three JRA terrorists directed by the PFLP to commit a massacre at the Lod Airport in Israel, killing 26 and injuring almost 80. The terrorists used assault rifles and hand grenades in the attack against mostly Christian pilgrims and had trained in PFLP camps in Lebanon in preparation for the assault.

In the United States, domestic terrorism poured out from the unrest of politics in the 1960s. Among the most significant of American leftwing terrorist analogues were the Weather Underground and the Symbionese Liberation Army (SLA). The Weather Underground took their name from the lyrics of a popular Bob Dylan song, "Subterranean Homesick Blues," which said "You don't need a weatherman to know which way the wind blows." Established at the University of Michigan in Ann Arbor, the group effectively was a militant wing of the Students for a Democratic Society (SDS), a New Left organization in American politics most noted for its anti–Vietnam War activism and protests during the Democratic National Convention in 1968. In July 1969 the Weathermen went to Cuba to meet with North Vietnamese officials and discuss how to create a domestic war front in the United States (U.S. Senate 1975, 142). Back in the United States, the Weathermen sought to "Bring the war home" through "Days of Rage" in

October. This consisted of rioting, but the effort was unsuccessful as fewer rioters attended than expected and there was a heightened law enforcement response. Hundreds were arrested, and the lackluster outcome of the attempt compared to the response that members expected drove the Weathermen underground. By May 1970 the group declared war on the United States and turned to a terrorist campaign of bombings. Early targets included courthouses, universities, police stations, the U.S. Capitol building, and the Pentagon. During the 1970s most Weather Underground actions were limited to the east coast, Midwest, and some in the San Francisco Bay area, and by 1982 operations ceased.

In California, a far-left Chicano militant group named *Venceremos* (Spanish for "We will overcome") engaged in activism and facilitated a prison break to try and free a member's boyfriend. The group ambushed and shot the two prison guards transporting the prisoner, killing one and wounding the other. A major part of the group's activism was its prison outreach. One of those counseled by Venceremos activists was Donald DeFreeze, who escaped from prison in 1973 and took refuge in Venceremos safe houses before ultimately founding his own group, the Symbionese Liberation Army (SLA).

Looking to the urban guerilla model, the SLA had black nationalist aims fused with leftwing ideology: Members wished to overthrow the capitalist system and all its perceived pillars, including the prison system, education system, and even monogamous relationships. In 1973 members of the group assassinated Marcus Foster, the African American superintendent of Oakland's schools. Two of the group's members were arrested and convicted of the crime, and the SLA set about winning their release by taking a hostage to exchange.

The SLA targeted publishing heiress Patricia Hearst and kidnapped her from her Berkeley apartment in 1974. Nevertheless, the SLA was unable to secure the release of their comrades and turned to demanding food aid for Oakland's poor. Hearst was not released by the SLA despite her family following the group's wishes in distributing food, and she subsequently became an accomplice of the group after being subject to repeated sexual assault and brainwashing. Hearst participated with the group in robbing a bank in San Francisco, and the SLA subsequently moved south to Los Angeles. There their safehouse was discovered by police, leading to a shootout with automatic weapons that ended with their safehouse catching on fire and the death of all members who were in it, including DeFreeze. Hearst was among the rest of the group that was not in the safe house and was later captured.

This broad phase of leftwing terrorism was aided by the rise of instantaneous mass media. The preferred methods of bombings, assassinations, kidnappings, and hijackings garnered instant and global coverage. Most targets were domestic in nature, but there was a high degree of international cooperation among and between groups. Consistent with the beliefs of terrorists during the anarchist phase, communist terrorists saw their role as jumpstarting what they saw as inevitable workers' revolutions. Thus, mobilization was the key purpose for the violence perpetrated. In practice, the societies that leftwing terrorists targeted in the 1970s were not as class-conscious as their Marxist worldviews allowed. Groups found ways to cooperate based on their shared ideology, but the populations that they relied upon to realize the revolution were not as ripe as they expected. In reality, these groups' use of violence alienated any broad base of support from the population. Moreover, the entire urban guerilla concept proved operationally limited since the counterterrorist units of the state had an easier time penetrating these urban networks than had their base of operations been in rural areas (O'Neill 2001, 44–47).

Terrorism for Antiglobalism

The fourth phase of terrorism concerns violence undertaken for various radical rightwing ideologies and was prevalent in the 1990s. A broad theme during this time was white nationalism and violent opposition to multiculturalism and immigration.

In the United States, bombings of abortion clinics were a regular occurrence as well as assassinations of abortion doctors and other clinic employees. Seven individuals were killed in that kind of political violence over the decade, with several more injured. Groups like the Army of God claim a religious justification for the actions in defense of the unborn and tactically promoted a leaderless model by providing information to like-minded individuals about targeting and techniques for conducting attacks. Group and individuals who adhere to the Christian Identity movement are considered antigovernment and the radical rightwing. Despite claiming to be religious, they are racially motivated more than religiously so. Despite the name, ideologically those in the Christian Identity movement claim that whites are the lost tribes of Israel, and that Jews are Satanic imposters who have since taken control of the government to establish a "New World Order." White supremacy and antigovernment sentiment drive the ideology, which is in stark contrast to the religious practice of mainstream Christians around the world who see the church in universal and not in racial terms.

The deadliest rightwing terror attack in the modern era was the Oklahoma City bombing in 1995 described earlier. The motive for the bombers in that attack, Timothy McVeigh and Terry Nichols, was antigovernment sentiment and retribution for perceived abuses during the Ruby Ridge and Waco standoffs. The following year, Atlanta's Centennial Park was bombed during the Summer Olympic games by Eric Rudolph, killing two and wounding over 100. Rudolph subsequently bombed two abortion providers as well as a lesbian bar in the American South. Rudolph's stated aim for the Atlanta attack was to counter globalization, which he saw as paving the way for a socialist one-world government.

Although prominent in the 1990s, rightwing terrorism has not dissipated in the contemporary era nor is restricted to cases in the United States. In 2011 Norwegian Anders Behring Breivik killed 77 and wounded over 300 in and around Oslo using a mixture of firearms and bombings. He specifically targeted a Norwegian leftwing political party's island youth camp, gaining access by masquerading as a police officer. Breivik has since declared adherence to the Viking religion of Odinism, with white nationalism and anti-Islam as key pillars in his beliefs and writings. In 2019 Australian mass shooter Brenton Tarrant killed 51 and injured 40 with a variety of firearms, specifically targeting two mosques in Christchurch, New Zealand. Tarrant espoused white supremacist and anti-Islamic views.

The United States recently has seen an uptick in the mass-casualty events committed by white nationalists. In 2015 white supremacist Dylan Roof shot nine African American congregants dead in the Emanuel African Methodist Church in Charleston, South Carolina. In 2018, a white nationalist and anti-Semite targeted Pittsburgh's Tree of Life synagogue, killing 11 with firearms. In 2019, Patrick Crusius shot and killed 23 Hispanics and injured an additional 23 in a Wal-Mart in El Paso, Texas. His purported aim was to incentivize Hispanics to leave the country so that they would no longer participate politically. In generalizing rightwing terrorism, the main strategy is intimidation, and the most recent tradecraft in conducting attacks is by way of mass shootings.

As with other periods, the measures and means of terrorism in the 1990s until today are not the sole preserve of rightwing terrorists. During the 1980s and 1990s anarchist Theodore Kaczynski mailed a total of 16 bombs to American academics and corporate figures. Three were killed and 23 were injured by the "Unabomber" over the course of his attacks before he was captured by the FBI in 1996. At the Republican baseball practice for the annual congressional charity baseball game in 2017, a leftwing terrorist shot House Majority Whip Steven Scalise and three others before being neutralized by police. In 2019 just hours after the El Paso shooting, Connor Betts killed nine in a mass shooting in Dayton, Ohio. Betts self-identified as a Satanist, leftist, and a backer of the Antifa movement (Knight and Golick 2019).

Notably, terrorists during this period broadly shared the same ideology but did not tend to work through close-knit, established organizational hierarchies. The attackers for the most part acted alone or in limited numbers and were highly decentralized when they did nominally belong to an organization. For instance, the Army of God was officially leaderless. The decentralized nature of the more recent attacks in the late 2010s was even more extreme, such that ideologically "inspired" individuals were the main perpetrators and not active members of specific groups.

Terrorism for Religious Purification

The fifth and most recent phase is that of religious terrorism. As the Cold War ended the number of groups whose political ideologies were a function of their religious beliefs increased. The case of Aum Shinrikyo earlier in the chapter is one example and demonstrates the mass destruction sought by such apocalyptic groups. The greatest share of violence in recent decades is due to ideologically Islamist militant and terrorist groups. Moreover, compared to earlier waves of terrorism, the religious wave is marked by strategies of attrition and annihilation. Mobilization is still important, but the main push for such groups is to use terrorism as a means of killing as many as possible using mass murder and suicide attacks. To revisit Brian Jenkins' contention that terrorism is theater, the attacks on September 11 demonstrated that terrorists not only wanted a lot of people watching, but they also wanted a lot of people dead. By and large, religiously motivated terrorists see life as dispensable and do not seek to influence, coerce, or "win" citizens over, as other groups do. The best contemporary example is the universe of Salafi-Jihadist terrorist groups who are responsible for nine of the top fifteen deadliest terror attacks since 1978.

Salafi-Jihadism's first contemporary examples hail from domestic terrorism in the North African Arab countries of Algeria and Egypt in the 1990s (Hafez 2003, 113–137). Terrorists in these countries derived their influence from a network of jihadists established during the 1980s as Arab fighters moved to Afghanistan to aid Afghan Mujahedeen ("holy warriors") in their war against Soviet occupation. The efforts to organize the "Afghan Arabs" was largely orchestrated by a Palestinian religious scholar named Abdullah Azzam, known as the "Father of Global Jihad" who worked with Osama bin Laden to establish al Qaeda as the first mainstream Salafi-Jihadist group with global reach. After the Soviet war in Afghanistan ended, many Afghan Arabs returned to their home countries such as in Algeria and Egypt and established cells. Al Qaeda has since spawned numerous offshoots in the Middle East, Asia, and Africa. Salafism derives its name from the *salaf*, or original companions of the Prophet Muhammad and their immediate successors in the 7th century Arabian Peninsula.

Salafism is a variant of Sunni Islam that sees Islamic practices since the time of these companions as having been corrupted. Thus, it is a fundamentalist ideology in seeking a return to the original practice of the faith. Importantly, it derives many of its interpretation from *hadith*, which are the recorded sayings of Muhammad. The heavy emphasis on hadith is in contrast to but not the exclusion of Islam's holy text, the Quran, as a key source of influence. For Salafists, Islam requires "protection and promotion" of the faith in the form of the following principles: the absolute oneness of God (*tawhid*), God's sovereignty over politics through religious law (*sharia*), loyalty to God and disavowal of that which opposes Him, and the excommunication of other Muslims from the faith (Maher 2017, 15). It is important to note that Salafists are not necessarily jihadists who seek violence to achieve their aims.

Salafi-Jihadis are those Salafists who believe it is incumbent on Muslims to fight literal war against nonbelievers (the house of war; *dar al-Harb*) in order to expand the abode of Islam (house of submission/peace; *dar al-Salam*). The goal of these organizations is the reestablishment of the caliphate, an Islamist government ruled by Islamic law, or *sharia*. For Salafists, democracy is inherently un-Islamic because it appeals to the will of the people for legitimacy rather than to God's will. Salafi-Jihadis see democracy and other forms of non-Islamic governance as polytheistic idolatry (*shirk*).

In the realm of political Islam, Salafi-Jihadism is distinct from mainstream Islamic practice regarding the notion of excommunication. This is a serious charge that can only be processed by a credentialed imam through a religious edict. In most contemporary Salafi-Jihadist views, however, the mainstream clerics are seen as corrupted, and they believe that any Salafi can make such a determination. This is a huge point of controversy that separates Salafi-Jihadists from mainstream Sunni Muslims.

In practice, Salafi-Jihadi groups regularly kill Muslims with the justification that their deaths are sanctioned collateral given the needs of jihad, but as is more often the case by declaring them to be heretics per the tenets listed previously. In Salafi-Jihadi circles, this "disbelief" is seen as an even worse offense than those who are deemed infidels ("unbelievers"). Unbelievers can be seen as enemies living in ignorance, whereas disbelievers are seen as traitors masquerading as Muslims. It is not that mainstream Islamic practice ignores disbelievers, but rather that in practice there is a more institutionalized and judicious process for designating a professing Muslim to be a disbeliever. In practice Salafi-Jihadists wage war against Arab regimes in the Middle East, who although governed by Muslims are seen as disbelievers who support Western countries.

In practice, Salafi-Jihadism is aided by the justification for the use of suicide attacks. Popularized by Palestinian militant groups in the 1990s like Hamas, the attacks are portrayed not as suicide but as "martyrdom operations," and the attackers are afforded all the attendant spiritual benefits of dying for the faith. Globally, Salafi-Jihadist violence is the deadliest form in contemporary terrorism when measuring fatalities and casualties. A few cases of attacks that span the globe are instructive.

The Middle East has long been the focus of Salafi-Jihadists terrorists. Many attacks were carried out in the course of ethnic violence between Sunni and Shi'a in Iraq in the late 2000s; however, one case stands out for its level of carnage. The Yazidis are one of Iraq's many ethnic communities who inhabit the north of the country and speak Kurdish. Notably, Yazidi religious practice involves the worship of a fire deity that has historically placed them at odds with Muslims. In April 2007, Yazidi villagers in Bashiqa, Iraq stoned to death a 17-year-old in an honor killing. The girl's crime was her conversion to Sunni Islam as part of her engagement to a Sunni Arab man. Sunni terrorists unleashed a series of terrorist attacks against Yazidis; the last and most devastating was in August 2007, when al Qaeda in Iraq bombed the Yazidi villages of Til Ezer and Siba Sheikh Khidir using 4,000 pounds of high explosive mixed with a fuel tanker. The massive explosion killed over 500 and wounded 1,500, making it the fifth deadliest attack in history (Cave and Glanz 2007).

Al Qaeda in Iraq later morphed into the Islamic State, which in the summer 2014 expanded out of east Syria into western Iraq. After conquering significant swaths of northern and western Iraqi territory, the Islamic State targeted Yazidis for mandatory religious conversion, massacring 3,100 and forcing 6,800 women and girls into sexual slavery (Cetorelli et al. 2017, 1–2). Many survivors fled to Mount Sinjar, where Kurdish ground forces and U.S.-led airpower ultimately saved the Yazidis from further violence.

Iraq has tragically proven to be the site of repeated mass-casualty terrorism carried out by the Islamic State. In June 2014, Islamic State forces captured the Iraqi military base at Camp Speicher. Approximately 7,500 unarmed Iraqi cadets were taken prisoner, and Islamic State militants singled out the Shia and non-Muslim cadets for execution (Arango 2014). Estimates range from 1,095 to 1,700 Iraqis murdered over the course of the massacre. In July 2016 during the Islamic holy month of Ramadan, an Islamic State terrorist drove a suicide truck bomb into the Karrada district in Baghdad, killing nearly 400 individuals and wounding hundreds more. Karrada was known for its upscale shopping and heavy Shia population (Basu 2017). The attack took place shortly after Islamic State militants had been driven from their stronghold in Fallujah by Iraqi and allied international forces.

In Africa, mass casualty attacks by Salafi-Jihadists are among the deadliest on record. As multinational counterterror operations pressured Salafi-Jihadi groups in the Middle East, groups like al Qaeda and the Islamic State expanded into sub-Saharan Africa to take root on the western and eastern sides of the continent. The two most prominent groups are al Shabaab ("the youth") in Somalia and Boko Haram ("Western education is forbidden") in Nigeria. Both groups conduct insurgent attacks against their respective country's security forces as well as mass-casualty terrorism within their regions. Al Shabaab has generally maintained its cohesion, and the group pledged an oath of loyalty to al Qaeda in 2012. Conversely, Boko Haram pledged loyalty to the Islamic State in 2015 but then fractured into two major different factions, the main force that remains allied with the Islamic State as the Islamic State West African Province (ISWAP) and a minority faction that opposed the union and was more indiscriminate in its targeting of civilians (International Crisis Group 2019, 7–9). In 2021 the ISWAP faction effectively defeated the minority rivals. Both Boko Haram and al Shabaab have a history of terrorist attacks, and one example for each illustrates the tremendous damage they have inflicted.

Boko Haram made its mark attacking civilians early in its operational lifespan, demonstrating that mass violence need not require high explosive bombs. In May 2014, its militants massacred over 300 Nigerians in the northeast towns of Gamboru and Ngala using assault rifles and rocket propelled grenades (Nossiter 2014). Eight months later militants overran the Nigerian army base at Baga, then launched a rampage into the village and its surrounding area. Estimates vary widely; however, locals assert that up to 2,000 were killed in the violence (Egbejule 2016). Three years later in the Horn of Africa, a terrorist from al Shabaab drove a truck bomb into the

Hodan district of the capital city Mogadishu. The explosion fused with a nearby fuel tanker truck to magnify the effects of the 800 pounds of explosives, killing almost 587 Somalis and injuring hundreds more (U.S. Department of State, 2018).

In Europe and Eurasia, Salafi-Jihadi terrorism is on the rise. In addition to the al Qaeda attacks described earlier in the chapter, Russia was the target of Chechen Islamists in 2004 when the school at Beslan was raided. Members of the Riyad us-Saliheen Martyr's Brigade (RSMB) took over 1,000 people hostage. Russian forces stormed the school, and in the ensuing chaos 334 hostages were killed by a mix of gunfire and explosions, most of whom were children. Almost 800 were injured, and many casualties were due to the frontal assault by Russian forces in the rescue attempt, while many others died in explosions by terrorists wired with explosives using dead-man's switches. Russia had long faced militant actions by Chechen nationalists; however, the Beslan school siege was motivated primarily by Salafi-Jihadi ideology as RSMB seeks to establish an Islamic emirate in the Caucasus.

Western Europe has also been a victim of various Salafi-Jihadi groups, with France as a special case. Chronicling the progression of terror in the country requires a return to Algeria in north Africa. After Algerian independence in 1962, the former militant group the FLN established a single-party regime in the following decades. In response to domestic pressures, the FLN leadership adopted a new constitution in 1988 that made provisions for political liberalization and the recognition of a rival Islamist party, the Islamic Salvation Front (FIS).

In December 1991, the FLN hosted elections it thought it would handily win only to find its new rival leading in the returns. Rather than accede to the results, the secular FLN government directed the military to cancel the elections through a coup, which initiated the Algerian Civil War. The next ten years pitted the secular FLN's government forces against the FIS's militant wing, the Islamic Salvation Army (AIS). In 1994, a terrorist group called the Islamic Armed Group (GIA) splintered from the FIS, having judged the FIS to be too moderate. In the following years, GIA terrorists massacred hundreds of civilians in rural Algeria, which had been strongholds of the FIS. Among the worst of these massacres were in the villages of Rais and Betalha in 1997. In many regards the Salafi-Jihadist GIA and its atrocities served as a precursor to the Islamic State in Syria and Iraq some 15 years later. The GIA's influence later fizzled out after these atrocities and as the peace process took root between the FLN and FIS.

One of the key Salafi-Jihadist groups in North Africa today, Al Qaeda in the Islamic Maghreb (AQIM), was the eventual successor of the GIA. Over the course of its operational life, the GIA targeted France as well as the Algerian government and its citizens. On Christmas Eve in 1994, four GIA terrorists hijacked an Air France flight in Algeria with scheduled service to Paris. The reported aim of the GIA terrorists was to crash the aircraft into the Eiffel Tower. The initial standoff started on the tarmac in Algeria, but eventually the plane was given permission to fly to Marseilles to take on fuel, and it was there that French National Police forces raided the plane. The counterterrorist operation killed the four hijackers at the cost of three passengers but saved the lives of 229 passengers and crew. France continues to lie in the crosshairs of Salafi-Jihadists. In November 2015, Paris was brought to a standstill by a coordinated set of suicide attacks and mass shootings by the Islamic State. Nine terrorists targeted a soccer match, theater, and restaurants, and the combined attacks killed 130 and injured nearly 400. The given motive for the attack was retaliation for French military participation in operations against the Islamic State in Syria and Iraq. In subsequent years, Islamic State terrorists have killed 106 French citizens in a mix of shootings, stabbings, bombings, and vehicular homicides.

South Asian countries have further been victimized by Salafi-Jihadi groups launching mass casualty terrorist attacks. Pakistani military intelligence working with LeT and Indian jihadists are suspected behind the bombing of Mumbai's railway system in a 2006 terrorist attack, deploying seven coordinated pressure cooker bombs on various trains. The explosions killed over 200 individuals and injured over 700 (Raj and Sengupta 2006). The explosives used in the bombs featured RDX, a common compound used in military explosives with limited civilian applications (Tankel 2014, 6). More recently, a Sri Lankan offshoot of the Islamic State suicide-bombed three churches and three hotels in Sir Lanka on Easter Sunday in 2019. The attackers coordinated their strikes with eight suicide bombers to inflict the carnage, with the combined death toll at 269 and over 500 individuals injured (British Broadcasting Corporation, 2020). Among the dead were 45 children, most of whom were participating as part of the Easter services.

Due to counterterrorism efforts by the United States and allied governments since 2001, key Salafi-Jihadist organizations have been on the defensive. Over time their influence has diffused, with the latest trend seeing ideologically inspired individuals commit attacks in the name of the idea or an organization. The threat matrix has shifted in many ways from the large, prepared, and devastating attacks of September 11 to piecemeal acts of terror inspired by the ideology and generally called for by leaders but not specifically directed by them. Although numerous instances abound, three cases from the last decade illustrate this.

Recent cases of Salafi-Jihadist domestic terrorism showcase the emphasis on seeking mass casualties over policy coercion. Brothers Dzhokhar and Tamerlan Tsarnaev bombed the finish line at the 2013 Boston Marathon with pressure cooker devices. Three were killed while over 250 were injured by the blast and shrapnel. The brothers were inspired by al Qaeda to undertake attacks on their own in support of the group's aims, and followed directions on bomb construction outlined in one of the regional affiliates' online magazines (Khan 2013). In December 2015 in the city of San Bernardino, California, married couple Syed Farook and Tashfeen Malik attacked Farook's workplace holiday party using semi-automatic firearms and pipe bombs, killing 14 civilians and wounding 22 before later dying in a shootout with police. Farook was an American citizen of Pakistani descent, and Malik was a Pakistani citizen who had spent most of her life in Saudi Arabia. The couple had met online and married in Saudi Arabia in early 2014 before Malik immigrated to California on a fiancée visa. As with the Tsarnaev brothers, the couple had been inspired by Salafi-Jihadis groups, and Farook even posted a pledge of loyalty to the Islamic State on social media during the attack (Whitcomb and Hosenball 2015). Six months after the San Bernardino attack, Omar Mateen shot 49 people dead in a mass shooting at a gay nightclub in Orlando, Florida. Mateen was an American citizen of Afghan descent who called 9-1-1 to pledge allegiance to the Islamic State during the attack.

Upon review, the terrorist acts of Salafi-Jihadists are geared toward large mass casualty attacks, and these attacks are truly global in their span. Nearly every continent has been affected by terrorism in the name of this ideology for the purpose of advancing the caliphate. Radicalization is a notable concern, as Salafi-Jihadists have spread well beyond the Middle East into South and Southeast Asia, Africa, Europe, and North America.

Salafi-Jihadists are animated by political objectives couched in their religious ideology that expansively defines their opponents and seeks their annihilation. That is to say that unlike the more limited and "secular" aims of past terrorists such as national liberation groups who see terrorism as an instrument to change their target's behavior, the use of terrorism by religious fanatics is uncompromising. Like the anarchists, Salafi-Jihadists seek to destroy the current political orders that stand. Unlike anarchists, they endeavor to replace it with a global Islamic caliphate. There is a sense that in other types of terrorism, terrorists are mindful of the counter-productive actions regarding casualties. With national liberation movements, violence was frequently used to garner attention for political aims and to coerce opponents into changing policy. Using too much violence, on the other hand, might enhance the resolve of the target population rather than sway it to appeasement. Religious terrorists by and large have no such hesitation about using mass violence, which they view as being instrumental to destroying their adversary. Given the desire to cause as much death and destruction as possible based on the means at hand, analysts fear the implication of Salafi-Jihadists and apocalyptic groups obtaining and deploying weapons of mass destruction in the pursuit of their religiously inspired aims.

It's All About Politics

In studying terrorism, the non-state nature of the perpetrators and civilians as victims are important elements, as is the use of violence. However, it is politics that is the overarching framework that distinguishes terrorism from other forms of violence. Terrorism is political violence at a sub-state level, but understanding the political motivations of terrorists and their beliefs is a prerequisite to designing effective counterterrorism strategies.

In reviewing the major phases of modern terrorism, four broad ideologies are evident. First, anarchist and leftist violence emphasizes mobilization to overthrow the political and economic system as the key aim. In terms of tradecraft, these groups utilize assassinations, bombings, kidnappings, and hijackings. The later theory of the urban guerilla was based on a strategy of provocation, but in practice the repressive reprisals that were in turn expected to drive a wedge between the population and the government were limited. Second, national liberation movements used violence to intimidate and provoke their opponents. More so than anarchists and leftists, these struggles are defined by insurgent actions with terrorism as a means in support of that aim. Those fighting for ethnonationalist reasons are among the most driven and historically enjoy a wider base of support than leftwing movements that organize along class-conscious lines. Third, rightwing terrorists seek to intimidate their opponents based on policies be they narrowly or broadly defined. For example, rightwing attacks have focused on the narrow policy of abortion, but many also encompass broader notions of white nationalism. Compared to the practice of other forms of terrorism, rightwing terrorists tend to be diffuse and broadly leaderless in their organization, with terrorists wed more to the idea more than any individual or hierarchy promoting them. In terms of tradecraft, rightwing terrorists rely mostly on shootings, with a limited number of bombings as well. Finally, religious terrorism seeks the aims of attrition and annihilation of its opponents. Mobilization can be a factor, but this wave is marked more by the broad instruments and wide scope of violence pursued. Many religious groups have sought or expressed interest in acquiring weapons of mass destruction, and the tradecraft of such groups involves attempts at mass murder and/or suicide attacks.

This chapter established a concrete definition of terrorism and reviewed the elements that factor into it. Additionally, the content in the chapter applied this definition to contemporary examples to illustrate cases of terrorism and distinguish them from other forms of violence. Finally, the chapter provides a brief review of major epochs of terrorism based on the differing ideologies of groups. After reviewing these periods, a comparison of their qualities yielded insights into the aims and tradecraft. With this foundation established, the next chapter will consider key problems, controversies, and solutions regarding terrorism.

References

Abrahms, Max. 2012. "The Political Effectiveness of Terrorism Revisited." *Comparative Political Studies* 45, no. 3 (March): 366–393.

Anglo-American Committee of Inquiry. 1947. *Supplement to Survey of Palestine*. Washington, D.C.: Institute for Palestine Studies.

Arango, Tim. 2014. "Escaping Death in Northern Iraq." *New York Times*, September 3, 2014. https://www.nytimes.com

/2014/09/04/world/middleeast/surviving-isis-massacre
-iraq-video.html.

Basu, Moni. 2017. "In Iraq, Thousands of Terrorism's Victims
Go Unnamed." *CNN*, January 12, 2017. https://edition
.cnn.com/2017/01/12/world/iraq-terrorism-faceless
-victims/index.html.

British Broadcasting Corporation. 2011. "The 38-Year
Connection Between Irish Republicans and Gaddafi."
February 23, 2011. https://www.bbc.com/news/uk
-northern-ireland-12539372.

British Broadcasting Corporation. 2020. "Sri Lanka Attacks:
Easter Sunday Bombings Marked One Year On." April 21,
2020. https://www.bbc.com/news/world-asia-52357200.

Cave, Damien and James Glanz. 2007. "Toll Rises Above
500 in Iraq Bombings." *New York Times*, August 22, 2007.
https://www.nytimes.com/2007/08/22/world/middleeast
/22iraq.html.

Cetorelli, Valeria, Isaac Sasson, Nazar Shabila, and Gilbert
Burnham. 2017. "Mortality and Kidnapping Estimates for
the Yazidi Population in the Area of Mount Sinjar, Iraq, in
August 2014: A Retrospective Household Survey." *PLoS
Medicine* 14, no. 5 (May 9): 1–15. https://www.ncbi.nlm.nih
.gov/pmc/articles/PMC5423550/pdf/pmed.1002297.pdf.

Clausewitz, Carl von. 1989. *On War.* Translated by Michael
Eliot Howard and Peter Paret. Princeton: Princeton
University Press.

Cronin, Audrey Kurth. 2003. "Behind the Curve:
Globalization and International Terrorism." *International
Security* 27, no. 3 (Winter 2002/03): 30–58.

Egbejule, Eromo. 2016. "The Massacre Nigeria Forgot: A
Year After Boko Haram's Attack on Baga." *The Guardian*,
January 9, 2016. https://www.theguardian.com/world
/2016/jan/09/nigeria-baga-massacre-boko-haram
-1-year-on.

Fleming, Marie. 1980. "Propaganda by the Deed: Terrorism and Anarchist Theory in Late Nineteenth-Century Europe." *Studies in Conflict & Terrorism* 4, no. 1–4: 1–23.

Fletcher, Holly. 2012. "Aum Shinrikyo." Council on Foreign Relations Backgrounder. Last updated June 19, 2012. https://www.cfr.org/backgrounder/aum-shinrikyo.

Frohne, Lauren, Corinne Chin, and Ramon Dompor. 2020. "'The Uprising': Watch How Seattle's Protests Have Evolved." *Seattle Times*, July 4, 2020. https://www.seattletimes.com/seattle-news/watch-the-uprising/.

Gallup. 2020. "Terrorism." Accessed October 15, 2020. https://news.gallup.com/poll/4909/terrorism-united-states.aspx.

Ganor, Boaz. 2002. "Defining Terrorism: Is One Man's Terrorist Another Man's Freedom Fighter?" *Police Practice and Research* 3, no. 4 (December): 287–304.

Goldberg, Jeffrey. 2002. "In the Party of God." *New Yorker*, October 28, 2002. https://www.newyorker.com/magazine/2002/10/28/in-the-party-of-god-2.

Green, Sara Jean. 2020. "CHOP Shooting Suspect Fled Washington State, Prosecutors Say; Warrant Issued for His Arrest." *Seattle Times*, August 6, 2020. https://www.seattletimes.com/seattle-news/crime/arrest-warrant-issued-for-chop-shooting-suspect-who-prosecutors-say-fled-washington-state/.

Gutman, David and Sydney Brownstone. 2020. "'Everybody down!': What Happened at the Shooting That Killed a Teenager and Led to CHOP's Shutdown." *Seattle Times*, July 8, 2020. https://www.seattletimes.com/seattle-news/everybody-down-what-happened-at-the-chop-shooting-that-killed-a-teenager-and-led-to-the-areas-shutdown/.

Hafez, Mohamed. 2003. *Why Muslims Rebel: Repression and Resistance in the Islamic World*. Boulder: Lynne Rienner.

Hoffmann, Bruce. 2006. *Inside Terrorism*. New York: Columbia University Press.

Horne, Alistair. 1978. *A Savage War of Peace: Algeria 1954–1962*. New York: The Viking Press.

Horsley, Richard A. 1979. "The Sicarii: Ancient Jewish 'Terrorists.'" *Journal of Religion* 59, no. 4 (October): 435–458.

International Crisis Group. 2019. "Facing the Challenge of the Islamic State in West Africa Province." Report 273. May 16, 2019. https://d2071andvip0wj.cloudfront.net /273-facing-the-challenge.pdf.

Jenkins, Brian M. 1974. *International Terrorism: A New Kind of Warfare*. Rand Paper P-5261. Santa Monica: The Rand Corporation.

Jensen, Richard B. 2014. *The Battle Against Anarchist Terrorism*. Cambridge: Cambridge University Press.

Jones, Seth G. 2020. "Who Are ANTIFA, and Are They a Threat?" Center for Strategic and International Studies Critical Questions. Last modified June 4, 2020. https:// www.csis.org/analysis/who-are-antifa-and-are-they-threat.

Karmon, Ely. 2000. "German and Palestinian Terrorist Organizations: Strange Bedfellows: An Examination of the Coalition." IDC Herzliya International Institute for Counter-Terrorism. Last modified May 10, 2000. https:// www.ict.org.il/Article.aspx?ID=1623#gsc.tab=0.

Khan, Azmat. 2013. "The Magazine that 'Inspired' the Boston Bombers." *Frontline*, April 30, 2013. https://www .pbs.org/wgbh/frontline/article/the-magazine-that-inspired -the-boston-bombers/.

Kilcullen, David C. 2013. *Out of the Mountains*. Oxford: Oxford University Press.

Knight, Cameron and Keith Biery Golick. 2019. "Dayton Shooting: What We Know About the Gunman's Politics." *USA Today*, August 7, 2019. https://www.usatoday.com /story/news/2019/08/07/dayton-shooting-what-do-we -know-connor-betts-politics/1943289001/.

Leighton, Marian K. 2014. "Strange Bedfellows: The Stasi and the Terrorists." *International Journal of Intelligence and Counterintelligence* 27, no. 4: 647–665.

Maher, Shiraz. 2017. *Salfi-Jihadism: The History of an Idea.* London: Penguin Books.

Meinhof, Ulrike. 2009. "The Urban Guerilla Concept." In *The Red Army Faction: A Documentary History. Volume 1: Projectiles for the People,* edited by J. Smith and Andre Moncourt, 83–105. Oakland: PM Press.

Merriman, John M. 2016. *The Dynamite Club: How Bombing in Fin-de-Siècle Paris Ignited the Age of Modern Terror.* New Haven: Yale University Press.

Mihm, Stephen. 2016. "America in the Grip of Terrorism (and the fateful year is 1886)." *The Kansas City Star,* September 22, 2016. https://www.kansascity.com /opinion/opn-columns-blogs/syndicated-columnists /article103333377.html.

Mueller, John and Mark G. Stewart. 2018. "Terrorism and Bathtubs: Comparing and Assessing the Risks." *Terrorism and Political Violence 33*(1): 138–163.

Nossiter, Adam. 2014. "Islamist Militants Kill Hundreds of Civilians in Northeastern Nigeria." *New York Times,* May 7, 2014. https://www.nytimes.com/2014/05/08/world/africa /islamist-militants-kill-hundreds-in-northeastern-nigeria.html.

O'Neill, Bard. 2001. *Insurgency & Terrorism: Inside Modern Revolutionary Warfare.* McLean: Brassey's.

Polo, Marco. 1929. *The Travels of Marco Polo the Venetian.* Translated by William Marsden. London: J.M. Dent. https://archive.org/details/marcopolo00polouoft/page/74 /mode/2up.

Raj, Saritha and Somini Sengupta. "Series of Bombs Explode on 7 Trains in India, Killing Scores." *New York Times,* July 12, 2006. https://www.nytimes.com/2006/07/12/world /asia/12india.html.

Rapoport, David. 1992. "Terrorism." In *Routledge Encyclopedia of Government and Politics Volume 2*, edited by Mary Hawkesworth and Maurice Kogan, 1049–1080. London: Routledge.

Rapoport, David C. 2004. "The Four Waves of Modern Terrorism." In *Attacking Terrorism: Elements of a Grand Strategy*, edited by Audrey Kurth Cronin and James M. Ludes, 46–73. Washington, DC: Georgetown University Press.

Roberts, Michael. 2010. "Killing Rajiv Gandhi: Dhau's Sacrificial Metamorphosis in Death." *South Asian History and Culture* 1, no. 1 (January): 25–41.

Stone, Andrea. 2002. "Military's Aid and Comfort Ease 9/11 Survivors' Burden." *USA Today*, August 20, 2002. http:// usatoday30.usatoday.com/news/sept11/2002-08-20 -pentagon_x.htm.

Tankel, Stephen. 2014. "The Indian Jihadist Movement: Evolution and Dynamics." National Defense University, Institute for National Strategic Studies, Strategic Perspectives No. 17, July 2014. https://inss.ndu.edu /Portals/68/Documents/stratperspective/inss/Strategic -Perspectives-17.pdf.

Trump, Donald (Trump Twitter Archive V2). 2020a. "The United States of America Will Be Designating ANTIFA as a Terrorist Organization." Twitter, May 31, 2020. https:// www.thetrumparchive.com/?searchbox=%22The+United +States+of+America+will+be+designating+ANTIFA+as +a+Terrorist+Organization.%22.

Trump, Donald (Trump Twitter Archive V2). 2020b. "Domestic Terrorists Have Taken Over Seattle." Twitter, June 10, 2020. https://www.thetrumparchive.com/?searchbox =%22Domestic+Terrorists+have+taken+over+Seattle%22.

U.S. Department of Defense. 2001. *Distribution of Personnel by State and Selected Locations (M02-2001 Personnel)*

DoD Military and Civilian Personnel by State – Sep. 30, 2001. Washington, D.C.: Government Printing Office. https://www.dmdc.osd.mil/appj/dwp/rest/download ?fileName=M02.zip&groupName=pubSelectedLocations.

U.S. Department of State. 2018. "United States Stands with Somalis on Anniversary of October 14 Attack." Embassy to Somalia Press Release, October 14, 2018. https:// so.usembassy.gov/united-states-stands-with-somalis-on -anniversary-of-october-14-attack/.

U.S. Department of State. 2019. "Designation of the Islamic Revolutionary Guard Corps." April 8, 2019. https://www .state.gov/designation-of-the-islamic-revolutionary-guard -corps/.

U.S. Senate. 1975. *The Weather Underground: Report of the Subcommittee to Investigate the Administration of the Internal Security Act and Other Internal Security Laws of the Committee on the Judiciary, 94th Congress, First Session.* Washington, D.C.: Government Printing Office.

Weber, Max. 2019. *Economy and Society: A New Translation.* Translated by Keith Tribe. Cambridge: Harvard University Press.

Whitcomb, Dan and Mark Hosenball. "FBI Investigating California Massacre as 'Act of Terrorism.'" *Reuters,* December 4, 2015. https://www.reuters.com/article /us-california-shooting-isis-idUSKBN0TN1SR20151204.

2 Problems, Controversies, and Solutions

Terrorism is fundamentally a form of political violence. Perpetrators of such violence have done so for a range of differing political motives. Consequently, attempted solutions for dealing with terrorism require comprehending the political dimension of terrorism and its associated controversies. Politics is the foundation of terrorism studies, but the study of politics is complex. To help better understand these issues and how they influence one another, scholars focus both on the origins and growth of terrorism and on governmental responses to the threat of terrorism. These "problem sets" are examined at the individual, organizational, and system levels.

The Problems Posed by Terrorism

To assess the problems associated with terrorism, it is worth noting the levels of analysis in social science literature. One of scholar Kenneth Waltz's major contributions to the field of international relations was outlining how understanding a

---

Static barriers are one approach governments can take to curtail attacks by members of terrorist groups by denying them access points for attacks. Here a member of Israel's security forces patrols in Bethlehem near a part of the security barrier separating Israel and the West Bank. Scholars noted a significant decline in the number of people killed by Palestinian militant groups after the barrier was erected. While such guarded walls have an obvious security benefit to the side erecting them, they also can be politically contentious by denying or complicating the movement of peoples and goods who are not affiliated with militant actors. (Rrodrickbeiler/ Dreamstime.com)

complex topics like war requires understanding whether actors or agents are operating at the individual, state, or international levels (Waltz 1959, 225–238). For terrorism, problems at the individual level concerns the beliefs and worldviews that motivate terrorists, while at the organizational level it pertains to the differences in scale between the terrorist group versus the state. Finally, the systemic level demonstrates how changes in the social, political, and economic conditions can create a more permissive environment for terrorist actors to flourish.

Problems of Prevention at the Individual Level

The first level considers the political orientation of an *individual*. This is very much a function of the individual's worldview, which encompasses one's experiences in life and beliefs that they hold. It also encompasses one's broader sense of justice and right and wrong, both of which are important in shaping individual concepts of morality and acceptable behavior. Outlining the relationship between identity and ideology clarifies this dynamic. Identity pertains to addressing who an individual is and how they see themselves in the world. An individual maintains multiple distinct identities (not personalities) based on gender, age, geography, ethnicity, language, citizenship, family position, and so forth.

Identities are not necessarily exclusive, but individuals can be thought of as positioning these identities into a hierarchy based on priority even if such a hierarchy may be unconsciously formed. One's paramount form of identity creates the building blocks of an ideology, which is a system of ideas and ideals that prescribe how a society is to be ordered and how power is to be used within it.

Ideologies are comprehensive. They extend beyond individual identities and worldviews to viewpoints on how the world should be structured and ordered to advance desirable policies and goals and mitigate undesirable ones. This underscores the transition from objective to subjective views, that is, from observing and understanding the world to positing and pursuing what is good in it.

Consequently, terrorism as a form of political participation is an outgrowth of both shared identity and ideology. It is unique, however, in that the expression of the ideology specifically promotes coercion through violence as a legitimate way to pursue its aims.

This understanding leads to the first problem of terrorism: It is rooted in ideas that can never be fully eradicated. This is because the use of terrorism first begins as ideas within an identity framework that ultimately coalesces into a political ideology. These ideas in turn form ideologies that may come to see violence as justified in their pursuit.

As the previous chapter noted, historically there four major ideologies associated with terrorism in the modern era, these being leftist, nationalist, rightist, and religious. Notice that although the definition of terrorism is objective, the political beliefs that an individual holds are subjective and frequently a source of contention in any society. Optimally societies seek to resolve political issues and differences through prescribed institutional processes, informally seen as the "rules of the game." Everyone by virtue of their worldview holds political beliefs, but clearly not every individual with such beliefs seeks terrorism as a means to pursue those aims. The overwhelming majority of people in the United States and other nations support their political beliefs through lawful means of participation like writing elected representatives, campaigning for candidates, donating time and money to favored candidates and groups, and voting.

The processes by which those holding political beliefs seek violence as a means of carrying them out is deeply psychological. It also leads to the realization that because identity, ideas, and political ideology are at the root of a terrorist's motivation, the phenomenon can tragically never be eradicated. Terrorists frequently operate as groups or organizations and can be reinforced by them, but the decision to participate in a group and commit such violent attacks is made at an individual level. Much is often made in discussions of attempting to isolate and eliminate the root causes of terrorism, but to truly do so at an individual level would require the totalitarian policing of all ideas and thought: a frightening proposition for those who desire living in a free and open society (Wilkinson 1977, 121). Moreover, giving a state such totalitarian power invites government-directed violence against its citizenry.

A second problem associated with the individual level of the ideology is that it can dictate the degree of destruction sought by a group. Terrorist acts are about inflicting death and damage as well as causing fear, but how these manifest can vary based on beliefs. Compared to the political beliefs of most others, terrorists holding extremist beliefs do not have a large political constituency—which explains why they resort to terrorism instead of the political process. By and large, groups that have more expansive goals for societal change are deadlier compared to those that pursue more limited political goals. Ethnonationalist groups tend to be more secular with their goals such as territorial liberation through the establishment of a country, the desire for regional autonomy within a country, or a narrow change in policy on a single issue. Ideologically the fact that aims are more limited means they tend to have more realistic outcome goals than their counterparts, and violence used for coercion will tend to be more measured since using too much violence might serve to mobilize the civilians who they seek to scare against them.

Alternatively, terrorists driven by religious beliefs tend to be more expansive in their aims, frequently seeking a complete restructuring of society. Consequently, their propensity for violence is often limited by their capacity rather than their ambition. Of all ideologies of terrorism, only religiously motivated terrorists have used or sought to use weapons of mass destruction. In addition, conventional attacks from terrorists acting on their radical religious beliefs account for a significant share of fatalities from terrorism worldwide.

Of the top 10 deadliest terrorist attacks around the world in 2019, over 77% of the fatalities were attributed to groups with a religiously-based ideology (Institute for Economics & Peace 2020, 10–11). Out of all perpetrator groups who had more than 100 attacks in the year, over 94% of their fatalities were caused by religiously based organizations (National Consortium for the Study of Terrorism and Responses to Terrorism 2020, 4). At a tactical level, their radical beliefs also make them more likely to give up their lives in carrying out attacks. Notably, nearly every terrorist group that has used suicide attacks in its tradecraft has had some component of religion as part of its ideology, mostly in the form of Salafi-jihadism.

Problems of Prevention at the Organizational Level

The next level of analysis is the organizational level that accounts for dynamics within a group or state. Terrorist groups are usually smaller and often more nimble than the state law enforcement and national security forces. A terror group does not need a large membership in order to have a devoted core of operatives.

For instance, a student interested in organizing an event can probably do so with greater speed and efficiency if they work with two other friends rather than 15 others to make the event a reality.

The same logic applies to terrorist and counterterrorist forces. Terrorist groups are smaller than the states that they operate against—but the breadth and scope of potential civilian targets the government must protect against terrorist attack is huge. Conversely, the infrastructures that terrorists use, such as hidden safehouses and training camps, are spread about and fewer in number.

This presents clear problems for counterterrorism efforts of governments who are often forced to be reactive to terrorist attacks. Organizational factors surrounding terrorist groups also have effects on their overall lethality. Researchers note, for example, that the larger and more religious a terrorist group is relative to others, the deadlier the group is likely to be (Hou, Gaibulloev, and Sandler 2020, 221). Research also indicates that groups that more cohesively network with one another are comparatively deadlier than those that do not (Horowitz and Potter 2014, 215).

The final level of analysis is the systemic level, where the actors and their broader environmental elements interact. These structural and societal factors tend to focus on change and dislocation, causing conditions that can exacerbate the likelihood of terrorism arising. The problems related to the rise of terrorism at a systemic level have to do with the limited effect that policy can have on such vast structural forces.

Problems of Prevention at the Systemic Level

Poverty and Terrorism

Two of the most heavily studied causes of terrorism, for example, are the related forces of poverty and economic inequality. Many policymakers and other observers have suggested that a lack of economic development makes the dispossessed and unemployed masses more likely to resort to violence to improve their situation. Yet empirical research suggests that economic factors alone do not sufficiently account for cases of political violence (Jager 2018). Studies carried out by economist Alan Krueger and political scientist James Piazza, for example, note the lack of a clear connection. Piazza reviewed a variety of economic measures, including gross domestic product (GDP) growth, unemployment, inflation, measures of income inequality, the Human Development Index score, and even access to nutrition (Piazza 2006, 168–170). His statistical analysis demonstrated no significant relationship between any of those variables and acts of terrorism as measured by the number of incidents or the number of casualties. In fact, Krueger's research noted that most profiles of terrorists indicate that on average they are from middle-class or higher socioeconomic backgrounds with greater educational attainment than many of their peers in society (2007, 32–44).

The notion that terrorism is caused by poverty alone may be rooted in conflating insurgency and terrorism. In the former, violence is used by a non-state actor against state security forces for political purposes in a civil conflict. With terrorism, the violence is directed against civilians. Guerilla warriors who fight in insurgencies often are from rural and comparatively underdeveloped backgrounds, and insurgent movements typically enjoy greater popular support in their specific areas of operation than outright terrorist groups do in their societies.

There are a great many poor countries in the world today, but acts of terrorism are rare events in most of them. Historical evidence also suggests that poverty alone does not typically account for an increase in domestic terrorism. In the United States, for example, poverty was statistically most prevalent in the 1930s during the Great Depression, but records do not show any notable increase in terrorism during this period. The country *did* see an increase in certain kinds of violent crime in the form of bank robberies and Prohibition-related mob violence, but these acts were criminal in nature and not politically motivated. In other words, conditions of poverty do tend to bring increases in crime, but such conditions have not been linked to increased terrorist activity.

Collective Perception and Terrorism

The theory of "relative deprivation," meanwhile, posits that political violence such as terrorism arises when a group perceives a difference in the goods and conditions it has and the goods and conditions it feels it is due (Gurr 1970, 4–12).

This theory is related to those that focus on poverty as a driver of terrorism because both are rooted in personal emotional and psychological attitudes about one's material status. The model then shifts from the group's perception of grievance to the viability of taking political action, followed by the state's response to organized political activity by discontented citizens.

Scholars have also explored whether other distinct factors, such as weak or failing governments, provide substantial opportunities for terrorist organizations to carry out attacks and other destabilizing activities. Research by Bridget Coggins found that generally weak states are not more or less prone to suffer from international or domestic terrorist attacks unless they are in the middle of an armed conflict that spans their borders. However, she found that failing states experiencing fundamental political collapse do see more instances of both types of terrorism, irrespective of any cross-border conflict (Coggins 2015, 476–477).

Terrorism in Changing Systems

Moving beyond raw levels of economic or political underdevelopment, scholars have further addressed the structural factors associated with states in transition. Samuel Huntington critiqued prevalent theories of modernization that anticipated that economic and political development would be generally peaceful. Writing during the 1960s, Huntington noted how violence and instability plagued many governments despite modernization. He argued that this dynamic "was in large part the product of rapid social change and the rapid mobilization of new groups into politics coupled with the slow development of political institutions" (1968, 4). In other words, societies were enduring higher levels of dislocation and violence because the new political demands of emerging groups had yet to catch up to the old governmental arrangements. Unlike theories rooted in outright poverty or state failure, this model envisions instability during transition periods from one status to another.

Huntington's framework further outlines how the increasing pace of social and technological change due to globalization can affect the prevalence of terrorism. For instance, radical or fringe ideas can expand with dizzying speed as online communities coalesce now to a greater extent than ever before. The printing press was seen as one of the most monumental inventions in human history because of how it impacted identity. Mass production of the written word broke down geographic barriers and expanded the sense of community peoples from different backgrounds and circumstances gained through nationalism. Benedict Anderson argues that the rise of nationalist movements would not have taken place without this technology and its effect of creating "imagined communities" (Anderson 1991, 37–46).

In the digital age identity-formation is magnified through the creation of online communities and rapid advances in communications technology. Today a variety of subnational or transnational identities exist that have the potential to mobilize and potentially radicalize individuals. Notably, the terrorist who carried out a mass shooting of worshippers at two New Zealand mosques on March 15, 2019, livestreamed his attack on Facebook (Wakefield 2019). Five months later, a terrorist committed a similar attack in an El Paso Walmart while citing the New Zealand attack as an inspiration for the attacks. This attacker also posted a manifesto online prior to the attack (Embury-Dennis 2019).

Terrorism in Changing Cultures

The impact of structural factors can also be the product of broader indirect socioeconomic traits at the system level. Scholar Michael Mousseau argues that globalization heightens the clash between traditional clientalist practices and market civilization, producing social anarchy that can manifest as terrorism (Mousseau 2003, 6). Clientalist systems are based on personal trust within a limited and prescribed circle, where identity based on kinship and ethnicity is dominant. By contrast, market societies are contract-based; trust is based on the contract rather than any individual who is a party to it. In the market framework, institutions such as laws, property titles, and recognized capital all require impersonal trust to work effectively.

This assertion better explains the prevalence of terrorism in developed societies as much as underdeveloped ones, since economic development is not perfectly correlated with market civilization. For instance, a country such as Greece or Italy may be part of the market-based West but feature many traits associated with clientalist systems. Mousseau makes the argument that although Nazi Germany was thoroughly modern, it was very much clientalist in operation. Mousseau contended that ideologies based on leftism, fascism, nationalism, and religion all exemplify clientelism and are expressly antimarket. In his view, both al Qaeda's desire to establish a Muslim caliphate and attacks by antiglobalization rioters against corporate business offices and properties share deep antimarket viewpoints.

Networking with Other Terrorists or States

A final system-level problem entails the ability of some terrorist groups to forge connections with similar organizations. Although the state is nearly always more powerful than the terrorist group it combats, broader geopolitical circumstances can provide fertile ground for terrorist groups to enlist support from other groups or states sympathetic to the cause. Terrorist groups may be conducting attacks in pursuit of their localized outcome goals, but frequently such groups cooperate through contacts and global networks they have developed due to shared ideology or affinity.

During the Cold War, various leftwing and ethnonationalist groups such as the Provisional IRA, Japanese Red Army, and Basque ETA jointly trained at camps in southern Yemen (Sterling 1981). More recently, various Islamist-jihadist groups have linked in a transnational network to share expertise and resources (Acosta and Childs 2013, 52–62). This diffusion of expertise and tradecraft is aided by advances in travel and technology, further complicating the efforts of counterterrorist forces.

For instance, until the early 21st century suicide attacks were restricted to cases in the Middle East and a few exceptional ones by the Liberation Tigers of Tamil Elam (LTTE) in Sri Lanka. After the tactic spread through identified network ties, however, suicide attacks by Salafi-Jihadist groups appeared in sub-Saharan Africa via al Shabaab in 2007 and Boko Haram in 2011.

The state sponsorship of terrorism is another challenge at this systemic level of analysis. State governments sometimes use terrorism as a means of effecting policy against an adversary state while retaining a degree of plausible deniability. In these scenarios, the state benefits politically from supporting terrorist activities against opponent—while also denying any support because the assistance is provided secretly. Moreover, it is difficult to identify and thus prevent such forms of state assistance because terrorism tradecraft emphasizes covert means to successfully execute an attack. Governmental security services are adept at the practice of unconventional tradecraft and can thus provide valuable equipment, training, intelligence, and assistance in planning and carrying out attacks. In other circumstances, a bordering state may assist in terrorist activities by providing safe haven for terrorist groups operating next door.

Examples of state sponsorship of terrorism are numerous. The Libyan government under Moammar Qaddafi provided the Irish Republican Army with Semtex plastic explosives that enhanced the scope of their bombings against British targets in the late 1980s. There is also evidence of the Soviet Union and Cuba using diplomatic pouches to smuggle weapons to groups that they supported, such as the Palestinian Liberation Organization (Cline and Alexander 1984, 43–49).

Empirical research suggests that terrorist groups that have a state sponsor live longer than those that do not, as long they do not have a safe haven (Carter 2012, 146). This effect, however, was largely the product of the Cold War and did not significantly extend to the period after 1991. Carter's key finding was that terrorist groups who are more reliant on a foreign state for support are more susceptible to failure, whereas groups that are less dependent are more survivable. This is because a state that is using its support of a group as an instrument of its own policy may find it useful to halt or attach conditions to their continued support in order to influence the group's policies and actions. The state may very well "sell out" the terrorist group and its cause if it becomes advantageous to do so. Carter's study is focused on the duration of terrorist groups; it does not address how state sponsorship affects the lethality of those groups.

A Complex Phenomenon: The Limits of Prevention

Evidently looking for possible root causes of terrorism at the individual, organizational, and systemic levels demonstrates how varied these influences are and how broad they can be. Unfortunately, there is not a single all-encompassing explanation for why terrorism occurs—which would make a solution much easier to find. The following section discusses the capacities and limitations of national security policy responses to the threat of terrorism, as well as considerations of their political side effects.

Problems of Response

Once an established terrorist group has initiated an attack or a campaign, the state's political leadership and security forces are under immense internal and external pressure to react and counter it. These responses can entail a raft of problems at the organizational level, including coping with the duration of terrorist campaigns, maintaining popular support from citizens, and disciplining responses to avoid harming innocent people.

Terrorist actors reflect a wide range when it comes to their operational lifespan. Some groups expire soon after formation while others persist for decades. For instance, a West German group called *Kommando hau weg die Scheisse* ("Get Rid of the Excrement Command") launched its only attack in 1986 (setting fire to a Daimler-Benz facility) and then effectively ceased to be, while the Ku Klux Klan was founded in 1866 and has undergone various evolutions through to the present day (Schmid and Jongman 1988, 554).

Research studies have found that most groups edge toward the shorter end when it comes to longevity, with only 30% of terrorist groups surviving past their first year of existence (Young and Dugan 2014, 12). Despite such high attrition, however, the median lifespan of a group is approximately eight years (Cronin 2009, 212–213). Still, eight years can feel like an eternity to civilians under the constant threat of terrorist attack.

As a form of political conflict the timeline for ending terrorism is frequently drawn out and not immediate. The drawn-out nature of terrorist campaigns means that quick solutions are messy and unlikely to work, and the strategic interaction for responses shows how the extreme minority of terrorist actors manage to inconvenience the masses through enhanced security measures.

Moreover, groups can always change tactics and targets if security forces make progress in countering earlier methods. Thus terrorist groups can seek to outlast a government through attrition, seeking to wear down its citizens to the point that they become willing to concede or negotiate a more favorable outcome. A terrorist group devoted to its outcome goals may continue the pace of operations at the expense of its own security. On the other hand, a group looking to increase its survivability may follow process goals in a more deliberate and cautious fashion. The reduced number of attacks that usually accompanies the latter is a positive effect, but the population remains vulnerable to future attacks from the group.

The same dynamic regarding counterterrorism approaches applies to states as well as terrorist leaderships. In democratic systems the leaders of a government will be challenged by rival political figures and parties who will seek to critique their performance as part of election campaigns. Governments may respond to this pressure in ways that are politically expedient to fend off such challenges—as opposed to taking the most effective steps from a counterterrorism perspective. For instance, critics can charge a government that responds swiftly to attacks with disregarding civil liberties on the one hand, or they can charge a government that responds in a more measured fashion with being "soft" on terrorism. Seeking reelection for leaders or their parties over sound counterterrorism policy might seem irresponsible, but staying in office can be a powerful motivator for lawmakers.

However, rapid responses are often imprecise and can have outsized influences on later dynamics in the conflict. Terrorists do not abide by international norms when they specifically target civilians, for example, yet the state must abide by certain boundaries of conduct in order to maintain domestic and international standing. In fact, some terrorist strategies are specifically geared toward provoking harsh reactions by the state to mobilize supporters and recruit members (Kydd and Walter 2006, 69–72).

For terrorist groups that start as radicalized and unpopular fringe groups in society, these tactics can be effective in building a constituency beyond what they ordinarily would achieve. For some heterogenous states, ethnonationalism can tempt states to act broadly against ethnic or nationalist communities of the same identity rather than specific perpetrators drawn from that community. The conflict between the government of Turkey and the Kurdish Worker's Party (PKK) in southeast Turkey is a notable case. PKK operatives have waged a decades-long conflict against the government of Turkey to create an independent Kurdish nation. At one point a tenuous ceasefire in the conflict was shattered when PKK militants executed unarmed Turkish soldiers and five civilians in the May 1993 Bingöl massacre (Marcus 2007, 214). In late 1993, Kurdish PKK militants and Turkish Army forces clashed, resulting in the death of Turkey's regional military commander. In October 1993 the Turkish Army undertook reprisal attacks against Kurdish civilians during the Lice massacre, killing 30 and injuring over 100 while setting fire to much of the city (Ron 1995, 120).

The "Troubles" in Northern Ireland

Indiscriminate violence need not come from the state to have harmful effects on a burgeoning conflict. A case in point can be found in the 1969 riots in Northern Ireland. The spark for what came to be popularly known as "the Troubles" can be traced to the August marching season celebrated by many Protestants across Northern Ireland. In 1969 a broad Catholic civil rights movement formed with its own organized marches throughout the territory driven by calls for socioeconomic change. In the city of Derry, the local police force of the Royal Ulster Constabulary (RUC), backed by unionist Protestants who wished to remain a part of the United Kingdom, used forceful crowd control measures to break up what were deemed illegal marches by the authorities. The unrest led to rioting and spread to other parts of the territory including West Belfast where Catholics and Protestants engaged in combat. As part of the violence unionist Protestant mobs burned down flats in the Catholic Bombay Street neighborhood. The violence created such anarchy that the British Army was deployed to Northern Ireland during Operation Banner to try and maintain order between the factions, albeit at great cost in the succeeding decades of the Troubles. Over 20,000 British soldiers were deployed in the territory during the 1970s at the height of the operation.

A significant political outcome of these 1969 riots was the rise of the Provisional Irish Republican Army (IRA) faction to eclipse the Official IRA. Much of the rationale given for the increasing popularity of the Provisionals was to have a self-defense force for Catholic neighborhoods, since the Official IRA had failed to prevent the burning of Bombay Street. The Provisionals even took this development into their identity, indicated by the group's phoenix logo denoting it as "rising from the ashes." Despite the increased recruitment and clout of the Provisional IRA due to the self-defense rationale, the group soon engaged in insurgent actions against the British Army as well as terrorist actions against Northern Irish and British civilians during the Troubles. In both the Turkish and Northern Irish cases, violence was widespread as an intimidation or reprisal tactic served to embolden terrorist groups.

Conversely, heavy-handed or excessive displays of force by the state can engender antigovernment sentiment. Federal U.S. law enforcement actions at Ruby Ridge, Idaho, and Waco, Texas, in the 1990s dramatically bolstered antigovernment sentiment among members of the political far right.

The Siege of Waco

The 1993 Waco siege began after agents from the Bureau of Alcohol, Tobacco, and Firearms (ATF) attempted to raid the Branch Davidian compound for possession of illegal weapons. The Branch Davidians at Waco were an offshoot of Seventh Day Adventism whose leader David Koresh considered himself the final prophet and sought to prepare his followers for the apocalypse. Members of the cult had been tipped off to the raid and repulsed the agency in a gun battle that left four agents and five cult members dead and scores more wounded. The gun battle marked the beginning of a 51-day siege at the compound by the Federal Bureau of Investigation (FBI), who took over operations in Waco in the wake of the ATF raid.

However, the militarized law enforcement actions before and during the siege, which included using National Guard helicopter overflights and armored vehicles to surveil the compound, reinforced the apocalyptic beliefs held by the cult members. When the siege ended cult members set fires to the compound, killing 76 members.

One consequence of this tragedy was an increased interest in the field of forensic theology, in which religious studies scholars help law enforcement understand and respond to the religious beliefs that drive some individuals or groups to carry out criminal or terrorist acts (Grey 2004, 44–46).

Terrorist Timothy McVeigh later cited the events in Waco as the motivation for his role in bombing the federal building in Oklahoma City, the deadliest case of domestic terrorism in the United States. The Oklahoma City bombing was intentionally timed to coincide with the second anniversary of the end of the Waco siege (Linder, n.d.).

The September 11 Attacks

When foreign-born terrorists carried out the September 11, 2001, attacks organized by Osama bin Laden, the U.S. government made it clear that al Qaeda and its radical affiliates were the enemy—not Muslims, most of whom were horrified by the attack. President George W. Bush noted that Muslims in the United States were victimized by the attacks just as much as any other Americans. He also emphasized that "The face of terror is not the true faith of Islam" (Bush 2001). Nonetheless, American law enforcement reported an increase in attacks on innocent American citizens of Middle Eastern and South Asian descent in the aftermath of the 9/11 attacks, but the statement by the president sent a signal at the national level that such criminal actions were wrong and would not be tolerated. Following the attacks law enforcement officials made concerted efforts to work with religious leaders in American Muslim communities to identify potential domestic security threats in their congregations (Schanzer et al. 2016, 6–7).

Responding to Terrorism

Terrorism presents government and security officials with many quandaries about the appropriate response to the killing and intimidation of innocents. The leading controversies pertain to the motivation for terrorism, its efficacy as a political tactic, the best and most appropriate counterterrorism security measures, debates about whether democracies are more or less vulnerable to domestic terrorism, and balancing the constitutional rights of news organizations and American citizens with the mandate to protect America from threats.

Why Do They Do It? Strategy Versus Psychology
Terrorists as Strategically Motivated

A fundamental debate with respect to terrorism is the primary motivations of terrorists. Most economists and many political scientists adopt a rational choice approach to the study of terrorism by analyzing the relative costs, risks, and benefits that groups or states perceive with different strategies. Morality aside, these models presume terrorists will act in ways that maximize their aims to secure their political objectives.

Alternatively, psychologists assert that the primary driver is not strategic or even due to the aims of the ideology, but rather a psychological conflict at the individual level that is seeking a group-based outlet (Borum 2004).

Scholar Martha Crenshaw argues that terrorism generally follows a logic and is a strategic choice by groups seeking to advance their political aims. For her, terrorism is an example of strategic bargaining, with each development serving as a scoring "round" in a series of games between the state and the group (Crenshaw 1998, 22). Her perspective does not see terrorists as irrational individuals who blindly and randomly commit violence. Scholars holding this view further argue that terrorist groups follow five major logics or strategies: attrition, intimidation, provocation, spoiling, and/or outbidding (Kydd and Walter 2006, 59–89). Advocates of this view believe governments should focus on figuring out what strategy a terrorist group is pursuing and then act accordingly to counter it.

In the case of *attrition,* the group seeks to wear down the government and population until they capitulate. It is a classic blackmail dynamic. By contrast, an *intimidation* strategy is one in which terrorists use the threat of violence as a form of psychological warfare. *Provocation* strategies seek to goad the state into overreacting on an issue, turning the tables of public perception against the government. For example, if a governmental response to terrorist activity is widely seen by the population as unduly harsh or unfairly indiscriminate, popular support for the government could decrease—precisely what the terrorist group wants.

The last two strategies pertain to the constituencies a terrorist group claims to represent. The first of these are strategies of *spoiling*; these strategies apply to cases where the terrorist group has competitors on its own side who are seeking a separate settlement or accommodation with the government. In this case terrorist strikes are designed to sink such agreements from coming to fruition, usually because the group carrying out the attacks opposes the terms of any possible agreement. Finally, *outbidding* strategies are meant to prove a group's devotion to a cause and rally supporters. In this context it refers to the efforts of terrorist groups to carry out attacks and other activities to outmaneuver political moderates and attract the attention and admiration of potential recruits.

Terrorists as Psychologically Motivated

Unlike most political scientists who ascribe rational choice assumptions to terrorists, scholar Jerrold Post argues that models based on strategic motivations of terrorism have the direction of causality wrong. In his view, terrorists do not engage in their behavior as an instrument to seek political goals, but rather adopt political goals as a justification for engaging in violence that they find desirable. In his words: "Individuals are drawn to the path of terrorism in order to commit acts of violence," and this participation is due to psychological forces associated with an identity crisis (1998, 25). For Post, most terrorists either act out of hostility to or loyalty toward their parents.

Post argues that people from abusive families are more likely to join terrorist groups out of a hatred for their parents—a hatred displaced to the state as a larger authority figure. But Post asserted that love and loyalty for one's parents can also radicalize people, if they believe that their parents have been persecuted or mistreated by the government. As Post summarizes, "for some, becoming terrorists is an act of retaliation for real and imagined hurts against the society of their parents; for others, it is an act of retaliation against society for the hurt done to their parents" (1984, 243). He further elaborates that attacks are not strategically timed due to external considerations as asserted by Crenshaw, but rather are internally motivated as a release of tension within a group meant to justify its existence (1998, 36).

For Post, terrorist leaders who fail to act while a group goes underground quickly lose the support of their adherents, and so they need to execute attacks to remain viable. In other words, attacks are strictly meant for the process goal of survival and have little to no bearing on outcome goals, which are irrelevant. Consequently, Post does not expect terrorist groups to readily enter negotiations but rather to frequently try and spoil any negotiations that do take place. This is because solving the political issue would remove their reason for existence as a group, and the group is what the members see as their defined identity. Removing the stated cause as an issue then eliminates the leading psychological means by which the terrorists in the group attempt to manage their own identity issues.

Does Terrorism Actually Work?

Does terrorism actually pay for groups that carry out such acts? Many scholars have studied this issue over the years. Scholars Andrew Kydd and Barbara Walter argue that terrorist tactics such as bombings, hijackings, and kidnappings "can be surprisingly effective in achieving a terrorist group's political aims" (2006, 49).

Of course, some terrorist groups are more dangerous than others. Most terrorist groups do not succeed in achieving their political goals. Even if groups do not achieve their full outcome goals, however, engaging in well-executed and deadly acts of terrorism is seen as a way to at least *advance* those stated goals. For instance, a group seeking independence for a territory from the nation state may not achieve independence, but it could eventually obtain a greater level of autonomy and greater self-governance. Accordingly, scholars who subscribe to this theory believe political actors with limited influence have greater incentive to engage in the behavior to better their political situation with violence since they do not gain much traction within the political system.

Not all scholars agree with this analysis. Max Abrahms critiques such scholarship with his own research design that differentiates between terrorist campaigns and guerilla campaigns when looking to the success that a group achieves. His data analysis notes that out of 125 total campaigns by terrorist and/

or insurgency groups, only 38 obtained at least partial concessions related to their issue (Abrahms 2012, 374). Recall that terrorist cases are where the targets are civilian whereas guerilla cases connote insurgency with the targets being the security forces of the state such as military or national police. After distinguishing between the two, he notes that 36 of those 38 campaign successes went to groups engaged in guerilla campaigns. Thus, the lion's share of the successes had to do with target selection (Abrahms 2012, 374–375).

Abrahms suggests that terrorist campaigns tend to lead to the political right gaining power in targeted countries since they advocate for more forceful response to terrorism than leftist parties that comparatively tend to favor concessions (381). Additionally, he argues that the bargaining dynamic that figures so prominently in the strategic perspective does not hold with respect to civilian populations. Populations do not pressure their governments to engage in dialogue with terrorist groups in light of the heinous violence against civilians. This is because bargaining requires a degree of trust, and terrorist actions are seen as so extreme and outside the milieu of what is acceptable that populations opt for harsh responses rather than political engagement.

If, as scholars like Brian Jenkins argue, terrorism is theater, then communication is critical; and although attacks generate media exposure about the violence, that coverage does not usually translate into increased public support for their cause. Usually, the reverse is true.

Terrorism by Suicide Attack

A related controversy in terrorism studies is the motivation of a specific subset of terrorism pertaining to suicide attacks. Robert Pape adopts a strategic perspective in arguing that such cases of terrorism have had some success in ejecting occupying forces from foreign countries (Pape 2005, 23).

One frequently cited example in this regard concerns an October 1983 suicide attack sponsored by Iran that killed 307

U.S. Marines and French paratroopers in Beirut, Lebanon, where they had been deployed as part of an international peacekeeping force. In the aftermath of the attack in Beirut, all peacekeeping forces were removed from the country.

Assaf Moghadam critiques Pape's methodology, noting that it does not distinguish between targets that are security forces versus those that are noncombatants. He thus argues that Pape's findings are not a true reflection of suicide *terrorism* (Moghadam 2006, 710–712). If looking only to the latter cases that fit most definitions of terrorism, then Pape's findings no longer hold. Moghadam further identifies how Pape's methodology does not use attacks but rather aggregated campaigns and also counts all attacks related to a city in a day as a single attack, even if they featured multiple bombers striking in a coordinated fashion. Taking stock of additional suicide attack data, Moghadam advances an explanation for why groups adopt suicide attack tactics: the globalization of martyrdom due to the shared religious ideology of Salafi-Jihadists, who are the most frequent practitioners of the tactic (720–723). Additional analysis of comprehensive suicide attack data bolsters Moghadam's claim that the targets of most suicide attacks are overwhelmingly domestic, not directed against foreign occupiers, and are predominantly conducted by Islamist groups against Muslim targets (Acosta 2016, 182).

How Severe of a Threat Is Terrorism?

The motivations and effectiveness of terrorism are important factors, but there is additional controversy as to the extent to which terrorism poses a threat to a population and/or government. Many policymakers and scholars contend that terrorism is a significant menace that demands a strong response. According to scholar Audrey Cronin, "In the twenty-first century, terrorism has become a threat to the fabric of the Western liberal state, thanks to its lethality and an unprecedented access to powerful weapons, its strong transnational character, its perceived legitimacy (and in some quarters), its connection to other types of violence, and its potential to compel states to undermine themselves through their responses" (Cronin 2009, 6). Cronin asserts that effective exploitation of terrorism chips away at the legitimacy of the nation-state system, and that social and technological changes are increasing the lethality of terrorist acts.

Others are not convinced that terrorism is consequential or a high-priority threat for developed states in the West, and thus advocate for minimalist policy responses. Analysts in this school statistically look at terrorism compared to public health menaces or natural disasters. These critics charge that on balance the ratio of failed or foiled plots vastly exceeds those that are successful, and they assert that homeland security efforts and expenditures vastly outweigh the actual risk posed by terrorism (Mueller and Stewart 2012, 84–87). By their count, in the decade since September 11, 2001, Islamist extremists successfully carried out only seven of 50 attempted attacks in the United States, but most of these successful attacks were minimal in the damage they inflicted due to limited aims or capabilities.

In particular, Mueller and Stewart's calculations suggest that there would need to be at least 333 attacks in a year to justify the $75 billion in security spending in the two decades after the September 11 attacks (106–107). Critics of their work contend that such a cost–benefit approach fails to include all relevant factors since it is not a truly experimental design, particularly in accounting for the impact of counterterrorism policy responses. One scholar argues that the reduction in successful attacks by Islamist militants such as al Qaeda after 9/11 had a great deal to do with offensive actions taken against its leadership and sanctuaries (Nordan 2010, 6). No one can truly know how many potential terrorist attacks were thwarted by these efforts. As one Israeli scholar put it: "Fighting terror is like fighting car accidents: one can count the casualties but not those whose lives were spared by prevention" (Luft 2003, 3).

Can Deterrence Strategies End Terrorism?

Deterrence is a long-studied phenomenon in literature on strategic coercion, and so it is studied in many contexts besides terrorism, including warfare and nuclear weapon policymaking. It is a concept where an actor considering a given action weighs the anticipated costs of that action and decides against acting if the cost of taking the action will be too high. The concept is of great interest to counterterrorism practitioners who seek to deter terrorist groups from striking. Nonetheless, the applicability of deterrence to terrorist cases is heavily debated and ties directly into how rational or strategic terrorists are.

For deterrence to work the actor must be assumed to be rational; that is to say that it must be capable of understanding the punishing response it will receive after an attack. Deterrence requires that terrorist groups (1) have something of value that can be threatened (such as political power, life, or freedom from imprisonment), (2) truly understand the threat to it, and (3) find the state's threats of retaliation to be credible.

Deterrence is a more effective counterterrorism strategy for some terrorist groups than others. Religiously motivated terrorists may not value their lives on earth as much as the spiritual gains they believe they will harvest from carrying out violent acts against their faith's perceived enemies. In such cases, much of the leverage associated with deterrence may not hold.

Even those with more secular aims may not find the state's threats concerning and might be willing to bear the punishments, particularly in light of their perceived injustice that justifies terrorism in their eyes. Put simply, a group's leadership must psychologically feel fear for deterrence to work, but the very act of engaging in terrorism can imply a sense of fearlessness of the consequences given the risks.

Finally, for deterrence to work a group must hold something that is dearly valued. Some groups, however, have such rigid and radical ideologies that they press on regardless of the likelihood of eventual reprisals. Part of the justification for the offensive nature of President George W. Bush's Global War on

Terrorism after 9/11 was that terrorist groups like al Qaeda, unlike past state adversaries like the Soviet Union, could not be deterred with threats of death since they were willing to commit suicide as part of their attacks to inflict mass carnage (Broad, Engelberg, and Glanz 2001, A1). Additionally, as a non-state actor, they may have safe havens but lack formal territory and governance over it. Put another way, they do not stand to lose control since they do not have it in the first place.

Despite these concerns, scholars Paul Davis and Brian Michael Jenkins argue that the logic of deterrence can at least partially work in even these difficult cases. While not using the word *deterrence*, they assert that terrorist actors can be influenced by the broader ecosystem that sustains them. This includes suppliers, recruiters, quarters of a respective population, and sources of religious and moral support (Davis and Jenkins 2002, 15). These enabling elements are part of the terrorists' support network, but individually they are often not as dedicated or committed to the cause as the actual terrorist practitioners. This makes them vulnerable to influence or coercion in order to halt whatever support they are providing.

Terrorism and Rational Choice

Scholars using rational choice models to assess deterrence in terrorism cases advance interesting and counterintuitive policy recommendations. Swiss economists Bruno Frey and Simon Luechinger take such a rational choice view. Assuming that terrorists are rational actors, they map the relative benefits and costs that a group faces as supply and demand curves. The cost side entails the planning and risk required to conduct attacks, and the benefits curve for a terrorist group relies on media coverage, destabilizing the political system, and disrupting the economy (Frey and Luechinger 2004, 511). According to their logic these actions increase the benefits to a group and will make a government more likely to settle a political issue in favor of that group, whether that entails giving greater political participation or redistributed rents. Just as how the forces of increasing supply and reducing demand drives prices down, conceptually "raising the price" of terrorism should yield less of it when the costs increase and the benefits are reduced.

Moreover, the benefits for terrorists are assumed to decline with successive attacks because the attacks have less of an effect on the targeted population. After mapping out the influence of the factors that affect these two dimensions, Frey and Luechinger (2004) arrive at a theoretical equilibrium point for the intensity of terrorism at a given time. Based on this theory the policy options for counterterrorists revolve around increasing the costs to terrorist actors, which is deterrence, or by reducing the benefits that terrorists obtain from their actions. According to these economists, the conundrum is that a deterrent approach by counterterrorists rooted in punishment often serves to simultaneously increase the benefits of terrorism rather than reduce them. This is because responses to terrorism typically encourage the centralization of governmental power and spending in the form of the military-industrial complex, the hardening of capital cities, and more media exposure for the attacks that are carried out. Paradoxically, this centralization raises the benefits to terrorists for successfully attacking them in addition to increasing the costs.

On net Frey and Luechinger assert that governments may encounter more terrorism because of their counterterrorism policies. They contend that the solution is to decentralize government such as with federalism, as well as encourage freer markets. Both approaches should serve to reduce the centralization in the society and thus make hitting any individual target less of a reward as opposed to a single high-profile target in a capital city. They also advocate exploring options that reward terrorists who renounce violence with reduced sentences and money to split them off from the rest of the group, whereas deterrence may force groups to bind closer together in the face of the hardships. The authors admit that the largest obstacles to this approach are that fanatics may be immune to cost–benefit calculations, and that offering inducements may actually encourage terrorism by causing political groups to adopt terrorist attacks and quickly stop once concessions had been obtained. Empirical analysis of this theory noted that its predictions were not born out politically, but there was evidence that greater financial decentralization by local governments corresponded with fewer instances of terrorism (Dreher and Fischer 2010, 990–992).

Are Democracies More Vulnerable?

A related controversy over terrorism is the degree to which political regime type matters. For Frey and Luechinger, decentralization makes a society more immune to terrorism. Even though not all democracies are decentralized, power is more distributed than in autocratic systems such as dictatorships or regimes controlled by a single party. Scholars of terrorism have long been interested in the differences that regime types might have on the likelihood or severity of terrorism. Earlier scholarship supposed that democracies were more vulnerable to terrorism because democracies' commitment to civil liberties limited their use of force (Crenshaw 1983, 18).

For Crenshaw, terrorists are rational actors who understand that democracies are limited in how violent they can be in their responses, and so groups consciously target them. Robert Pape came to the same conclusion about the exposure of democracies to suicide terrorism because "democracies are often thought to be especially vulnerable to coercive punishment" (Pape 2005, 44–45). That is to say that democracies not only are presumed to be more constrained in their reprisals against terrorists but also less able to sustain punishment from terrorist attacks. Autocracies are not thought to be swayed by mounting casualties against their citizens and so are presumed to make less desirable targets. Later scholarship has cast doubt on these assertions regarding democracies' susceptibility to terrorism.

Max Abrahms reviewed data concerning both domestic and foreign terrorist attacks and compared the regime type of the target for each attack. His analysis found that autocratic countries have about the same number of terrorists incidents as partial and fully free regimes combined (Abrahms 2007, 232). Moreover, the distribution of fatalities by regime type was even more skewed toward autocracies with the combined casualties from partially and fully free regimes amounting to approximately half the number of fatalities incurred by autocracies. Moreover, his analysis indicates that autocratic countries overall are more likely to adjust policy when faced with terrorism than democracies. This is because rather than give in to terrorist blackmail, the populations of politically free countries are motivated to fight terrorists as enemies of their liberal systems and the value they place on civil liberties.

There are analogues in international relations research, where scholars of the democratic peace theory noted that democracies tend not to fight one another but fight against illiberal regimes with great regularity and intensity (Bueno de Mesquita et al. 1999, 792–793). Abrahms also contends that civil liberties are not a weakness for counterterrorists but actually a strength that prevents indiscriminate reprisals. These are important because terrorist campaigns can last years, and it is essential to enlist the help of moderates from within the terrorists' broad community to alienate the extremists rather than alienate moderates and bolster the support for terrorists.

Returning to Mueller and Stewart's argument that security responses to terrorism are disproportionate to the actual threat it poses, Abrahms treats this as evidence that free political regimes want to defeat terrorist actors so passionately that they are willing to bear such costs and burdens (Abrahms 2007, 247). Put another way, democracies are thought to go to greater measures to destroy terrorist opponents precisely because those opponents reflect the most illiberal traits of using violence against innocents despite having the means to petition their grievances in the free political system.

More recent statistical analysis portrays a more complicated set of findings. Researchers identified an inverted-U shaped relationship between the political freedom of a country and the number of terrorist incidents in it. Most research methods are oriented toward assessing linear relationships with either increases or decreases; however, researchers identified that full autocracies and full democracies saw fewer attacks but that countries in the transitional zone between the two were the most vulnerable. This nonlinear relationship sees anocratic regimes, or those that have some traits of both autocratic and democratic regimes, as having the highest number of terrorist attacks (Gaibulloev, Piazza, and Sandler 2017, 511). This finding for terrorism tracks with previous scholarship that found the same inverted U to apply to cases of civil war and suggests that unconsolidated regimes are at the greatest risk of political violence.

How Should the Media Behave?

Thus far the review of controversies had touched on what motivates groups, if they can be deterred, and how vulnerable regime types are. That is to say that organizational and institutional factors are addressed that consider the supply side of the phenomenon. Still, terrorist aims hinge upon communicating their message through their violent acts, and the media is a critical player despite not possessing any elements of force the way terrorists and states do. Controversies over media ethics and the effects that coverage has on terrorist dynamics are an important element for the demand side of the equation.

Journalists have it as their professional task to share the news, and some even see their profession as a public service. Terrorist attacks are certainly newsworthy. Concerns arise over the degree that coverage is sensationalistic as opposed to reporting the facts of an event. The old adage that "if it bleeds, it leads" means that politically motivated violence such as bombings, assassinations, and kidnappings all generate headlines and enjoy widespread coverage. Moreover, as one scholar argues, "Journalists amplify, arbitrate, and create their own rhetoric about terrorist acts" (Picard 1989, 5). That is to say that the way that journalists report on terrorist events influences the message received by an audience. With amplification the media's reporting gives a voice to the terrorist perpetrators, and it is controversial because of concerns that amplifying the terrorists' message rewards the violent medium as an effective means of communication.

For instance, certain terrorist actors make a point of video-taping their kidnaping or hostage victims to elicit emotional reactions in hopes of obtaining the ransom payment that they demand. Should media organizations air these videos (Sambrook 2006, 167–168)? For governments these videos complicate their counterterrorism efforts by generating domestic political pressure to act swiftly, and they also give terrorists a platform that they desire. Conversely, such content is part of the news story. In other circumstances, members of the media can easily be swayed to parrot either the terrorist position or that of the government in their coverage. Many organizations have internal guidelines that aim to avoid being used to further aims of the subjects that they report on; however, controversies still abound.

How Does the Media Behave?

One example of controversy is self-censorship or censorship for security reasons versus honoring the principle of free information in news reporting. Israeli researchers noted that during the 2006 war with the militant group Hezbollah in Lebanon, reporters adopted the goals of the state and self-censored as a form of protecting national security (Elbaz and Bar-Tal 2019, 7). Research suggests that al Qaeda attacks follow a pattern of reporting in major U.S. media outlets, with each additional minute of coverage on a 30-minute news program statistically corresponding to an additional attack in the subsequent week. Interestingly, the results noted that low coverage saw an actual decline in future attacks rather than a simple postponement of those attacks (Jetter 2017, 20).

Journalistic practices related to terrorism vary, with some outlets changing their policy to intentionally not publish the names and photos of terrorists to prevent their idolization by acolytes or copycats. In other circumstances, governments institute partial censorship to specifically prohibit the media from broadcasting messages from terrorist group leaders or their associated political representatives. This was the case in the United Kingdom starting in November 1988 when Prime Minister Margaret Thatcher sought to deny the Irish Republican Army "the oxygen of publicity" as part of its terrorist campaign against the United Kingdom over Northern Ireland (Frankel 1990). If a leader of the IRA or its political wing Sinn Fein issued any statements, the British press had to make provisions to have voice actors "revoice" those statements or simply avoid reporting on them altogether. These specific bans ended after the Good Friday Accords were signed by the two sides in the conflict; however, the controversies apply well beyond. Less than a month after the July 7, 2005, terrorist attack by al Qaeda against British transportation targets in London, the British Broadcasting Corporation's *Newsnight* program featured an interview of two Salafi-Jihadists who argued that they supported the terrorist attacks and found them to be justified, and that they would not work with authorities to foil a terrorist plot if they knew of one. Section 19 of the UK's Terrorism Act of 2000 allows authorities to obtain information from journalists regarding terrorist actors, and the law was used to demand materials related to the interview after the show aired. The editors refused to give the authorities the materials sought, arguing that the interview did not provide material support or information about planned attacks. The episode highlighted the free speech clash between authorities seeking to limit the reach of those who support terrorists versus the press arguing that their journalism was necessary to understand the thinking of some British Islamists (Sambrook 2006, 172).

The case of the jumpers from the September 11 attack is also telling about the conflict between free speech and the ethics of reporting. Major media organizations purposefully did not air footage of the individuals trapped at the top of the World

Trade Center buildings who decided to end their lives by jumping to escape a death by fire. In some instances, journalists on the ground intentionally did not shoot that footage on camera, such as one French cameraman who refused to capture flaming victims on 9/11 because "no human being needs to see this" (Mogensen 2008, 39). In other contexts besides 9/11, the controversy over showing the effects of terrorism is significant. Take for instance debates about including the grisly injuries and human remains of victims. It is common for media to not show these images out of sensitivity to the families of victims. Salafi-Jihadist groups in particular regularly use execution videos, such as with murdered *Wall Street Journal* reporter Daniel Pearl whose 2002 beheading was videotaped and distributed by his al Qaeda murderers.

Conversely, others voice concerns that withholding such imagery serves to sanitize the violence to the benefit of terrorists, preventing viewers from seeing the full impact of terrorist actions. In May 2002 CBS News reporter Dan Rather aired a 30-second excerpt from the Daniel Pearl video against the protestations of Pearl's widow, justifying the decision based on the need to understand the propaganda war (Collins 2002). Others contend that showing especially graphic or horrifying imagery can create a violent response by viewers against those seen to be associated with attackers. Additionally, ethical concerns arise over how to cover developments related to a story. Both al Qaeda and the Islamic State regularly made use of recruitment videos and periodicals to glorify their cause of jihad against Western targets. Yet the release of these videos falls under part of the story of the coverage.

Journalists are in the unique position to arbitrate the language surrounding attacks. Government officials seek to stigmatize terrorists for their actions and so use terminology to that effect in their press releases. Journalists aiming to remain neutral are put in a position to either amplify this perspective or to describe events using more dispassionate terms. Journalists are frequently not experts in news that they cover, and without access to security officials who are busy coordinating the response to attacks they often rely on former officials who have their own biases. Moreover, journalists have an incentive to not ruffle the feathers of governmental officials to cut off that supply of sourcing in the immediate aftermath of an attack because information is initially scarce, and audiences are in search of answers (Elbaz and Bar-Tal 2019, 8).

Finally, journalists can create rhetoric based on the medium used, and short segments often do not offer context surrounding the issues. Members of the media are often able to establish a narrative surrounding events; however, key figures can be misunderstood or misrepresented in order to fit a narrative that proves more sensationalist than the facts may warrant. The crux of controversy is that media is a business that is usually aided by sensationalism through increased ratings, but abiding by the norms of journalistic integrity can produce an impartial but comparatively blander treatment of dramatic but grisly content (White 2020, 22). Additionally, the news media is a competitive industry with reporters in a race to be the first to break a story. In this environment the incentive is to run with available facts early despite the real possibility of errors as information is still coming in.

New Media and Terrorism

The spread of social media has also raised issues due to its effects on reporting of terrorist attacks. Because nearly everyone has a smartphone with video cameras, eyewitnesses to events are able to capture footage and upload viral videos for broad viewership. Legacy media institutions are essentially cut out of this loop and frequently play catch-up to obtain such footage. The implications are that established ethical norms internal to mass media institutions are less applicable due to the "democratization" of reporting through various means of social media (White 2020, 20).

A new controversy about social media and terrorism pertains to censorship. Traditional media sources like print media

and television have long been part of the debate over censorship and how it clashes with free speech provisions, but unlike
traditional media various social media platforms are used not
only to share or report news but also as a vehicle for groups
to organize. In the immediate aftermath of the January 6 riot
at the U.S. Capitol in Washington, D.C., many tech companies broadly banned or censored conservative sub-channels
and platforms, with the best example being the Parler social
media site. The justification for the bans was that organizers
were using or would use the platforms to plot violent attacks.

The censorship actions are controversial on two counts.
First, there are debates as to whether the blanket removal or
limitations of groups based on general political identity is an
effective means of curtailing violence since most users on these
sites and platforms were not connected to the events of January 6. Most of those present at the U.S. Capitol on January 6
had organized using Facebook, and there is evidence that Parler submitted information that it monitored on the site to the
FBI before January 6 (Banares 2021). Counterterrorism efforts
broadly applied against a population can have negative consequences; for instance, banned users suspect that the punitive
measures were taken against them for their political beliefs.
There is worry that such measures might drive individuals
toward radicalization by affirming the arguments of repression
made by extremists.

Second, banning entire platforms can have tactical implications for counterterrorists by forcing users who do have ill
intent to seek alternative platforms, which reduces their ability to coordinate in great numbers but makes it more difficult
for law enforcement to monitor those channels for signs of
planned activity. It may well be that smaller cells of extremists using new platforms that law enforcement are less familiar with would be more likely to plan and initiate a successful
terrorist attack than activity planned on larger platforms that
stand a better chance of being foiled due to more effective and
established monitoring. This clash between centralization and

decentralization and its effects on survivability versus capability are wide and apply to several other contexts beyond terrorism.

Civil Liberties and International Terrorism

One of the most controversial aspects of dealing with terrorism concerns the clash between security and civil liberties. Liberal democracies value the freedoms enjoyed by citizens regarding their speech, right to assemble, and privacy. A notable example from the United States is the Uniting and Strengthening America by Providing Appropriate Tools Required to Intercept and Obstruct Terrorism (USA PATRIOT) Act passed by Congress in 2001 just 45 days after the 9/11 attacks. The legislation's intent was to empower security officials with the means to better tackle foreign terrorist actors operating domestically in the United States along with domestic conspirators. Proponents of the law argued that the measures were necessary to protect Americans from terrorist actions and better match the law with the technologies and tradecraft used by terrorists.

Among the many elements of the law were the authorization of warrants that applied to multiple districts rather than officials requiring warrants be obtained for each individual district tied to terrorism-related activities. Similarly, the law also allowed for "roving" wiretaps where warrants could be obtained for a subject of surveillance that covered all their devices rather than the legal standard of basing them on precise platforms such as a specific phone line. These changes in law were justified as necessary to combat terrorists who made use of regular travel and switching of devices as part of their procedures (U.S. Department of Justice, n.d.).

The law also allowed for delayed-notice search warrants in what some term "sneak-and-peek" warrants. These warrants allow authorities to begin surveillance on a subject's property or effects without informing them until a later time, and these provisions were included to prevent a terrorist suspect under surveillance from being tipped off. The logic is similar to law enforcement officials who argue for "no-knock" warrants because notifying the subject might cause them to destroy evidence or put arresting officers' lives in danger. Citing the national security nature of terrorism, the law made use of the infrastructure of the existing Foreign Intelligence Surveillance Act of 1978 (FISA). That law created the Foreign Intelligence Surveillance Court (FISC), which is drawn from 11 judges from across the federal judiciary's 94 districts. Nonetheless, at the time of publication the current composition of the FISC has all 11 judges drawn from districts that are east of the Mississippi River (U.S. Foreign Intelligence Surveillance Court, n.d.).

True to its name, the intent behind the creation of the court was to have a legal structure in place to authorize the surveillance of foreign intelligence agents operating in the United States. At the time the law was passed the main threats were from communist spies operating in the United States, and surveillance was authorized by warrants signed by FISC judges. The proceedings in the FISC are kept secret from the public due to the need to protect the sources and methods used to identify and surveil the spies. Disclosing these methods to the public in court proceedings would compromise such important avenues of information by allowing spies to adopt countermeasures.

The Patriot Act broadened FISA law to include authorizing surveillance of individuals not tied to foreign governments, such as terrorists. The primary controversy is that the FISA process originally focused on the subject of surveillance as an agent of a foreign power, with this being the "primary" purpose for the government to seek surveillance. However, the revisions in the Patriot Act downgraded the government's standard to "significant" purpose, enabling the government considerable latitude in defining when to use its powers. Moreover, the rate of rejection for FISA warrant applications is exceedingly small, leading some to charge the courts with exercising weak oversight. Between 2002 and 2017 the overall rejection rate for all presented FISA warrants was 0.31% (Electronic Privacy Information Center 2021).

Yet another controversial aspect of the law was that pertaining to National Security Letters (NSLs). These letters are issued by the FBI to demand records about an individual under investigation from persons, companies, and public agencies. They are also accompanied by a gag order that prevents whoever receives the letter from telling anyone about it for national security reasons. Those who do not comply or inform others, even close family, are threatened with criminal prosecution under the law. Moreover, the letters for records are issued by those at the rank of Special Agent in Charge, a rank held by the leader of each of the FBI's 56 different field offices. Moreover, they are not subject to any authorization from judges the way that a warrant is. Finally, the records collected from NSLs are stored by the FBI, subject to database searches, and available to U.S. prosecutors. One government report noted that there is no way to tell whether information collected under the auspices of counterterrorism is then used in criminal cases unrelated to terrorism (U.S. Department of Justice 2016, 123).

Critics contend that the measures are intrusive and violate Americans' Fourth Amendment rights, and that the legal justifications for counterterrorism are not matched by the overwhelming use for securing non-terrorism criminal convictions (American Civil Liberties Union 2023). Critics cite data showing that between October 2009 and September 2013 the number of sneak and peak warrants grew by a factor of 2.8, and that only 0.56% of the total 31,541 warrants during this period were used for terrorism cases (Tien 2014). The bulk of the warrants were used in narcotics investigations. Additionally, legal challenges to NSLs in the courts have deemed parts of them unconstitutional in not providing a means for the NSL recipients to contest the orders.

Civil Liberties and Domestic Terrorism

The most recent controversy pertains to domestic terrorism legislation in the United States. In August 2019, Democratic party lawmakers introduced the Confronting the Threat of Domestic

Terrorism Act. Thirteen days after the January 6, 2021, riot at
the U.S. Capitol, legislators introduced House Resolution 350,
the Domestic Terrorism Prevention Act (DTPA). The first bill
would have created a specific criminal statute in U.S. federal
law for domestic terrorism, whereas the more recent legislation
would create dedicated offices in the Department of Homeland Security, Department of Justice, and the Federal Bureau of
Investigation to monitor, investigate, and prosecute domestic
terrorism. The bill also calls for the creation of an interagency
fusion center focused on domestic terrorism along with federal
training for state and local law enforcement officials.

Proponents of the legislation argue that extremists are a new
and rising threat, and that the U.S. government needs tools
and channels to counter it. Advocates also contend that since
there is no U.S. federal law against domestic terrorism, it is
necessary to stigmatize political extremists and proactively prevent them from conducting attacks. Many cite the events of
January 6, 2021, at the U.S. Capitol as demanding a stronger
response to political violence from domestic actors, and charge
that domestic cases receive less attention than efforts to thwart
foreign terrorist organizations and plots. Moreover, proponents
argue that the passage of the Patriot Act in 2001 to deal with
the threat of foreign terrorism serves as a successful model for
dealing with the threat.

Critics of these legislative attempts contend that current hate
crime and homicide laws are adequate to deal with extremists
and that the optimal means to handle such cases is through
criminal law. Despite the lack of a specific domestic terrorism
statute, the Oklahoma City bomber Timothy McVeigh was
charged with eight counts of homicide against federal agents
along with three other charges related to using a weapon of
mass destruction, and he was sentenced to death after conviction for those crimes.

Researcher Brian Michael Jenkins cautions against the adoption of domestic terrorism legislation on pragmatic grounds
(Jenkins 2021a). He assesses that existing law is sufficient to

deal with the issue, contends the terminology is imprecise, and argues that politically it might create more violence than it would prevent. Citing the case of January 6, Jenkins notes that 90% of those arrested for their participation on January 6 were not members of known extremist groups. Drawing comparisons between domestic and foreign terrorism, Jenkins argues that "Jihadist ideology, with few exceptions, gained very little traction in America's Muslim communities. In contrast, the beliefs driving today's domestic extremists are deeply rooted in American history and society" (Jenkins 2021b). Jenkins fears exacerbating political divides due to the difficulty of specifically defining domestic extremism at such a politically polarized time. This is because ideology and speech, absent violent acts, are protected by the First Amendment. Law enforcement officials echo similar sentiment in understanding the difference concerning what is lawful and what is not. FBI director James Wray testified to the Senate Judiciary Committee that "Our focus is on the violence. We don't, we the FBI don't investigate ideology no matter how repugnant. We investigate violence" (Wray 2019, 1:00:24).

Solutions for Countering Terrorism

Compared to the state, terrorism is a weapon of the materially weak who are nonetheless radical and willing to use violence against noncombatants in pursuing their political aims. Terrorism is complex as seen in the levels of analysis from broad structural characteristics through organizations down to individual motivations. Consequently, how states seek to counterterrorists is highly varied and subject to constant debate regarding its efficiency. Among the leading approaches are accommodationist policies of negotiation, offensive policies of decapitation and repression, defensive approaches involving static barriers and homeland security, society-based approaches of population resilience, and approaching the issue from a criminal justice lens versus one of national security. These approaches are not all necessarily exclusive, but they are broadly distinct methods of tackling terrorism.

Negotiations

The first policy approach entails the state negotiating with the terrorist group. Politically this policy is risky, as government leaders expose themselves to charges from domestic rivals that they are weak on terrorism and are appeasing the terrorists' use of force. This is all the more telling given that many governmental leaders state that they will not negotiate with terrorists. Politics aside, appeasement is precisely the logic at play when a negotiation strategy is undertaken in earnest since it is rewarding the terrorists' coercion. That said, governmental leaders may prefer reaching accommodation if they consider the stakes of the issue to be restricted and if engaging in talks with the terrorist group effectively ends the issue. The example of paying for the return of hostages exemplifies this. Typically these negotiations are carried out in secret since the terrorist group wants the money or material they frequently demand, and government leaders want to secure the safe return of the hostages for their families without media fanfare. Many European governments regularly pay ransoms for hostages, and al Qaeda and its regional affiliates have regularly used it as a sustainable source of funding (Callimachi 2014).

Even states like Israel that have a strong reputation for battling terrorism do engage in dialogue with Palestinian terrorist groups when it involves the return of captured soldiers or their remains. The most famous such instance was the 2011 prisoner exchange between Israel and Hamas, where Israel released over 1,000 Israeli Arabs and Palestinians from prison, including hundreds convicted for terrorist offenses. This was done in order to secure the return of captured soldier Gilad Shalit (Mitnick 2011). Shalit had been held in Hamas captivity for over five years after militants captured him in a Gaza-based cross border raid in 2006. His case garnered significant publicity in Israel, and close to 80% of surveyed Israelis approved of the deal (*Ynet News* 2011). Proponents maintain that terrorists have power by virtue of their actions, and thus an unwillingness to consider negotiation does not change that fact or the reality of the situation (Simonsgaard 2016, 46).

In other contexts, negotiations can lead to political settlements when the terrorist group renounces militancy as part of the bargain and commits to the political process. Neumann elaborates that governments must only enter into negotiations with a terrorist group after it has declared an end to the use of violence where negotiations are the start of a conflict resolution process that closes off avenues for a continuation of violence (Neumann 2007, 133). In this case negotiations are more than just a transactional return of hostages, and the 1998 Good Friday Agreement is one example. Tensions remain high in Northern Ireland between unionists who wish to remain a part of the United Kingdom and republicans who want to unite with the Republic of Ireland; however, the Good Friday framework between the two countries also involved political parties in Northern Ireland tied to terrorism, such as the IRA's political wing Sinn Fein and the Progressive Unionist Party representing the loyalist Ulster Volunteer Force (UVF) militia.

There are other advantages for a state to engage in negotiations, primarily with an eye toward obtaining tactical intelligence about the group as well as strategically using negotiations to split groups into separate factions or to pit rivals against one another (Cronin 2009, 37). This kind of "divide and conquer" strategy worked for the United Kingdom in the deliberations for the Anglo-Irish Treaty of 1921 that effectively ended the Irish Independence War. The treaty stipulated that all of Ireland, except Northern Ireland, would become a free state, but this free state would be a dominion of the United Kingdom. This split the leadership of Irish republicans and led to the Irish Civil War in the new Irish Free State. Michael Collins and the state's National Army military forces did not like the dominion status but felt that having a self-governing Ireland was a pragmatic step for the republican cause, whereas the antitreaty "Old" Irish Republican Army led by Eamon de Valera considered the treaty to be a betrayal of the cause by splitting Ireland and still falling under royal dominion. Ultimately the IRA was defeated in the war, and the case illustrates how a state's use of negotiations can drive a wedge between extremists and relative moderates representing one of the sides in a conflict.

All told, negotiations have limited places in the counterterrorist toolkit but are often not the first or most frequent option pursued. Their success requires terrorists with limited and more secular goals, such as regional autonomy, and so they are ill-suited for the growing number of terrorist groups who are motivated by religious or apocalyptic ideologies. Moreover, negotiations are often not popular among the public, who see terrorists as uncivilized for using violence as their form of political expression and so do not understand using a more civilized response like negotiations to reward their terror. Critics of policies of engagement contend that negotiation legitimizes the behavior of terrorists when those groups should be ostracized and punished. For Wilkinson, negotiations and concessions undermine the authority and legitimacy of the government, which should be preserved above all else (Wilkinson 1986, 296–298).

Offensive Measures: Decapitation and Repression

Nearly every counterterrorism approach entails some form of offensive action on the part of the state; however, the specific strategy can vary. Specific strikes undertaken against terrorist leaderships, called decapitation strikes, are hotly debated in the literature with respect to their effects on curtailing terrorism. The logic of such strikes is that "cutting the head off the snake" of the terrorist group will remove all direction, causing disarray within the ranks and ultimately leading to collapse of the group. Detractors argue that whenever a leader is removed, another is often ready in the command chain to assume control and continue operations. They also argue that killing a leader can serve to make them into a martyr that will accelerate a terrorist group's popularity rather than curtail it.

Examples of successful decapitation strikes are plentiful, with contemporary cases involving American airstrikes against Islamic State leader Abu Bakr al-Baghdadi in 2019 and al Qaeda in the Arabian Peninsula leader Qasim al-Raymi in 2020. Not all decapitation strikes are conducted as airstrikes, as the killings of al Qaeda leader Osama bin Laden in 2011 and al Qaeda in the Islamic Maghreb (AQIM) leader Abdelmalek Droukdel by American and French special forces, respectively. In fact, decapitation approaches can take numerous forms, and not all are lethal. Although lethal strikes by unmanned aerial vehicles ("drones") are widely referenced, the technique can also take nonlethal forms to include a leader's capture and arrest or even capture followed by execution. Operationally the nonlethal approaches are more difficult to undertake due to the intelligence required, and they can place special forces operators at far greater risk than standoff attacks. A May 2017 attempt to capture a deputy of the al Shabaab leadership in Barii, Somalia ended in the death of a U.S. Navy SEAL and the withdrawal of his team (Stewart and Sheikh 2017). Although difficult, these methods are not impossible, and in 1999 the leader of the PKK, Abdullah Ocalan, was captured by Turkish National Intelligence in Kenya.

The research on decapitation effects is presently mixed as to the effects, with one scholar looking at insurgent movements finding that decapitation leads to a 25–30% probability of a group's defeat as well as a reduction in the number of attacks (Johnston 2012, 77). Evidence cited as counterarguments are that the bureaucratic orientation of a terrorist group determines how effective such strikes are, with larger and more established terrorist groups with religious ideology being the most survivable (Jordan 2014, 38).

Another offensive approach available to counterterrorists is based on broadly attacking the environments where terrorists draw support. If a decapitation approach is a surgical instrument available to policymakers, then repression is a cudgel. Political repression is the use of force to control or subdue political activity and expression, and the logic of this means is to inflict punishment on the collective of peoples who might support the aims of a group to deter them from doing so. Examples would be the state's government banning political parties, imprisoning individuals for supporting opposition figures, enforcing censorship or banning the press, forbidding free speech or symbols of political movements, and even dictating dress and grooming standards to minimize cultural representation.

When force is used widely and without constraint, it can have significant and decisive effect. The People's Republic of China under Communist Party control has long repressed its ethnic Uighur and Tibetan populations. The regime imprisons over a million Uighurs in concentration camps, administers a surveillance state, conducts arbitrary detentions, removes parents from their children to be raised in state-run institutions, forces reeducation, promotes sexual assault against women, has destroyed thousands of mosques, and prevents cultural and religious expression in what amounts to cultural genocide (Maizland 2021). Despite this widespread repression, evidence of terrorist attacks undertaken by Uighurs against Chinese remains limited in comparison to other regions of the world.

The brutality of China's "salt the earth" repression and occupation is untenable and unethical for most liberal democratic regimes. Moreover, research suggests that repression is not altogether effective at limiting terrorism. Cross-national time-series evidence from 149 countries from 1981 until 2006 suggests that the use of repression by the state tracks with an increase in the number of terrorist attacks, although the effects depend on the type of repression. Scholar James Piazza found that repression targeting electoral self-determination, religious freedom, and labor rights had the most substantial impact on seeing more subsequent attacks by terrorist groups (2017, 113–114). Stated simply, the state's broad and indiscriminate use of force against an entire population makes more enemies than it limits terrorists and their sympathizers. In a pragmatic sense it is highly inefficient and resource-intensive to occupy entire populations and implement broad laws against political expression; however, the greater use of information technology and big data may be changing the equation regarding what authoritarian states can do to their citizens.

Defensive Measures: Static Barriers and Homeland Security

States interested in battling terrorism also have defensive measures to draw from. These can be broken down into the use of static barriers and policies related to homeland security.

Although sometimes controversial, physical barriers have historically proven to be effective security measures. Hadrian's Wall in northern England secured the northern flank of the Roman Empire for some 300 years, and the Great Wall of China's various fortifications lasted some 2,000 years. Barriers can be expensive to construct and defend, but in limited geographical areas can be worth these expenses for the security they provide members of the state. They will not work in every context as a counterterrorism tool, but two examples are worth noting.

Israel endured a record number of terrorist attacks from various Palestinian terrorist groups in 2002, and in that year the state began construction on a security barrier around the West Bank. It now generally follows the Green Line barrier; however, controversially, there are areas where the security barrier extends across the line into the disputed territory where Israeli settlements have been constructed. Palestinians oppose the structure, but it proves widely popular in Israel due to its success in curtailing the number of Palestinian terrorist attacks against Israeli targets. Scholars Avi Dicter and Daniel Byman note that the Samaria region was the deadliest point of entry for Palestinian terrorists into Israel but that 90% of fatalities there between 2000 and 2005 were from attacks before the barrier was completed (2006, 7). They also noted a 60% decline in fatalities from the southern Judea region. The success of the barrier at its intended purpose is so extensive that ground-based terror attacks in Israel today are a rare occurrence.

In Europe the case of Northern Ireland is also instructive, where "peace line" barriers were established within the city of Belfast and other cities in the region at the start of the Troubles in 1969. The barriers were built around sectarian neighbor-hoods to separate Catholic nationalists from Protestant union-ists to minimize sectarian violence between the communities (Grattan 2020). Notably, the barriers feature tall fencing to prevent projectiles from being thrown over, and access between the neighborhoods in Belfast is facilitated by controlled gates that close at designated curfew times. Despite their imprint on the cityscape the majority of Northern Irish prefer that they remain standing. A total of 78% of survey respondents stated they would like the walls to remain as they are, with some changes, or would like to see them come down at some time in the future (Byrne et al. 2015, 21). Only 14% of respon-dents stated that they wanted the walls to come down now, and this is all the more interesting given that the Northern Ireland executive made it a goal to remove all walls by the year 2023.

Looking at the Israeli and Northern Ireland cases, the barri-ers provide clear security benefits for citizens if the goals are a reduction in overall violence. That said, they still prove contro-versial when considering the economic and normative dimen-sions apart from security. Critics contend that barriers harm the economic opportunities of individuals to conduct trade, as well as assert the barriers are a form of collective punishment against the free movement of those who are not inclined to participate in terrorist violence. There are other cases where the physical geography will simply prohibit seeking a physical bar-rier as a viable option.

Physical barriers are a clear example of an attempt at defen-sively tackling terrorism and constitute one form of home-land security. Homeland security is "a unified national effort to prevent and deter terrorist attacks, protect and respond to hazards, and to secure the national borders" (Reese 2013, 8). Homeland security encompasses more than just law enforcement officials manning customs and border checkpoints; it also considers the role of first responders acting to contain or minimize the effects of an attack. In that sense it is defensively active by emphasizing prevention, but also defensively passive by responding to any attack that is successful. Homeland security plays an important role as a solution to terrorism, but it alone has a key limitation in relying solely on defense and response that effectively cedes the initiative to terrorists. Aside from the elements dealing with intelligence and border protection, homeland security tends to emphasize the necessity of "clean-up" for attacks that make it through rather than preventing them in the first place.

While not a physical security element the way law enforcement and emergency first responders are, the resilience of the population is no less important as a component of homeland security. The population of countries that have long exposure to terrorists waging campaigns can develop a societal strength against the harms inflicted in attacks by becoming collectively resigned to the reality of their situation. Counterterrorism and homeland security measures can minimize the number of attacks and the damage they inflict, but inevitably terrorists will successfully strike, and the population's resilience to the expectation of strikes can be an important form of coping with it.

One of the benefits is that terrorism can begin to lose its core function of seeking to coerce through fear. Populations that are collectively less fearful of terrorist strikes continue with the status quo as an element of resolve. In both the Israeli and Northern Ireland cases, this resolve was one aspect of homeland security. The Provisional IRA's terror campaigns as part of the Troubles were extensive, including a number of attacks against civilian targets in England in the 1980s and 1990s. Despite the Provisional IRA's bombing campaign against targets in the United Kingdom, the population generally followed a restrained approach, and society treated the attacks as news-worthy but not societally crippling (Lowe 2017). Similarly, Israeli resilience in the 1990s and early 2000s to Palestinian terrorist attacks is based heavily on organization at the community level (Elran 2017). Population resilience aids counterterrorism efforts by lessening the perceived gains that terrorists expect from coercing the population with violence. Carrying on with a "stiff upper lip" also has a benefit of fostering national unity in the face of adversity caused by terrorism, as opposed to sending a signal of division that might reward terrorists. The caveat is that these efforts require patience and endurance by the population and are a resignation to continued violence with no expectation that it will end in the near future.

Counterterrorism Mindset: National Security or Criminal Justice?

The last items covered with respect to countering terrorism determines the mindset by which the state approaches the issue. In a broad sense there are two avenues of pursuit, one that emphasizes a national security framework and another that adopts a criminal justice approach.

A national security framework is one general approach a state can adopt in seeking to counterterrorism. National security is "the ability of national institutions to prevent adversaries from using force to harm [citizens] or their national interests" and in practice justifies greater license for the actions of the state to maintain security (Sarkesian, Williams, and Cimbala 2013, 2). Historically it entails matters related to the preparation for and conduct of war with threats that are primarily directed by other states. The stakes in national security are high since they pertain to the survival of the state by preventing severe attacks and invasion while also protecting critical interests abroad, such as the flow of resources to the economy. Terrorism has historically been a challenge to states that demanded a response but was not considered a typical national security threat until the age of weapons of mass destruction elevated the concern over the damages that terrorists could inflict. The September 11 attacks in particular were instrumental in leaders reassessing the type of threat that terrorists posed.

One facet of the national security framework is the exception it makes in the debate between security and civil liberties because the stakes are so high. Note from earlier in this chapter how the 1978 Foreign Intelligence Surveillance Act (FISA) was passed to provide authorities greater powers that do not fall under conventional accountability; the courts that FISA created hold deliberations in secret. Some of the tools permissible in a national security framework are aggressive interrogation measures, the use of targeted killings against leaders or operatives, and persistent intelligence collection. Because the threats traditionally came from powerful states and were foreign, security is valued above civil liberties protections.

A notable example of this framework applied to terrorism is the Patriot Act as well as the Guantánamo Bay military detention camp at the naval base bearing the same name. The base is legally owned by the government of Cuba but is leased to the United States, and this location is central to the role the detention camp has fulfilled since its opening in January 2002. After 9/11 captured enemy combatants such as Taliban and al Qaeda operatives were sent to the camp for detention but did not maintain legal rights as prisoners of war, which are afforded to members of the armed forces of states during war. The detainees were also not granted access to the legal process for those in the United States.

The Bush administration asserted that since the detainees were not housed in the United States, they were not subject to American laws and the writ of *habeas corpus* outlined in Article I of the Constitution. This legal principle roughly translates as "the court demands a prisoner be brought before them" and means that those accused of a crime must appear in court to determine the legality of their detention, to hear the charges brought against them, and to initiate the legal process of a trial if their detention is legal. Without this principle an individual can be held indefinitely by the government without ever being charged or having a trial. Per the U.S. Constitution the writ of *habeas corpus* can only be revoked during rebellion or invasion; for example it was suspended by President Abraham Lincoln in 1861 during the American Civil War.

In the case at Guantánamo Bay, detainees were instead subject to military commissions where they were represented by military lawyers and judged by panels of U.S. military officers. The commissions did not have the same legal protections for defendants that American citizens and U.S. military members have. Nearly 800 detainees were sent to the facility since its opening in 2002. In 2008 the U.S. Supreme Court ruled in *Boumediene v. Bush* that detainees were entitled to *habeas corpus* through federal courts with respect to their detention, with the courts possessing the ability to order the release of detainees. However, the ruling did not end use of the Guantánamo facility, and those whose cases did appear before federal judges and were deemed to be lawfully held continued in their detention.

In January 2017, newly elected president Obama promised to close the detention camp at Guantánamo Bay within a year but did not do so by the end of his presidency. Controversially, the administration greatly expanded the use of drone strikes in the Afghanistan theater; some critics allege this was done to prevent the capture of Taliban and al Qaeda members to avoid the legal quandary altogether (Roberts 2013). Nevertheless, the Obama administration initiated policies to release detainees deemed nonthreatening and to also transfer others back to the governments of their home countries. By the end of his presidency the detainee population at Guantánamo declined from 214 to 60 (McCarthy 2018). President Trump vowed to keep the facility open; however, over the course of his presidency the detainee population further declined to 40, where it remains as of 2022. In February 2021 the Biden administration pledged to close the detention camp before leaving office (Spetalnick, Hunnicutt, and Stewart 2021). Most members of Congress and the American people support the facility because they do not want to see the alternative of detainees entering American courts and serving prison terms in U.S. facilities or see the detainees released, since some have gone on to attack U.S. forces (Opinion Research Corporation International for Cable News Network 2016, 2).

Another controversial element seen in a national security approach to terrorism is extraordinary rendition. This policy seeks to skirt the detention laws of a host nation by capturing terrorists and transferring them to covert sites in other nations that do not have such laws. Reporting on these practices suggests that "enhanced interrogation" like water boarding, cited by critics as torture, were regularly used (Murray 2011, 18). In most cases the interrogations were conducted by contractors to the CIA, and critics see the policy as damaging the government's reputation and moral standard with respect to human rights, whereas supporters see it as a powerful tool to stop known terrorists before they can conduct their attacks and also obtain intelligence about impending attacks.

All told the national security approach to terrorism views the non-state practitioners as an enormous threat that justifies extraordinary measures to pursue, prevent, and punish terrorists. The legal framework sees terrorists as a special category of enemy of the state that is not subject to the laws that govern citizens of a state, nor the practices pertaining to treatment of captured members of an opponent's armed forces. Because of the legal gray area regarding the status of international terrorists and their disdain for norms against targeting civilians, the state asserts wide latitude to deal with the threat. Since terrorism is at its core a form of political violence like war, those advocating a national security response contend that the response measure should be as extensive as the powers wielded by the state when at war.

By contrast, a criminal justice approach focuses on processes and an established rule of law. In this model the stakes are seen as considerably less than a core threat to the entire nation, and the mindset regarding methods is less rooted in emergency measures and more regarding procedure and codified law. The framework here seeks foremost to preserve the law and order that the state apparatus is based upon to protect its standing while still punishing violators of the law who commit murder. In the criminal justice mindset a terrorist is seen more as a criminal and less a threat to national security, and so punishments can be under statutes related to homicide or special laws pertaining to terrorism.

In a criminal justice approach, the impetus is on securing convictions for crimes and thus the collection and presentation of evidence is paramount for legal proceedings at trial. One challenge here is that trials inevitably require the methods used to obtain the evidence regarding a plot be disclosed. From an accountability standpoint the jurors or justices in an independent legal system need to understand how evidence was collected, yet doing so divulges the sources and methods that can hamper their effectiveness for future use. Moreover, legal proceedings do not always produce just results, and as with some criminals the act of sending a terrorist to trial is no guarantee that they will be convicted. In that manner a national security approach of detaining an especially dangerous terrorist is especially enticing from the perspective of the state that need not risk their release. Additionally, opting for a criminal justice approach and the reliance on trials can give committed terrorists a very public and lengthy platform to promote their cause.

One of the strongest arguments made from a criminal justice approach concerns the approach to interrogation. In contrast to the deeply adversarial approach taken using a national security mentality, interrogators operating from a criminal justice mindset typically seek to befriend the subject in order to glean information. George Spiro, the FBI's interrogator for Saddam Hussein, obtained a surprising amount of information from the former dictator in the course of his engagement that was based on building rapport (Connett 2011). FBI agent Ali Soufan testified to the U.S. Senate's Judiciary Committee about his success using the "Informed Interrogation Approach" of the U.S. Army field manual when applied to al Qaeda member Abu Zubaydah and contrasted it with the harm and ineffectiveness of the "harsh" interrogation approach used by CIA contractors (2009).

The two mindsets presented illustrate the fundamental conundrum between security and civil liberties. In practice governments do not wholly commit to one approach over the other, and it is easy to see the difficulties inherent in weighing the merits and demerits of each. A framework devoted solely to criminalizing terrorism can harm the methods used to interdict them before they can strike, although it diminishes critiques of secret action and abuses by the state. Conversely, a national security approach that values total security over any legal accountability can erode the trust that citizens have in the system. Managing the preferred balance between the two is an exercise that an informed and critically thinking electorate will have to navigate.

References

Abrahms, Max. 2012. "The Political Effectiveness of Terrorism Revisited." *Comparative Political Studies* 45, no. 3 (March): 366–393.

Abrahms, Max. 2007. "Why Democracies Make Superior Counterterrorists." *Security Studies* 16, no. 2 (April–June): 223–253.

Acosta, Benjamin. 2016. "Dying to Survive." *Journal of Peace Research* 53, no. 2 (March): 180–196.

Acosta, Benjamin and Steven Childs. 2013. "Illuminating the Global Suicide-Attack Network." *Studies in Conflict & Terrorism* 36, no. 1: 49–76.

American Civil Liberties Union. 2023. "Surveillance Under the Patriot Act." https://www.aclu.org/other/surveillance -under-usapatriot-act.

Anderson, Benedict. 1991. *Imagined Communities: Reflections on the Origins and Spread of Nationalism.* London: Verso.

Banares, Ilya. 2021. "Parler Notified FBI of Violent Content Ahead of Capitol Riot." *Bloomberg*, March 25, 2021. https://www.bloomberg.com/news/articles/2021-03-25 /parler-notified-fbi-of-violent-content-ahead-of-capitol-riot.

Borum, Randy. 2004. *Psychology of Terrorism*. Tampa: University of South Florida.

Broad, William, Stephen Engelberg, and James Glanz. 2001. "Assessing Risks, Chemical, Biological, Even Nuclear." *New York Times*, November 1, 2001. https://www.nytimes .com/2001/11/01/us/a-nation-challenged-the-threats -assessing-risks-chemical-biological-even-nuclear.html.

Bueno de Mesquita, Bruce, James Morrow, Randolph Siverson, and Alastair Smith. 1999. "An Institutional Explanation of the Democratic Peace." *The American Political Science Review* 93, no. 4 (December): 791–807.

Bush, George W. 2001. "Remarks by the President at Islamic Center of Washington, D.C." September 17, 2001. https:// georgewbush-whitehouse.archives.gov/news/releases /2001/09/20010917-11.html.

Byrne, Jonny, Cathy Gormley-Heenan, Duncan Morrow, and Brendan Sturgeon. 2015. "Public Attitudes to Peace Walls (2015): Survey Results." Ulster University Research Commissioned by the Northern Ireland Department of Justice, December 2015. https://www.ulster.ac.uk/__data /assets/pdf_file/0015/224052/pws.pdf.

Callimachi, Rukmini. 2014. "Underwriting Jihad: Paying Ransoms, Europe Bankrolls Qaeda Terror." *New York Times*, July 29, 2014. https://www.nytimes.com/2014 /07/30/world/africa/ransoming-citizens-europe-becomes -al-qaedas-patron.html.

Carter, David. 2012. "A Blessing or a Curse? State Support for Terrorist Groups." *International Organization* 66, no. 1 (Winter): 129–151.

Cline, Ray S. and Yonah Alexander. 1984. *Terrorism: The Soviet Connection*. New York: Crane Russak.

Coggins, Bridget. 2015. "Does State Failure Cause Terrorism? An Empirical Analysis (1999–2008)." *Journal of Conflict Resolution* 59, no. 3 (April 2015): 455–483.

Collins, Padraig. 2002. "Footage of Pearl Murder Emerges on Web." *The Irish Times*, May 22, 2002. https://www.irishtimes.com/news/footage-of-pearl-murder-emerges-on-web-1.424665.

Connett, David. 2011. "From Beyond the Grave, Saddam Reveals All (Nearly)." *The Independent*, October 23, 2011. https://www.independent.co.uk/news/world/middle-east/from-beyond-the-grave-saddam-reveals-all-nearly-1732167.html.

Crenshaw, Martha. 1998. "The Logic of Terrorism: Terrorist Behavior as a Product of Strategic Choice." In *Origins of Terrorism: Psychologies, Ideologies, Theologies, States of Mind*, edited by Walter Reich, 7–24. Washington, D.C.: The Woodrow Wilson Center Press.

Crenshaw, Martha, ed. 1983. *Terrorism, Legitimacy, and Power: The Consequences of Political Violence*. Middletown: Wesleyan University Press.

Cronin, Audrey K. 2009. *How Terrorism Ends: Understanding the Decline and Demise of Terrorist Campaigns*. Princeton: Princeton University Press.

Davis, Paul and Brian Michael Jenkins. 2002. *Deterrence and Influence in Counterterrorism: A Component in the War on al Qaeda*. Santa Monica: Rand Corporation.

Dicter, Avi and Daniel Byman. 2006. "Israel's Lessons for Fighting Terrorists and their Implications for the United States." *The Saban Center for Middle East Policy at the Brookings Institution Analysis Paper 8*. https://www.brookings.edu/wp-content/uploads/2016/06/byman20060324.pdf.

Dreher, Axel and Justina Fischer. 2010. "Government Decentralization as Disincentive for Transnational Terror? An Empirical Analysis." *International Economic Review* 51, no. 4 (November): 981–1002.

Elbaz, Sagi and Daniel Bar-Tal. 2019. "Voluntary Silence: Israeli Media Self-Censorship During the Second Lebanon War." *Conflict and Communication Online* 18, no. 2. https://regener-online.de/journalcco/2019_2/pdf/elbaz-bar -tal2019.pdf.

Electronic Privacy Information Center. 2021. "Foreign Intelligence Surveillance Act Court Orders 1979–2017." Accessed June 14, 2021. https://epic.org/privacy /surveillance/fisa/stats/default.html.

Elran, Meir. 2017. "Societal Resilience in Israel: How Communities Succeed Despite Terrorism." *Foreign Affairs*, March 23, 2017. https://www.foreignaffairs.com/articles /israel/2017-03-23/societal-resilience-israel.

Embury-Dennis, Tom. 2019. "El Paso Shooting: 21-Year-Old Suspect Patrick Crusius 'Espoused Racist Tropes and Voiced Support for Christchurch Mosque Gunman.'" *The Independent*, August 4, 2019. https://www.independent .co.uk/news/world/americas/el-paso-shooting-suspect -patrick-crusius-white-supremacist-trump-texas-walmart -a9038611.html.

Frankel, Glenn. 1990. "British Media Ban on Terrorists Still Controversial." *The Washington Post*, October 21, 1990. https://www.washingtonpost.com/archive/politics /1990/10/21/british-media-ban-on-terrorists-still -controversial/c3ad1500-25ee-43b0-b740-6fcbd6c872a6/.

Frey, Bruno and Simon Luechinger. 2004. "Decentralization as a Disincentive for Terror." *European Journal of Political Economy* 20, no. 2 (June): 509–515.

Gaibulloev, Khusrav, James Piazza, and Todd Sandler. 2017. "Regime Types and Terrorism." *International Organization* 71, no. 3 (Summer): 491–522.

Grattan, Steve. 2020. "Northern Ireland Still Divided by Peace Walls 20 Years After Conflict." *The World*, January 14, 2020. https://www.pri.org/stories/2020-01-14 /northern-ireland-still-divided-peace-walls-20-years-after -conflict.

Grey, Stephen. 2004. "Follow the Mullahs." *The Atlantic Monthly* 294, no. 4 (November): 44–47.

Gurr, Ted Robert. 1970. *Why Men Rebel*. Princeton: Princeton University Press.

Horowitz, Michael C. and Philip B. K. Potter. 2014. "Allying to Kill: Terrorist Intergroup Cooperation and the Consequences for Lethality." *Journal of Conflict Resolution* 58, no. 2 (March 2014): 199–225.

Hou, Dongfang, Khusrav Gaibulloev, and Todd Sandler. 2020. "Introducing Extended Data on Terrorist Groups (EDTG), 1970 to 2016." *Journal of Conflict Resolution* 64, no. 1 (January 2020): 199–225.

Institute for Economics & Peace. 2020. *Global Terrorism Index 2020: Measuring the Impact of Terrorism.* https:// visionofhumanity.org/wp-content/uploads/2020/11/GTI -2020-web-1.pdf.

Jager, Avraham. 2018. "Does Poverty Cause Terrorism?" Research Brief, International Institute for Counter-Terrorism, Interdisciplinary Center Herzliya. https:// www.ict.org.il/images/Does%20Poverty%20Cause %20Terrorism.pdf.

Jenkins, Brian Michael. 2021a. "Five Reasons to Be Wary of a New Domestic Terrorism Law." *The Hill*, February 23, 2021. https://thehill.com/opinion/national-security /540096-what-exactly-is-the-definition-of-terrorism-and -four-other-reasons.

Jenkins, Brian Michael. 2021b. "Domestic Violent Extremists Will Be Harder to Combat Than Homegrown Jihadists." *The Hill*, January 31, 2021. https://thehill.com/opinion

/national-security/536637-domestic-violent-extremists
-will-be-harder-to-combat-than-homegrown.

Jetter, Michael. 2017. "Terrorism and the Media: The Effect
of US Television Coverage on Al-Qaeda Attacks." *Institute
of Labor Economics Discussion Paper Series* No. 10708
(April). https://www.econstor.eu/bitstream/10419
/161331/1/dp10708.pdf.

Johnston, Patrick. 2017. "Does Decapitation Work?
Assessing the Effectiveness of Leadership Targeting in
Counterinsurgency Campaigns." *International Security* 36,
no. 4 (Spring): 47–79.

Jordan, Jenna. 2014. "Attacking the Leader, Missing the
Mark: Why Terrorist Groups Survive Decapitation Strikes."
International Security 38, no. 4 (Spring): 7–38.

Krueger, Alan. 2007. *What Makes a Terrorist. Economics and
the Roots of Terrorism*. Princeton: Princeton University
Press.

Kydd, Andrew and Barbara Walter. 2006. "The Strategies
of Terrorism." *International Security* 31, no. 1 (Summer):
49–80.

Linder, Douglas. n.d. "Timothy McVeigh in Waco." Accessed
February 25, 2021. https://famous-trials.com/oklacity
/717-waco.

Lowe, Josh. 2017. "London Isn't Burning: How Britain's
History with the IRA Made It Resilient in the Face of
Attack." *Newsweek*, March 24, 2017. https://www
.newsweek.com/london-attack-ira-terror-threat-severe
-bomb-terrorism-573629.

Luft, Gal. 2003. "The Logic of Israel's Targeted Killing." *The
Middle East Quarterly* 10, no. 1 (Winter): 3–13.

Maizland, Lindsay. 2021. "China's Repression of Uyghurs in
Xinjiang." Council on Foreign Relations, March 1, 2021.
https://www.cfr.org/backgrounder/chinas-repression
-uyghurs-xinjiang.

Marcus, Aliza. 2007. *Blood and Belief: The PKK and the Kurdish Fight for Independence.* New York: New York University Press.

McCarthy, Niall. 2018. "Guantanamo's Shrinking Prisoner Population." Statista Charts. January 31, 2018. https://www.statista.com/chart/12741/guantanamos-shrinking-prisoner-population/.

Mitnick, Joshua. 2011. "Gilad Shalit Prisoner Swap: Why Netanyahu Agreed to 1,000 Palestinians for One Israeli." *The Christian Science Monitor*, October 12, 2011. https://www.csmonitor.com/World/Middle-East/2011/1012/Gilad-Shalit-prisoner-swap-Why-Netanyahu-agreed-to-1-000-Palestinians-for-one-Israeli.

Mogensen, Kirsten. 2008. "Television Journalism During Terror Attacks." *Media, War & Conflict* 1, no. 1 (April): 31–49.

Moghadam, Assaf. 2006. "Suicide Terrorism, Occupation, and the Globalization of Martyrdom: A Critique of Dying to Win." *Studies in Conflict & Terrorism* 29, no. 8 (2006): 707–729.

Mousseau, Michael. 2003. "Market Civilization and Its Clash with Terror." *International Security* 27, no. 3 (Winter): 5–29.

Mueller, John and Mark Stewart. 2012. "The Terrorism Delusion: America's Overwrought Response to September 11." *International Security* 37, no. 1 (Summer): 81–110.

Murray, Mark. "Extraordinary Rendition and U.S. Counterterrorism Policy." *Journal of Strategic Security* 4, no. 3 (2011): 15–28.

National Consortium for the Study of Terrorism and Responses to Terrorism. 2020. *Global Terrorism Overview: Terrorism in 2019.* https://www.start.umd.edu/pubs/START_GTD_GlobalTerrorismOverview2019_July2020.pdf.

Neumann, Peter. 2007. "Negotiating with Terrorists." *Foreign Affairs* 86, no. 1 (January–February): 128–138.

Nolan, Christopher, director. 2010. *Inception*. Warner Bros.

Nordan, E. Walker. 2010. "The Best Defense Is a Good Offense: The Necessity of Targeted Killings." August 24. *Small Wars Journal.* https://smallwarsjournal.com/jrnl/art /the-best-defense-is-a-good-offense.

Olson, Mancur. 1971. *The Logic of Collective Action: Public Goods and the Theory of Groups*. Cambridge: Harvard University Press.

Opinion Research Corporation International for Cable News Network. 2016. "CNN/ORC International Poll." March 4.

Pape, Robert. 2005. *Dying to Win: The Strategic Logic Suicide Bombing*. New York: Random House.

Piazza, James. 2017. "Repression and Terrorism: A Cross-National Empirical Analysis of Types of Repression and Domestic Terrorism." *Terrorism and Political Violence* 29, no. 1: 102–118.

Piazza, James. 2006. "Rooted in Poverty? Terrorism, Poor Economic Development, and Social Cleavages." *Terrorism and Political Violence* 18, no. 1 (March): 159–177.

Picard, Robert. "The Journalist's Role in Coverage of Terrorist Events." Presented at the Annual Meeting of the Speech Communication Association, San Francisco, California, November 18–21, 1989. https://files.eric.ed.gov/fulltext /ED312694.pdf.

Post, Jerrold. 1998. "Terrorist Psycho-logic: Terrorist Behavior as a Product of Psychological Forces." In *Origins of Terrorism: Psychologies, Ideologies, Theologies, States of Mind*, edited by Walter Reich, 25–40. Washington, DC: The Woodrow Wilson Center Press.

Post, Jerrold. 1984. "Notes on a Psychodynamic Theory of Terrorist Behavior." *Terrorism* 7, no. 2: (241–256).

Reese, Shawn. 2013. "Defining Homeland Security: Analysis and Congressional Considerations." Congressional

Research Service Report R42462, January 8. https://fas.org
/sgp/crs/homesec/R42462.pdf.

Roberts, Dan. 2013. "U.S. Drone Strikes Being Used as
Alterative to Guantánamo, Lawyer Says." *The Guardian*,
May 2, 2013. https://www.theguardian.com/world/2013
/may/02/us-drone-strikes-guantanamo.

Ron, James. 1995. *Weapons Transfers and Violations of the
Laws of War in Turkey*. New York: Human Rights Watch.

Sambrook, Richard. 2006. "Regulation, Responsibility and
the Case Against Censorship." *Index of Censorship* 35, no. 1
(February): 166–172.

Sarkesian, Sam, John Williams, and Stephen Cimbala. 2013.
U.S. National Security: Policymakers, Processes and Politics.
5th ed. Boulder: Lynne Rienner Press.

Schanzer, David, Charles Kurzman, Jessica Toliver, and
Elizabeth Miller. 2016. *The Challenge and Promise of Using
Community Policing Strategies to Prevent Violent Extremism:
A Call for Community Partnerships with Law Enforcement
to Enhance Public Safety*. Durham: Triangle Center on
Terrorism and Homeland Security. https://www.ojp.gov
/pdffiles1/nij/grants/249674.pdf.

Schmid, Alex and Albert Jongman. 1988. *Political Terrorism: A
New Guide to Actors, Authors, Concepts, Data Bases, Theories,
& Literature*. New Brunswick: Transaction Publishers.

Simonsgaard, Craig. 2016. "Negotiating with Terrorists:
The Way Forward." *Army War College Review* 2, no. 1
(February): 45–48.

Soufan, Ali. 2009. "Statement of Ali Soufan." Testimony to
the United States Senate Committee on the Judiciary,
May 13, 2009. https://fas.org/irp/congress/2009_hr
/051309soufan.pdf.

Spetalnick, Matt, Trevor Hunnicutt, and Phil Stewart. 2021.
"Biden Launches Review of Guantanamo Prison, Aims

to Close It Before Leaving Office." *Reuters*, February 12. https://www.reuters.com/article/us-usa-biden-guantanamo -idUSKBN2AC1Q4.

Sterling, Claire. 1981. "Terrorism: Tracing the International Network." *The New York Times Magazine*, March 1. https:// www.nytimes.com/1981/03/01/magazine/terrorism -tracing-the-international-network.html.

Stewart, Phil and Abdi Sheikh. 2017. "U.S. Navy SEAL Killed in Somalia Raid on Militant Compound." *Reuters*, May 5. https://www.reuters.com/article/us-somalia -security-usa/u-s-navy-seal-killed-in-somalia-raid-on -militant-compound-idUSKBN1811DV.

Tien, Lee. 2014. "Peekaboo, I See You: Government Authority Intended for Terrorism Is Used for Other Purposes." Electronic Frontier Foundation, October 26. https://www.eff.org/deeplinks/2014/10/peekaboo-i-see-you -government-uses-authority-meant-terrorism-other-uses.

U.S. Department of Justice. n.d. "The USA PATRIOT Act: Preserving Life and Liberty." Highlights of the USA PATRIOT Act. Accessed June 14, 2021. https://www .justice.gov/archive/ll/what_is_the_patriot_act.pdf.

U.S. Department of Justice, Office of the Inspector General. 2016. "A Review of the Federal Bureau of Investigation's Use of National Security Letters." Redacted—For Public Release. Accessed June 14, 2021. https://oig.justice.gov /reports/2016/NSL-2007.pdf.

U.S. Foreign Intelligence Surveillance Court. n.d. "Current Membership—Foreign Intelligence Surveillance Court." Accessed June 14, 2021. https://www.fisc.uscourts.gov /current-membership-foreign-intelligence-surveillance -court.

Ynet News. 2011. "Poll: 79% of Israelis Support Shalit Deal." October 17, 2011. https://www.ynetnews.com/articles /0,7340,L-4135847,00.html.

Young, Joseph and Laura Dugan. 2014. "Survival of the Fittest: Why Terrorist Groups Endure." *Perspectives on Terrorism* 8, no. 2 (April): 1–23. http://www.terrorismanalysts.com/pt/index.php/pot/article/view/334/669.

Wakefield, Jane. 2019. "Christchurch Shootings: Social Media Races to Stop Attack Footage." *BBC News*, March 16, 2019. https://www.bbc.com/news/technology-47583393.

Waltz, Kenneth N. 1959. *Man, the State and War: A Theoretical Analysis*. New York: Columbia University Press.

White, Jessica. 2020. "Terrorism and the Mass Media." *Royal United Services Institute for Defence and Security Studies Occasional Paper*. May. https://rusi.org/sites/default/files/terrorism_and_the_mass_media_final_web_version.pdf.

Wilkinson, Paul. 1986. *Terrorism and the Liberal State*. London: Macmillan.

Wilkinson, Paul. 1977. *Terrorism and the Liberal State*. London: Macmillan.

Wray, Christopher A. (2019, July 23). *Oversight of the Federal Bureau of Investigation*. Testimony to the United States Senate Judiciary, July 23, 2019 [Video]. Integrated Senate Video Player. https://www.senate.gov/isvp/?auto_play=false&comm=judiciary&filename=judiciary072319&poster=https://www.judiciary.senate.gov/assets/images/video-poster.png&stt=.

3   Perspectives

Violence Spurs Change, Yet Terrorism Is for Losers
Benjamin Acosta

Let's look at terrorism from a scientific perspective. As scholars, we must operationalize (a fancy word for "define") our variables. The word *terrorism* means *the use of violence against civilians in the pursuit of political gain* (Acosta and Childs 2013, 71). Simply put, terrorism refers to the murder of innocent people in hopes that those who rule or govern over the targets will respond favorably to the perpetrator's demands.

Under a scientific definition, let's put to bed the notion that "one man's terrorist is another man's freedom fighter."

Terrorism predominately classifies as a strategy of coercion. It is inherently authoritarian (precluding dialogue), dogmatic (precluding ideological negotiation), and extremist (as exemplified by the method). The terrorist strategies are highly lethal stories with an allegedly therapeutic ending: "We will stop murdering your innocents when you give us what we want (whatever that might be)."

A variety of diverse ideologies animates politics and thus political violence, including those that are leftwing, ethnonationalist, rightwing, and religious. Here police protect a building in downtown Portland from leftwing "Anti-Fascist" (Antifa) demonstrators. In July 2020 Federal law enforcement and Antifa rioters clashed in the areas surrounding the Mark O. Hatfield Federal Courthouse. (Alexander Oganezov/Dreamstime.com)

Political Violence Versus Terrorism

Violence underpins many pursuits of justice and injustice alike. Walking the gray line, violence can stamp a movement's hallmark of success, or just as frequently lead it to the ash heap of history.

Terrorism, on the other hand—the petty stepsister to political violence—tends to ignite a visceral response of resolve from those targeted.

From time immemorial, violence has reshaped borders, empowered emerging peoples and flourishing nations, and toppled long-lasting empires. Like any tool, perspectives on the "good" and the "bad" effects of violence largely depend on the ideologies of who's doing it and how they are doing it.

"Weapons Are the Ornaments of Men" . . .

Originally put: *"al-silah zinat al-rijal."* Al-Sayyid Musa al-Sadr, Lebanese-Shi'a populist and founder of the militant organization Amal, ate those words as he went mysteriously missing (Abu-Khalil 1985, 46), likely murdered by allies on behalf of enemies (Norton 1987, 54–55).

Acts of violence are neither moral nor immoral in isolation (Arendt 1970, 3; Kagan 1996, 569–573). The place of violence in the annals of human development does not differ all that much from the wheel, printing press, combustion engine, birth control, or the washing machine. "Bad" people use violence. "Good" people use violence. Even "bad guys" fighting for a "good cause" use violence. And, sometimes "good guys" fighting for a "bad cause" use violence.

From Swamp Warfare to Civil Rights

In the late 1770s and early 1780s, and in the pursuit of American independence from British oppression, patriot Francis Marion employed a new type of violence—*swamp warfare*—against the red-coat army (Bass 2017). Utilizing tactics learned from fighting in the French and Indian War during the two prior decades, Marion's militiamen killed many British soldiers and officers, looted their supplies, and generated a narrative of an "invincible American ghost-warrior force." Without the efforts of Marion and his men, many historians doubt whether the American revolutionaries, and the regular army under the command of General George Washington, would have succeeded against the mighty British Empire or garnered the support of the French, who aided significantly in the American ultimate effort to defeat the British.

This exemplifies the "little man" creatively using violence to defeat the "big man."

Even some who primarily embrace the tenets of nonviolent resistance acknowledge that violence—or the threat of violence—can effectively advance worthy goals. In *This Nonviolent Stuff'll Get You Killed: How Guns Made the Civil Rights Movement Possible*, Black American civil rights activist Charles Cobb emphasizes: "although nonviolence was crucial to the gains made by the freedom struggle of the 1950s and '60s, those gains could not have been achieved without the complementary and still underappreciated practice of armed self-defense" (Cobb 2014, 1).

Islamic Fundamentalism and Terrorism

In a completely opposite manner, for over a century, Palestinian militant organizations have targeted Jewish civilians in terrorist attacks, killing thousands of innocent men, women, and children in pursuit of territory deemed "Islamic" (Acosta 2010).

The extremely violent Palestinian *intifada* (1988–1994) and even more violent Palestinian *al-Aqsa* intifada a few years later (2000–2005) culminated in few gains for the Palestinian movement (Acosta and Ramos 2017, 232–247; Morris 2009, 149–150). The only primary end the Palestinian movement somewhat achieved resulted from the Israeli government in 2005, under the leadership of Prime Minister Ariel Sharon, giving in to the terrorist coercion and forcibly removing Jewish citizens from a small strip of well-established neighborhoods in Gaza.

Contrasting the guerrilla tactics of Marion and his patriots and the armed flank of the civil rights movement, the terrorism of the Palestinians has targeted unarmed civilians, leaving the Palestinian movement not only morally bankrupt but strategically flaccid.

Do Countries Gaslight?

Some observers criticize countries for carelessly tossing around the word *terrorism* to slur rebel populations, but then said countries exempt themselves from the same labeling during times of war. For example, think of the horror, if not terror, exacted upon civilians during World War II in Korea, Japan, China, the Dutch East Indies, Indochina, Germany, Hungary, Poland, the Soviet Union, and Yugoslavia, each of whom lost more than half a million civilians by the time the conflict was over (National World War II Museum 2021).

In a more recent example, war journalist Peter Brock reflects on NATO's air campaign in response to Serbian military actions in the territory of Kosovo:

> For seventy-eight straight days in early 1999, the United States—with token assistance from its puppet partners in NATO—bombed and re-bombed the independent, sovereign republic of Serbia. All agree that relatively few military targets were hit and that massive damage was inflicted instead upon innocent civilian populations in a punitive campaign where cruise missiles were launched and smart bombs were dropped by orders from [supposedly] intelligent generals in Brussels. (2005, vii)

What Do Your Actions Say About You? As an Individual? As a Movement?

Politics derives its meaning and goals from the starting point of the concept of identity. Political institutions, almost by definition, *exclude* certain groups. This is what Benedict Anderson means by "imagined communities" (1983). Upon foundation, institutions establish an "us," and they create a "them" (Acosta 2022). Some scholars illustrate that civil wars, wherein terrorism often occurs, provides more of an opportunity for individuals to mask personal vendettas in a shroud of collective goals (Harris 2006; Kalyvas 2009). Here, the us-versus-them dichotomy justifies violence both for the individual and thereby for those leading the larger organized movement.

The use of terrorism against targets often emboldens those targeted, making targets less likely to submit to coercive demands (Abrahms 2012). As such, terrorism usually only "works" as part of brute-force efforts such as the Taliban's summer 2021 offensive that seized control of Afghanistan. Brute-force warfare aligns with outcome goals related to the genocide, annihilation, ethnic cleansing, or other forms of the complete defeat of the enemy. It speaks volumes that entities and identity groups that employ terrorism tend to succeed only in pursuit of such vile goals.

References

Abrahms, Max. 2012. "The Political Effectiveness of Terrorism Revisited." *Comparative Political Studies* 45, no. 3: 366–393.

Abu-Khalil, As'ad. 1985. "Druze, Sunni and Shiite Political Leadership in Present-Day Lebanon." *Arab Studies Quarterly* 7, no. 4: 28–58.

Acosta, Benjamin. 2010. "Palestinian Precedents: The Origins of Al-Qaeda's Use of Suicide Terrorism and *Istishhad.*" In *Political Islam from Muhammad to Ahmadinejad: Defenders, Detractors, and Definitions*, edited by Joseph M. Skelly, 193–206. Santa Barbara: Praeger Security International.

Acosta, Benjamin. 2022. "Exclusionary Politics and Organized Resistance." *Terrorism and Political Violence* 34, no. 2: 341–363.

Acosta, Benjamin and Steven J. Childs. 2013. "Illuminating the Global Suicide-Attack Network." *Studies in Conflict & Terrorism* 36, no. 1: 49–76.

Acosta, Benjamin and Kristen Ramos. 2017. "Introducing the 1993 Terrorism and Political Violence Dataset." *Studies in Conflict & Terrorism* 40, no. 3: 232–247.

Anderson, Benedict. 1983. *Imagined Communities: Reflections on the Origin and Spread of Nationalism.* New York: Verso.

Arendt, Hannah. 1970. *On Violence.* New York: Harvest.

Bass, Robert D. 2017. *Swamp Fox: The Life and Campaigns of General Francis Marion.* Auckland: Papamoa Press.

Brock, Peter. 2005. *Media Cleansing: Dirty Reporting, Journalism and Tragedy in Yugoslavia.* Los Angeles: GMBooks.

Cobb, Charles E., Jr. 2014. *This Nonviolent Stuff'll Get You Killed: How Guns Made the Civil Rights Movement Possible.* New York: Basic Books.

Harris, William. 2006. *The New Face of Lebanon.* Princeton: Markus Wiener.

Kagan, Donald. 1996. *On the Origins of War and the Preservation of Peace.* New York: Anchor.

Kalyvas, Stathis. 2009. *The Logic of Violence in Civil Wars.* New York: Cambridge University Press.

Morris, Benny. 2009. *One State, Two State: Resolving the Israel/Palestine Conflict.* New Haven: Yale University Press.

The National World War II Museum. 2021. "Research Starters: Worldwide Deaths in World War II." Accessed September 9, 2021. https://www.nationalww2museum.org /students-teachers/student-resources/research-starters /research-starters-worldwide-deaths-world-war.

Norton, Augustus Richard. 1987. *Amal and the Shi'a: Struggle for the Soul of Lebanon.* Austin: University of Texas Press.

Benjamin Acosta *is the chief data officer at Arcturus Intelligence and previously worked for years in academia as a professor. Acosta has published peer-reviewed scholarly articles in the* Journal of Politics, Journal of Peace Research, International Studies

Quarterly, Terrorism and Political Violence, Studies in Conflict & Terrorism, Cooperation and Conflict, Middle East Journal, *and* Middle East Quarterly.

Why Terrorism Does Not Really Work
Max Abrahms

Does terrorism work? Of course, the answer depends on what we mean by "work." By definition, terrorism attracts attention and spreads fear beyond the immediate victims. So, if garnering attention and inspiring fear are the measures of success, then terrorism naturally has a hundred percent success rate. More than any other aspect, however, what distinguishes terrorism from other crimes is its presumed political motivation—be it establishing a national homeland, creating a caliphate, or spurring a communist revolution (Schmid 2012). If success is assessed in terms of whether the perpetrators achieve their strategic demands, then terrorism is a remarkably ineffective strategy.

Terrorism works better in theory than in practice. In theory, terrorism works as a political "communication strategy" (Pape 2006). Perpetrators supposedly commit attacks to call attention to their grievances and the costs of ignoring them. By inflicting pain on the population, the perpetrators signal to governments that their civilians will continue to suffer until political concessions are made. Terrorists themselves often describe their violence as a communication strategy. The head of the United Red Army, an obscure offshoot of the Japanese Red Army, explained: "Violent actions . . . are shocking. We want to shock people everywhere . . . It is our way of communicating with the people" (McKnight 1974, 168). Al Qaeda used similar language to characterize its violence. Osama bin Laden and his deputy Ayman al-Zawahiri described the September 11, 2001, terrorist attack as a "message with no words" which is "the only language understood by the West" (quoted in Abrahms 2005).

But in practice the violence seldom amplifies terrorist grievances. Historical accounts confirm that the far-left American group from the 1970s, the Weather Underground, could "bomb their names on to the front pages, but they could do next to nothing to make sure that the message intended by their bombings was also the message transmitted" (Schmid & de Graaf 1982, 111). The sociologist Charles Tilly likewise observed that American journalists did not grasp the political purpose of Chechen hostage-taking in the 1990s beyond "senseless acts" of violence (Tilly 2003, 237). As a RAND study noted in the 1980s, "Although terrorism is often described as a form of communication, terrorists are rather poor communicators" because "the violence of terrorism is rarely understood by the public" (Cordes et al. 1984, 1). Indeed, terrorists themselves frequently complain that their violence is misunderstood by the target country (O'Malley 2007).

Terrorism is a politically ineffective strategy precisely because it is a flawed communication strategy. Rather than focusing on the political demands, people tend to fixate on the extreme violence itself and infer from it that the perpetrators are unappeasable sociopaths committed to their destruction and thus poor candidates for political negotiation. To assess this thesis, I conducted the first large-n studies ever published to empirically assess whether terrorism works politically. I found that groups are significantly more likely to achieve their political demands when they direct their violence against military and other government targets rather than civilian ones (Abrahms 2006). Because it is generally understood as an anticivilian tactic, terrorism does not pay politically.

An illustrative example was Al Qaeda on September 11, 2001. Bin Laden said the point was to eject the United States from the Muslim world. In response to the watershed attack against American civilians, U.S. forces did the opposite by toppling the Taliban from power in Afghanistan, killing off numerous Al Qaeda leaders and occupying the country. The American response to September 11 demonstrates how terrorism tends to provoke target countries rather than coercing government compliance. Grinding down American forces in

Afghanistan, however, ultimately persuaded the U.S. military after two decades to withdraw in accordance with the 9/11 demands. This example underscores how target selection matters. Whereas attacks on military forces often coerce concessions, terrorist attacks on civilians tend to provoke governments into digging in their political heels and going on the offensive.

The negative relationship between terrorist attacks on civilians and government concessions remains statistically significant even after accounting for all sorts of other variables such as the strength of the perpetrators and the nature of their political demands (Abrahms 2012; see also Fortna 2015). In this sense, terrorism is not only a strategy for political losers, but a losing political strategy.

An interesting question is why people engage in terrorism when it seldom pays off politically. One possibility is that terrorists are simply irrational. The problem with this explanation is that most terrorists are typically understood as cognitively normal (Sprinzak 2000). Another explanation is that terrorists simply overestimate the likelihood of political success (Abrahms and Lula 2012) and then eschew attacks against civilians over time as the negative political effects of the terrorism become more apparent (Abrahms 2018). This explanation appears to have some merit, although many foreign terrorist organizations toil fecklessly for decades without political progress. A final possibility is that people may partake in terrorism for all sorts of personal reasons that can have surprisingly little to do with politics, such as for the social ties (Abrahms 2008), food, shelter (Tullock 1971), and power (Lichbach 1998). Terrorism can indeed help perpetrators achieve these "selective incentives," even if the tactic is ineffective or even politically counterproductive.

References

Abrahms, Max. 2005. "Al Qaeda's Miscommunication War: The Terrorism Paradox." *Terrorism and Political Violence* 17, no. 4: 529–549.

Abrahms, Max. 2006. "Why Terrorism Does Not Work." *International Security* 31, no. 2: 42–78.

Abrahms, Max. 2008. "What Terrorists Really Want: Terrorist Motives and Counterterrorism Strategy." *International Security* 32, no. 4: 78–105.

Abrahms, Max. 2012. "The Political Effectiveness of Terrorism Revisited." *Comparative Political Studies* 45, no. 3: 366–393.

Abrahms, Max. 2018. *Rules for Rebels: The Science of Victory in Militant History*. Oxford: Oxford University Press.

Abrahms, Max and Karolina Lula. 2012. "Why Terrorists Overestimate the Odds of Victory." *Perspectives on Terrorism* 6, no. 4/5: 46–62.

Cordes, Bonnie, Bruce Hoffman, Brian Michael Jenkins, Konrad Kellen, Sue Moran, and William Sater. 1984. *Trends in International Terrorism: 1982 and 1983*. Santa Monica, CA: Rand.

Fortna, Virginia Page. 2015. "Do Terrorists Win? Rebels' Use of Terrorism and Civil War Outcomes." *International Organization* 69, no. 3: 519–556.

Lichbach, Mark Irving. 1998. *The Rebel's Dilemma*. Ann Arbor: University of Michigan Press.

McKnight, Gerald. 1974. *The Mind of the Terrorist*. London: Michael Joseph Limited.

O'Malley, Padraig. 2007. *Shades of Difference: Mac Maharaj and the Struggle for South Africa*. New York: Penguin Books.

Pape, Robert A. 2006. *Dying to Win: The Strategic Logic of Suicide Terrorism*. New York: Random House.

Schmid, Alex P. 2012. "The Revised Academic Consensus Definition of Terrorism." *Perspectives on Terrorism* 6, no. 2: 158–159.

Schmid, Alex P. and J. de Graaf. 1982. *Violence as Communication: Insurgent Terrorism and the Western News Media*. Beverly Hills, CA: Sage.

Sprinzak, Ehud. 2000. "Rational Fanatics." *Foreign Policy* September-October 2000, no. 120: 66–73.

Tilly, Charles. 2003. *The Politics of Collective Violence.* Cambridge: Cambridge University Press.

Tullock, Gordon. 1971. "The Paradox of Revolution." *Public Choice* 11, no. 1: 89–99.

Max Abrahms is an associate professor of public policy and political science at Northeastern University, where he specializes in the study of terrorism. Abrahms has published extensively in leading academic and popular outlets such as International Organization, International Security, International Studies Quarterly, Security Studies, Comparative Political Studies, Harvard Business Review, Foreign Affairs, Foreign Policy, New York Times, Washington Post, USA Today, *and* Los Angeles Times. *His book,* Rules for Rebels, *explains why the conventional wisdom about the Islamic State was wrong. Abrahms regularly fields questions about the terrorism landscape in the news and for government agencies. He has held fellowships and other research affiliations with the Center for International Security and Cooperation at Stanford University, the Empirical Studies of Conflict project at Princeton University, the Dickey Center for International Understanding at Dartmouth College, the Council on Foreign Relations, the Combating Terrorism Center at West Point Military Academy, the Center for Cyber and Homeland Security at George Washington University, the Moshe Dayan Center at Tel Aviv University, the economics department at Bar Ilan University, the Observer Research Foundation in New Delhi, the political science department at Johns Hopkins University, and the Belfer Center at Harvard University.*

Without the Rule of Law, What's Left?
Kevork Kazanjian

Terrorism is inherently political. It is easy to fixate on the violent nature of terrorism as non-state groups target noncombatants, and this use of violence certainly separates terrorism from other forms of political behavior. However, the wider political context is also critical when assessing terrorism's effect and impact. Terrorism need not amass a large death count to have major ramifications in a society.

According to the Center for Strategic and International Studies (CSIS), only 25% of the nearly 900 defined terrorist attacks in the United States between the years 1994 and 2020 were defined as leftwing terrorism (Jones, Doxcee, and Harrington 2020). Based on CSIS measures, leftwing terrorism is among the least-concerning variants and rightwing terrorism is currently the most prolific. Although many of the reports from mainstream media sources and government agencies argue that the biggest terrorist threat within the United States comes from rightwing extremists, leftwing terrorism is more concerning to the United States because leaders in mainstream institutions have normalized this violence as acceptable, with tragic consequences for the rule of law. It would be a mistake to focus solely on measures of the number of attacks and their casualties and ignore how the normalization of violence by members of these groups directly challenges one of the bedrocks of a free society. This normalization of leftwing terrorism constitutes the greatest terrorism threat in the United States today.

To begin with, the CSIS statistics have validity issues since attacks by members of the "involuntary celibate" (incel) movement are coded as right-wing (Jones, Doxcee, and Harrington 2020). Incels are men who are hateful toward women due to their own inability to secure romantic relationships, but it is puzzling why violence by incels would be categorized as rightwing in nature. In fact, research shows that more involuntary celibates identify as leftwing (45%) in affiliation than rightwing (39%) (Costello et al. 2022, 387). Setting this aside, extremist ideology of any sort can mobilize tremendous violence and extreme manifestations of leftwing ideology is no different. Based on the statistical compilations of scholar R. J. Rummel (1994, 8), over 70% of the deaths tabulated by the top nine bloodiest dictators in the last century were at the hands of communists, with nearly 68% of this amount (over 88 million killed) at the hands of Lenin and Stalin in the Soviet Union and Mao Zedong in the People's Republic of China. The Khmer Rouge regime in Cambodia killed as many as 2 million of the country's 8 million people at the time. All violence is horrific regardless of the ideology that motivated it, but the greatest human suffering in the modern era hails from totalitarian governments, and particularly those motivated by leftwing ideology. Why might those adhering to Marxist ideology in these countries have committed such widespread violence against their own citizens?

At its core Marxist ideology is based on a materialist understanding of human affairs that sees conflict as the result of a class struggle between a capitalist ownership class with wealth and an impoverished working class. Moreover, it is utopian in its aspiration of ending the class struggle and sees the enlargement and empowering of the state as necessary to create harmony through forced equality of outcome, as opposed to the equality of opportunity. As those prior cases illustrate, unobstructed extremist left-wing governance assumes a totalitarian character and fanatical zeal that justifies violence against those who would block the power of the state to pursue the promised utopia. In the Russian, Chinese, and Cambodian examples, among others, not only did the governments commit mass murder, but their systems simply exchanged who the elites were in the society, leaving the bulk of citizens more impoverished than before their revolutions. Violence does not have to be carried out by those holding government power to have effect. In Peru between 1980 and 2000, the communist Shining Path group waged a campaign of terror and rebellion that is estimated to have killed over 18,000 people (Rendon 2019, 7).

The American experience is unique in that the United States globally fought against totalitarian regimes, combating fascist regimes in Nazi Germany and Imperial Japan in the 1940s, and then containing communist Soviet efforts to expand in the Cold War, which formally ended in 1991 with an American victory.

The efforts of the U.S. government were oriented against such extreme regimes motivated by their ideologies. Nevertheless, leftwing ideology expanded domestically in the 1960s with the rise of the "New Left" wave and a gradual expansion of politically leftist individuals in academia, mass media, and technology corporations.

The university is one of the most lopsided areas in terms of political representation. Of those who agree that politics on college campuses lean toward a political viewpoint, 77% said the lean was liberal versus 15% who said it leans conservative (Parker 2019). Data profiling the partisan identification of university faculty notes that on the low end there is a ratio of 4.5 Democrats per Republican in the subject of economics and on the high end 33.5 Democrats per Republican in the subject of history (Langbert et al. 2016). In none of the categories surveyed did Republican faculty outnumber Democrats. Other examples abound where workers in the media and big tech are also overwhelmingly leftwing in their politics (Pearlstein 2020; Call et al. 2022, 5). The lack of diversity in these influential sectors of society promotes leftwing ideology without the stabilizing presence of alternate perspectives.

Leftist influence reached a crescendo in recent years, and the most visible militant agitators are the many chapters of the popular leftwing organization Antifa, shorthand for anti-fascist. The name and flag are derived from the Soviet-aligned German Communist Party during the early 1930s. The most active contemporary American chapter started in Portland in 2007 and combines anarchist tactics with communist ideology. Berkeley chapters of the group first started organizing counterprotests to rightwing demonstrations, and the Portland elements have since advanced to using incendiary devices against the Federal Court House in Portland in July 2020. There Antifa operatives also attacked conservative journalist Andy Ngo for his reporting on the chapter's activities. In Washington state, an Antifa sympathizer attempted to bomb an Immigration and Customs Enforcement detention center in 2019 (Jones, Doxcee, and Harrington 2020, 7).

Antifa and others' biggest successes to date are normalizing leftwing political violence in the United States. In the year 2020, elements of the group supported the insurrection of the Capitol Hill Autonomous Zone (CHAZ) in Seattle, Washington, in June, and in August, Antifa conducted 100 days of "protest" in Portland, attacking the federal courthouse and federal law enforcement officers in the city. Notably, the sustained campaign was absent from most national level news, and in both cases, the local authorities failed to respond effectively. In Portland, dozens of militants were arrested only to be released by district attorneys who chose not to prosecute them for their violent criminal activity (Lambert 2021).

What makes leftwing extremism most dangerous today is that groups like Antifa have the support of many intellectuals, government officials, and members of the media. Looking back at the summer of 2020, massive protests and political violence raged across the United States in Minnesota, Washington, Oregon, California, and New York City following the killing of George Floyd. While most demonstrators were nonviolent in their protests, in many instances they were accompanied by those using violence. In May 2020, some of those arrested for violent actions in Minneapolis had their bail paid for by the staff of then presidential candidate Joseph Biden through donations to the Minnesota Freedom Fund (Lange and Hunnicutt 2020). One media outlet showcased a journalist standing across the street from a burning city block and labelled the protests "Fiery but mostly peaceful" (Concha 2020). Later in June, CNN opinion commentor Chris Cuomo stated, "Please, show me where it says protesters have to be polite and peaceful?" (*Cuomo Prime Time* 2020). Mr. Cuomo had apparently not read or understood the full text of the First Amendment to include the right of the people to "peaceably" assemble. According to RealClearInvestigation, despite over 16,000 arrests made over the course of the summer, over 90% of charges in major cities were dropped by district attorneys who refused to enforce the law, and property damages totaled over $1 billion (2022). More important than the direct costs is the double standard that now permeates society where there is not an equal treatment under the law for political conservatives. A clear example is the relentless prosecution of hundreds of unarmed and nonviolent persons who walked into the Capitol grounds after the initial violence on January 6, 2021, compared to how charges were dropped against the hundreds who participated in the 2017 riots that accompanied Donald Trump's inauguration (Khalil 2018).

The effects of diminishing the rule of law are not without consequence. Tragically, the weak response to the political violence of the summer of 2020 led to an increase in homicides nationally. Pressure for police departments to scale back police activity or defund departments was met by an increase in the homicide rate, a sharp reversal of the nationwide trend of year-on-year declines in murders across the country (Cassell 2020, 118). The number of murders in the United States in 2020 climbed to 21,570 and constituted a 30% increase from the previous year. It was the single largest increase on record (Reuters 2021). Until that year homicide rates had been on a notable downward trend since a peak in the early 1990s. Tragically, minority communities bore the brunt of this increased violence, likely due to limitations on policing and selective enforcement, and the yearly net increase of 4,900 murders from the previous year dwarfs the human cost of terrorism in the United States during the same period.

Leftwing terrorism may not be seen as prolific in any direct accounting of casualties, but the fact that it is tolerated produces a far wider impact than even that suffered by those who are directly victimized by it. It is not conducive to the stability of a democratic and free society.

References

Call, Andrew C., Scott Emett, Edlar Maksymov, and Nathan Y. Sharp. 2022. "Survey Evidence on Financial Journalists as Information Intermediaries." *Meet the Press* 73, nos. 2–3

(April–May): 101455. https://www.sciencedirect.com /science/article/abs/pii/S0165410121000707.

Cassell, Paul G. 2020. "Explaining the Recent Homicide Spike in U.S. Cities: The 'Minneapolis Effect' and the Decline in Proactive Policing." *Federal Sentencing Reporter* 33, no. 1–2 (October/December): 83–127. https://online .ucpress.edu/fsr/article/33/1-2/83/115494/Explaining-the -Recent-Homicide-Spikes-in-U-S.

Concha, Joe. 2020. "CNN Ridiculed for 'Fiery but Mostly Peaceful' Caption with Video of Burning Building in Kenosha." *The Hill*, August 27, 2020. https://thehill.com /homenews/media/513902-cnn-ridiculed-for-fiery-but -mostly-peaceful-caption-with-video-of-burning.

Costello, William, Vania Rolon, Andrew G. Thomas, and David Schmitt. 2022. "Levels of Well-Being Among Men Who Are Incel (Involuntarily Celibate)." *Evolutionary Psychology Science* 8, no. 4 (December): 375–390.

Cuomo Prime Time. 2020. Produced by Melanie Buck. Aired June 2, 2020, on Cable News Network (CNN). https:// twitter.com/SteveGuest/status/1267987525198585856.

Jones, Seth G., Catrina Doxcee, and Nicholas Harrington. 2020. "The Escalating Terrorism in the United States." *Center for Strategic and International Studies Briefs* (June 2020). https://csis-website-prod.s3.amazonaws .com/s3fs-public/publication/200612_Jones _DomesticTerrorism_v6.pdf.

Khalil, Ashraf. 2018. "Government Drops Charges Against All Inauguration Protesters." Associated Press, July 6. https://apnews.com/article/40e5eab2fd964098b8c60ed1 4de35398.

Lambert, Hannah Ray. 2021. "Protesters 'Emboldened,' Despite Tough Talk from Portland Officials." *KOIN News*, January 5. https://www.koin.com/news/protests /protesters-emboldened-despite-tough-talk.

Langbert, Mitchell, Anthony J. Quain, and Daniel B. Klein. 2016. "Faculty Voter Registration in Economics, History, Journalism, Law, and Psychology." *Econ Journal Watch* 13, no. 3 (September): 422–451.

Lange, Jason and Trevor Hunnicutt. 2020. "Biden Staff Donate to Group that Pays Bail in Riot-torn Minneapolis." *Reuters*, May 30. https://www.reuters.com/article/us -minneapolis-police-biden-bail/biden-staff-donate-to-group -that-pays-bail-in-riot-torn-minneapolis-idUSKBN2360SZ.

Parker, Kim. 2019. "The Growing Partisan Divide in Views of Higher Education." Pew Research Center, August 19. https://www.pewresearch.org/social-trends/2019/08/19/the -growing-partisan-divide-in-views-of-higher-education-2/.

Pearlstein, Joanna. 2020. "Tech Workers Lean Left, But Their Companies' PACs Play Both Sides." *Protocol*, February 25. https://www.protocol.com/tech-company-pacs-2019-2020.

Rendon, Silvio. 2019. "Capturing Correctly: A Reanalysis of the Indirect Capture-Recapture Methods in the Peruvian Truth and Reconciliation Commission." *Research and Politics* 6, no. 1 (January–March): 1–8.

Rummel, R. J. 1994. *Death by Government*. New Brunswick: Transaction Publishers.

"RealClearInvestigations' Jan. 6-BLM Side-by-Side Comparison." 2022. *RealClearInvestigation*, Accessed January 26, 2023. https://www.realclearinvestigations.com /articles/2021/09/09/realclearinvestigations_jan_6-blm _comparison_database_791370.html.

"U.S. Murders Soar Nearly 30% in 2020, FBI Reports." 2021. *Reuters*, September 28, 2021. https://www.reuters .com/world/us/us-murders-soar-nearly-30-2020-fbi -reports-2021-09-28/.

Kevork Kazanjian *has a master's degree in national security studies and is a political science instructor at Victor Valley College.*

Rightwing Terrorism: History and Trends
Simeone Miller

In 2009, the U.S. Department of Homeland Security warned of a potential surge in rightwing extremist attacks, with groups focused on contentious political issues such as illegal immigration and gun policy (U.S. Department of Homeland Security). According to the report these groups maintained an active interest in recruiting U.S. veterans who had served in Iraq and Afghanistan during the War on Terror (Beirich 2011).

Explanations for the anticipated surge were attributed to perceived grievances surrounding the 2008 economic recession and the election of the nation's first African American president (Beirich 2011). Following its leak, the report was criticized by some media outlets, veteran's groups, and Republican Party lawmakers who suggested that the Obama administration politically targeted conservative Americans. Consequently, the administration withdrew the report and directed reductions in the unit's staff unrelated to analyzing Islamist extremism (Smith 2011).

Concurrent with the assessment's projections, the United States saw a dramatic rise in domestic terrorist activity in the 2010s. From 1994 to 2020, there were over 893 domestic terrorist attacks. Of those 893 terrorist attacks, rightwing extremists accounted for 57% while leftwing, religious, ethnonationalist, and other forms combined accounted for 42.7% (Jones, Doxsee, and Harrington 2020).

Many of these attacks can be attributed to political and socioeconomic polarization. This was the case in the lead up to and during January 6 when an assortment of extremist organizations and individuals breached the U.S. Capitol in Washington, D.C., to prevent the certification of the 2020 presidential election results (Tucker and Mascaro 2021). The attack on the capitol highlighted how rightwing extremist ideology had intensified and diversified due to continued sociopolitical grievances, the COVID-19 pandemic, and the capacity for far-right groups to network (Sewell 2021).

Commentators noted that these trends in domestic terrorism are not unprecedented in U.S. history. Scholar Kathleen Belew notes how the modern norms of white supremacy and militant rightwing radicalism are based on Cold War–era perceptions of global communism being an existential threat to the future of Christianity (2018, 7–9). The American defeat in the Vietnam War motivated some veterans disillusioned by their country's loss to adopt radical beliefs (Belew 2018, 7–9).

The 1970s presented a renaissance of social activism via the New Left, with the gay rights movement as well as second-wave feminism. For the far right, these movements defined their worst fears. This led Vietnam War veterans on both sides of the political spectrum to be driven by both economic and social anxiety. These anxieties, also common to subsequent generations of men and women who served in the armed forces, eased the transition from the use of violence in war for wider political purposes to domestic attacks against civilian targets (Belew 2018, 7–9).

The most infamous example of violent rightwing domestic terrorism came in 1995 with the Oklahoma City bombing. Timothy McVeigh, one of the perpetrators of the attack, served in the 1991 Gulf War and had become radicalized after the Ruby Ridge incident, which began when U.S. Marshals sought to apprehend Randy Weaver at his remote Ruby Ridge, Idaho, cabin for a failure to appear in court for firearms-related charges. A shootout took place after the Weaver family's discovery of a Marshal surveillance team on their property, killing Marshal William Degan and Randy Weaver's son, Samuel. This led to a week-long standoff during which a federal agent shot and killed Weaver's wife, Vicki. After Weaver and his three daughters finally surrendered to authorities, it was discovered he had missed his court appearance because the court had issued him the wrong date to appear. The Ruby Ridge standoff subsequently became a rallying cry for the far-right militia movement.

After Ruby Ridge, McVeigh traveled to Waco, where he witnessed the ATF raid against the Branch Davidians' compound and passed out antigovernment literature (PBS 2017). After a law enforcement raid on the Branch Davidian compound in April 1993 triggered a standoff and ultimately a fire that claimed the lives of 76 Branch Davidians, McVeigh and fellow veteran Terri Lynn Nichols planned a violent attack against the United States as a response to what they perceived to be a tyrannical government that was persecuting gun owners (PBS 2017).

Originally, McVeigh and Nichols planned to assassinate U.S. Attorney General Janet Reno for her role in both Ruby Ridge and Waco (Gullo 2006). However, the duo gradually shifted their focus to targeting federal government offices (Thomas and Smothers 1995). Eventually they settled on the Murrah Building in Oklahoma City, which housed military recruiting offices as well as offices for the Drug Enforcement Agency (DEA) and the Bureau of Alcohol, Tobacco, and Firearms (ATF) (Lewis 2000). Two years after the Waco siege, the duo copied a 1983 Aryan Nations attempt against the building by using stolen fertilizer to create a truck bomb.

The 1995 attack in Oklahoma City shocked the American public in part because of the unprecedented nature of its intensity, with over 168 were killed and another 680 injured, but also because McVeigh and Nichols were American citizens and military veterans (Stammer and Hall 1995).

Since 1995, efforts by law enforcement agencies to effectively prevent rightwing terrorism have been complicated by civil liberty protections. One such example is the unpredicted 2019 mass shooting at a Walmart in El Paso, where the perpetrator killed 23 Hispanics in a race-based attack. According to the FBI, the perpetrator targeted Walmart shoppers because he wanted to prevent an invasion by immigrants at the U.S.–Mexico border (Dearman 2020). This was not the first or only instance where a rightwing terrorist used a firearm in the commission of their attack. In fact, most rightwing terrorists employ firearms in the commission of their crimes (Yablon 2017). This is a result of rightwing extremists amassing arsenals that they brandish in defiance of any measure that may restrict their

Second Amendment rights (Jenkins 2021). Therefore, policies that can reduce extremists' access to firearms potentially lead to standoffs between extremists and law enforcement, as well as allegations that the government is attempting to impede the rights of private citizens.

Since the tragedies at Ruby Ridge and Waco, federal law enforcement agencies have often employed greater restraint in pursuing cases to avoid escalating tensions. In 2014, officers of the federal Bureau of Land Management entered a weeks-long standoff against cattle ranchers and militia groups in Nevada. The standoff began after the ranchers had been grazing their cattle on federal lands without permits and government contractors were sent to seize the herds. At the height of the standoff, with militia and federal officers pointing weapons at one another, authorities withdrew to avoid escalating the situation (Lind 2016). This strategy from authorities caused zero casualties on either side. However, federal officers were unable to detain anyone involved. This highlighted a debate over whether the ranchers had been victims of authoritarian government or actual terrorists. In 2016 some of these same ranchers in the Nevada case were involved in another standoff with federal agents at a wildlife refuge in Oregon that led to the death of one rancher who violently resisted arrest, as well as the arrest and conviction of 16 others.

The debate has been revived in the aftermath of January 6 attack on the Capitol, given that there is no specific law against domestic terrorism. In the context of the Capitol breach, six individuals affiliated with the Oath Keepers group have been convicted of seditious conspiracy (U.S. Department of Justice 2023), and over 250 perpetrators were charged with assaulting or impeding law enforcement. Most of the nearly 1,000 people identified so far, however, have only been charged with low-level offenses such as trespassing and disrupting federal business (Gerstein and Cheney 2021; Johnson 2023).

Rightwing terrorism is not a new phenomenon, and its presence today is a reminder that extremism is a persistent force within the United States as it is outside of it. Terrorism motivated by rightwing ideology has evolved in recent decades to represent not just white supremacy but also antigovernment ideology and conspiracy theories which can appeal to individuals who do not identify with the political right.

References

Beirich, Heidi. 2011. "Inside the DHS: Former Top Analyst Says Agency Bowed to Political Pressure." *Intelligence Report*, June 17. https://www.splcenter.org/fighting-hate /intelligence-report/2011/inside-dhs-former-top-analyst -says-agency-bowed-political-pressure.

Belew, Kathleen. 2018. *Bring the War Home*. Cambridge: Harvard University Press.

Dearman, Eleanor. 2020. "Racism and the Aug. 3 Shooting: One Year Later, El Paso Reflects on the Hate Behind the Attack." *El Paso Times*, July 29. https://www.elpasotimes .com/in-depth/news/2020/07/30/el-paso-walmart -shooting-community-reflect-racist-motive-behind -attack/5450331002/.

Gerstein, Joshua and Cheney, Kyle. 2021. "Many Capitol Rioters Unlikely to Serve Jail Time." *Politico*, March 30. https://www.politico.com/news/2021/03/30/jan-6-capitol -riot-jail-time-478440.

Gullo, Karen. 2006. "McVeigh Wanted to Assassinate Reno." *ABC News*, January 7. https://abcnews.go.com/US/story?id =93454&page=1.

Jenkins, Brian. 2021. "Domestic Violent Extremists Will Be Harder to Combat Than Homegrown Jihadists." *Rand Corporation*, February 1. https://www.rand.org/blog /2021/02/domestic-violent-extremists-will-be-harder-to -combat.html.

Johnson, Arianna. 2023. "Jan. 6 Insurrection 2 Years Later: How Many Arrested, Convicted and What Price Donald

Trump May Still Pay." *Forbes*, January 5. https://www
.forbes.com/sites/ariannajohnson/2023/01/05/jan-6
-insurrection-2-years-later-how-many-arrested-convicted
-and-what-price-donald-trump-may-still-pay/.

Jones, Seth G., Catrina Doxsee, and Nicholas Harrington.
2020. *The Escalating Terrorism Problem in the United States.*
https://www.csis.org/analysis/escalating-terrorism-problem
-united-states. Washington, DC: CSIS.

Lewis, Carol W. 2000. "The Terror That Failed: Public
Opinion in the Aftermath of the Bombing in Oklahoma
City." *Public Administration Review* 60, no. 3: 201–210.
https://doi.org/10.1111/0033-3352.00080.

Lind, Dara. 2016. "Waco and Ruby Ridge: The 1990s
Standoff Haunting the Oregon Takeover, Explained." *Vox*,
January 5. https://www.vox.com/2016/1/5/10714746
/waco-ruby-ridge-oregon.

Nacos, Brigitte L. 2016. *Terrorism and Counterterrorism.* New
York: Routledge.

PBS. 2017. "Tracing the Roots of the America's Biggest
Domestic Terror Attack." Video, February 7. 2:35. https://
www.pbs.org/newshour/show/tracing-roots-americas
-biggest-domestic-terror-attack.

Sewell, Tia. 2021. "ODNI Assesses That Domestic Violent
Extremism Poses Heightened Threat in 2021." *Lawfare*,
April 12. https://www.lawfareblog.com/odni-assesses
-domestic-violent-extremism-poses-heightened-threat-2021.

Smith, Jeffrey R. 2011. "Homeland Security Department
Curtails Home-Grown Terror Analysis." *The Washington
Post*, June 7. https://www.washingtonpost.com/politics
/homeland-security-department-curtails-home-grown
-terror-analysis/2011/06/02/AGQEaDLH_story.html.

Stammer, Larry B. and Carla Hall. 1995. "Terror in
Oklahoma City: American Muslims Feel Sting of
Accusations in Bombing's Wake: Reaction: Talk of a

Middle East Link Led to Epithets Against the Ethnic Community. The Arrest of a Midwesterner Has Spurred a Collective Sigh of Relief." *Los Angeles Times*, April 22. https://www.latimes.com/archives/la-xpm-1995-04-22 -mn-57460-story.html.

Thomas, Jo and Ronald Smothers. 1995. "Oklahoma City Building Was Target of Plot as Early as '83, Official Says." *The New York Times*, May 20, 1–6.

Tucker, Eric and Lisa Mascaro. 2021. "Pro-Trump Mob Storms US Capitol in Bid to Overturn Election." Associated Press, January 5. https://apnews.com/article /congress-confirm-joe-biden-78104aea082995bbd7412a6e 6cd13818.

U.S. Department of Homeland Security. Office of Intelligence and Analysis. 2009. "Rightwing Extremism: Current Economic and Political Climate Fueling Resurgence in Radicalization and Recruitment." https://fas.org/irp /eprint/rightwing.pdf.

U.S. Department of Justice. 2023. "Four Oath Keepers Found Guilty of Seditious Conspiracy Related to U.S. Capitol Breach: Defendants Also Convicted of Felony Charges." Office of Public Affairs, January 23. https:// www.justice.gov/opa/pr/four-oath-keepers-found-guilty -seditious-conspiracy-related-us-capitol-breach.

Yablon, Alex. 2017. "In Attacks by Right-Wing Extremists, Guns Are More Likely Than Bombs to Kill and Injure." *The Trace*, June 7. https://www.thetrace.org/2017/06 /right-wing-extremists-attacks-guns-bombs/.

Simeone Miller is a candidate in the Social Sciences and Globalization M.A. program at California State University, San Bernardino, where he concentrates in conflict and peace studies. Previously he was a researcher at the Center for the Study of Hate and Extremism at the university.

Ethnonationalist/Separatist Groups
Anibal Serrano

Ethnonationalist/separatist groups are in direct conflict with the norms of the international system by using violence to challenge a state's sovereignty to obtain independence from a nation-state. The motivation for ethnonationalist/separatist terrorism is frequently based "in grievances such as injustice (real or perceived), discrimination, and marginalization suffered by a social or political minority" (Forest 2018, 74). Notably, ethnonationalist/separatist groups have a more domestic focus compared to other terrorist groups.

This dynamic is connected to the Westphalian nation-state system, which was created in 1648 by European statesmen who ratified the Treaty of Westphalia, making the "nation-states the primary institutionalized actors in a global system of relations" (Forest 2018, 75). However, in the ethnonationalist/separatist's perspective, their "grievances stem from what they characterize as oppressive action (or inaction) on the part of the government and/or the majority population" (Council on Foreign Relations n.d.). This form of terrorism can encompass different ideologies, but a shared trait is an emphasis on the identity of the ethnic group seeking separation compared to that of the government.

A significant difference between ethnonationalist/separatist groups and other terrorist labeled groups is the fact that they seek to "carve out a state for themselves from a larger country or annex territory from one country to that of another" (EUROPOL 2020, 54). Three cases of ethnonationalist/separatist terrorist groups from different regions illustrates their common features. The first group is the Euskadi ta Askatasuna (ETA, Basque Fatherland and Liberty) in Spain, the second is the Liberation Tigers of Tamil Eelam (LTTE) in Sri Lanka, and finally, the Kurdistan Workers' Party (PKK) in Turkey.

Euskadi ta Askatasuna

During the Spanish Civil War in 1937, the Nationalist forces led by Francisco Franco defeated Republican forces in the north of the country, including the Basque region. Just the year before, the Basques had obtained a Statute of Autonomy from the Republican government that allowed for a degree of self-governance. After Franco's victory, the statute ended, and Basques suffered under the Nationalist government. The state, for example, placed restrictions on the Basque language and cultural expression.

In this context, the ETA was established in 1959 as an outgrowth of a student movement inspired to create an "independent homeland in Spain's Basque region" (*BBC News* 2019). The group drew strength from the well-established cultural, ethnic, and linguistic interests of the Basque minority (Harmon 2012, 589). The violent ETA campaign that ensued for the next 59 years featured terrorist attacks against Spanish civilians, assassinations of government officials, and guerilla attacks against Spanish security forces. The group's continued survival was aided by using safe houses across the French border, where other Basques supportive of the group lived. Despite the violent efforts, the ETA was unsuccessful. The Basques did attain greater autonomy in 1979 following Franco's death, when the new democratic Spanish government recognized a new statute of autonomy. However, the ETA continued its violent campaign over the succeeding 30 years. An international peace conference in 2011 isolated Basque extremism, however, and set the ETA on the path to formal dissolution in 2018. The leader of the group was arrested in 2019 (Harmon 2012, 590–93).

Liberation Tigers of Tamil Eelam

The LTTE was formed in 1976 due to discontent of the minority Tamils based on their treatment by the Sinhalese following Sri Lankan independence in 1948. The group's formation was a direct response to mob violence against Tamil communities

(Richards 2014, 6–11). The LTTE fought the Sri Lankan government from 1983 to 2009 and aimed to create a Tamil nation that would function independently and without the majority-led Sinhalese Sri Lankan state (Hashim 2018, 336).

The LTTE used suicide bombings and assassinations as part of their campaigns. It also developed a conventional and sophisticated infrastructure, including specific uniformed armed forces and networks of funding and support from ethnic Tamils in India. The LTTE fought a multiphased civil war against the Sri Lankan military and used terrorism as one of its tactics in killing 4,000 civilians over its 33-year existence (Diaz and Murshed 2013, 288–289). Moreover, the LTTE engaged in violence against competing Tamil groups. In 2009 the LTTE was defeated by the Sri Lankan military after the former captured its territory in the north of the island. However, as Ahmed Salah Hashim mentions, "military victory does not equal political victory" (Hashim 2018, 345–346). The Tamil minority continues to reside in Sri Lanka, and nationwide protests against President Rajapaksa for his response to the country's post-COVID economic crisis did not widely feature ethnic Tamils, who fear they will be targeted for violence and further discrimination (Marsh 2022). The new government in Sri Lanka under President Wickremesing has stated, though, that national reconciliation is among its chief priorities.

Kurdistan Workers' Party

The Kurds are an ethnic minority group who have resided historically in regions of modern-day Iran, Iraq, Syria, and Turkey. The 1916 Sykes-Picot agreement split the Middle East into British and French zones of influence and created the boundaries of the region in the modern era (Ariav 2021).

After World War I, in the 1923 Treaty of Lausanne, the Kurds, who inhabited previous Ottoman territories, were scattered throughout Iran, Iraq, Syria, and Turkey (Ariav 2021). In this context, the PKK is the main Kurdish group fighting for separatism for Kurds in Turkey. The PKK was founded as a

Marxist-Leninist organization by Abdullah Ocalan in 1978 in an effort to establish a Kurdistan state independent of Turkey (Thomas and Zanotti 2019, 1). In 1984, Ocalan launched an insurgency from Syria into Turkey, beginning the hostilities between the PKK and the Turkish government.

Ocalan was captured in 1999 by Turkish agents, which ended the PKK–Turkish conflict for a time. In 2004, however, the PKK discarded the ceasefire and resumed its insurgency, and in 2019 Turkey's military invaded Kurdish-inhabited parts of northeast Syria. The Turkish government continues to consider the PKK an active challenge because of "(1) its 'democratic confederalism' with major Kurdish groups in Syria (PYD) and Iran (PJAK) seeking greater autonomy or functional independence, (2) financial and media support from the Kurdish diaspora in Europe, and (3) its military safe haven in the Qandil mountains [near the Iranian border]" (Zanotti and Thomas 2019, 1). The Turkish government fears Kurdish separatism in the southeast of Turkey.

As of January 2023, Turkey has blocked the admission of Finland and Sweden into the NATO alliance. Those two European governments sought entry into NATO following Russia's invasion of Ukraine, but Turkish officials charge the two countries with harboring PKK militants (Reuters 2023). From the Kurdish perspective, Turkish leaders deny Kurdish freedoms and use Kurds as a security scapegoat to unify various non-Kurdish political factions given the country's poor economic performance. Turkish government officials froze pro–Kurdish People's Democratic Party (HDP) bank accounts in the months leading up to May 2023 presidential election, asserting that the party had connections to militants (Toksabay 2023).

Major Themes and Key Takeaways

Ethnonationalist/separatist groups can be found in various regions worldwide, and they all aim to develop their autonomous territories within the international system. This is the main distinction between such groups. Notably, they engage in violence against the nation-states they operate within, clashing with the Westphalian international system they ultimately seek to join. In each of the three examples presented previously, the group was actively fighting a nation-state. The methods and capabilities might differ from organization to organization, but the ETA, LTTE, and PKK all operated (or continue to operate) with the same goal of creating a self-governed territory for their people.

Finally, some of the notable features of ethnonationalist/separatist groups underline the saliency of the potential threat they pose. These features are present throughout all three groups mentioned earlier. They include obtaining monetary and political support among co-ethnic groups across national borders; the interweaving of insurgent and terrorist acts that create complex dynamics for nation-states attempting to curtail their influence; and the usage of an identity framework centered on ethnicity/nationalism that is potentially more robust than other identity forms based solely on political ideology.

References

Ariav, Hagit. 2021. "Timeline: The Kurds' Quest for Independence." Council on Foreign Relations, February 22. https://www.cfr.org/timeline/kurds-quest-independence.

BBC News. 2019. "Timeline: ETA Campaign." *BBC*, May 16, sec. Europe. https://www.bbc.com/news/world-europe -11181982.

Council on Foreign Relations. n.d. "Terrorism: Reducing Threats Is a Major Challenge for Both Governments and Citizens." World 101 Global Era Issues. Accessed June 13, 2021. https://world101.cfr.org/global-era-issues/terrorism.

Diaz, Fabio Andres and Syed Mansoob Murshed. 2013. "'Give War A Chance': All-Out War as a Means of Ending Conflict in the Cases of Sri Lanka and Colombia." *Civil Wars* 15, no. 3: 281–305. https://doi.org/10.1080 /13698249.2013.842743.

EUROPOL. 2020. "European Union Terrorism Situation and Trend Report 2020." The European Union Agency of Law Enforcement Cooperation.

Forest, James J. F. 2018. "Nationalist and Separatist Terrorism." In *Routledge Handbook of Terrorism and Counterterrorism*, 1st ed., edited by Andrew Silke, 74–86. Abingdon, Oxon, New York: Routledge. https://doi.org /10.4324/9781315744636.

Harmon, Christopher C. 2012. "Spain's ETA Terrorist Group Is Dying." *Orbis* 56, no. 4: 588–607. https://doi.org /10.1016/j.orbis.2012.08.005.

Hashim, Ahmed Salah. 2018. "Liberation Tigers of Tamil Eelam (LTTE)." In *Routledge Handbook of Terrorism and Counterterrorism*, 1st ed., edited by Andrew Silke, 336–349. Abingdon, Oxon, New York: Routledge. https://doi .org/10.4324/9781315744636.

Marsh, Nick. 2022. "Sri Lanka: The Divisions Behind the Country's Unified Protests." *British Broadcasting Corporation*, May 4, https://www.bbc.com/news/world-asia-61295238.

Reuters World News. 2023. "Explainer: Why Is Turkey Blocking Sweden and Finland NATO Membership?" *Reuters*, January 27. https://www.reuters.com/world/why -is-turkey-blocking-swedish-finnish-nato-membership -2023-01-25/.

Richards, Joanne. 2014. "An Institutional History of the Liberation Tigers of Tamil Eelam (LTTE)." *The Centre on Conflict, Development and Peacebuilding*, 10, 92. http:// repository.graduateinstitute.ch/record/292651.

Thomas, Clayton and Jim Zanotti. 2019. *Turkey, the PKK, and U.S. Involvement: A Chronology.* Washington, D.C.: Congressional Research Service. https://crsreports.congress .gov/product/pdf/IF/IF11380.

Toksabay, Ece. 2023. "Turkish Top Court Freezes Pro-Kurdish Party Funds as Elections Loom." *Reuters Middle East News*,

January 5. https://www.reuters.com/world/middle-east
/turkish-top-court-blocks-pro-kurdish-hdp-bank-accounts
-state-media-2023-01-05/.

Zanotti, Jim and Clayton Thomas. 2019. "The Kurds in Iraq,
Turkey, Syria, and Iran." Washington, D.C.: Congressional
Research Service. https://fas.org/sgp/crs/mideast/IF10350
.pdf.

*Anibal Serrano graduated from California State University,
San Bernardino, with his M.A. in national security studies and
is a 2020–2021 American Political Science Association Diversity Fellow. Previously he was a 2018–2019 CSU Sally Casanova
Pre-Doctoral Scholar. Anibal's research lies at the intersection of
international relations and comparative politics, particularly
political violence, peace, and security. As a 2019 visiting student
at the University of California, Irvine (UCI), Anibal carried out
research assessing the application of international relations theories to non-state armed actors (NSAAs). Anibal looks forward to
continuing his research on the impacts that NSAAs have on international, national, and human security. He began his studies in
the Ph.D. program in political science at UCI in 2020 and has
presented and published in various outlets.*

Religious Terrorism
Tim Milosch

At first glance, religious terrorism appears to have faded as a
threat to the United States. After Al-Qaeda's September 11,
2001, attacks on New York and Washington, D.C., antiterror
efforts at the state, federal, and international levels appear to
have largely succeeded in keeping such mass casualty attacks
away from American shores. Meanwhile, political polarization
at home has led to greater concern over other forms of terrorism. According to data gathered by the Center for Strategic
and International Studies (CSIS), politically motivated terrorism, particularly rightwing terrorism, now constitutes the

larger number of terrorist threats in the United States (Jones and Doxsee 2020).

However, religious terrorism, particularly radical Islamist terrorism, accounts for more real harm done at the national and global level (Romano, Rowe, and Phelps 2019). It thus remains the more dangerous terrorist threat to the United States compared to other forms of terrorism given its track record, stated objectives, adaptability, and ongoing capacity to radicalize and recruit adherents from a global audience. Put simply, religious terrorism is more severe and enduring than its counterparts.

What Is Religious Terrorism?

Religious terrorism is distinct from other forms of terrorism, but that should not lead to overgeneralizations about the merits of a given religious tradition (Wibisono, Louis, and Jetten 2019). Religious terrorism is understood to be mass violence carried out against government and civilian targets to advance a particular religious and political agenda frequently derived from fringe and/or heretical doctrines within a religious tradition. Its objectives are often tied to faith in some future utopian state that its adherents believe themselves to be able to either bring about in the present or gain in the afterlife because of their terrorist actions. As such, religious terrorists often hold to extreme doctrinal positions within their religious tradition, often citing those positions as justification for their violence (Saiya and Scime 2015).

Al-Qaeda and its descendant groups like the Islamic State (ISIS) are good examples of this characteristic through their embracing a particularly radical view of the Islamic concept of *jihad* and marrying it to an equally extreme interpretation of the doctrine of *takfir* (Wright 2007). In Islam, *jihad* is used to describe both the struggle between people and groups as well as the inner struggle against one's own sinfulness. Terrorist groups like ISIS focus their followers' attention on the external practice of *jihad* as warfare against an unbelieving world. *Takfir*, a controversial doctrine deemed heresy by some Muslim scholars, states that violence against fellow Muslims is permissible if they are considered apostate ("Takfir" n.d.; Shahzad 2007; Wright 2007). By waging *jihad* on unbelievers and declaring Muslims not supporting their cause apostate, Islamist terrorist groups create a religious justification for carrying out acts of terrorist violence against anyone who opposes them.

How Is Religious Terrorism Different from the Other Forms of Terrorism?

Religious terrorism is distinct from other forms of terrorism primarily in its scope and level of violence (Ritchie et al. 2013). Because religious terrorism is fueled by religious extremism, groups typically do not negotiate or compromise, and they frequently display a willingness to use any means available to produce as much violence and death as possible. In a word, religious terrorism has a maximalist approach to violence.

Politically motivated terrorism is narrower in focus, often targeting a selected group of individuals and/or institutions. Leftwing terrorism of the 1970s, for example, often targeted property belonging to specific institutions; when these organizations killed people, those people were often specifically targeted. By contrast, religious terrorism tends to embrace collateral damage and seeks to maximize it. The CSIS report noted, for example, that although rightwing terrorist acts outnumber religious terrorist acts, the death toll is much higher from religious terrorism (Jones and Doxsee 2020).

Why Is Religious Terrorism More Dangerous?

Detractors of the view that religious terrorism is the more dangerous form of terrorism point out that the high death toll from religious terrorism in America is almost entirely due to a single event on a single day—the September 11 attacks (Jones and Doxsee 2020). Far from this being a reason to discount religious terrorism as more dangerous, it proves the point.

The attacks of September 11 were accomplished by a global network of logistical, tactical, and financial sophistication that was tied together by a shared system of belief. That shared system of belief allowed the Al-Qaeda ideology to be exported and rebranded into more extreme versions, which found even greater success in ISIS. ISIS was able to simultaneously develop a nascent state in Syria and Iraq while continuing to support and inspire terrorist attacks in the United States, notably in San Bernardino in 2015 and Orlando in 2018.

By contrast, terrorism motivated by political ideologies or even ethnonationalist interests is by definition narrow in scope, often finding recruits and targets within the same domestic population. Leftwing and rightwing terrorism in the United States have both tended to focus on domestic political issues and targets with an aim toward advancing a particular policy-level objective like stopping environmental degradation or gaining access to federal land for agricultural purposes. Rarely do such groups seek the complete destruction of the political system they inhabit, unlike religious terrorists.

By contrast, radical Islamist terrorist groups are global in their operational capacity and objectives. ISIS, in particular, has achieved a level of adaptability in operations, radicalization, and recruitment unseen in the modern era of terrorism. Its ability to radicalize and recruit fighters, then deploy them to conflict zones half a world away is an admittedly impressive achievement that creates a range of possibilities for attacks unavailable to more domestically focused groups.

Is There a Difference Between Islamist Forms of Terrorism and Other Forms of Religious Terrorism?

When discussing religious terrorism, this essay has focused on radical Islamist terrorism as a particularly visible and threatening form of religious terrorism. However, this distinction raises an important question: Is radical Islamist terrorism different from other forms of religious terrorism?

In some respects, Islamist terrorist groups are like other religious terrorist groups in terms of their ability to recruit and motivate followers, and the adoption and universalization of controversial doctrines within a religious tradition (Ranstorp 1996). In two critical aspects, though, radical Islamist terrorism distinguishes itself as a more dangerous form of religious terrorism (Romano, Rowe, and Phelps 2019).

First, the global scope of radical Islamic terrorist operations has led to innovations in terrorist financing, recruitment, and logistics, as well as making the attacks by such groups a global security concern rather than a more regional or local one. Second, the adoption of suicide attacks as a favored tactic by radical Islamist terrorist groups creates an aura of nihilistic invincibility around the groups, which achieves dual objectives of terrorizing victim populations and gaining recruits. The promise to suicide bombers is immediate martyrdom and access to paradise, rendering every such attack a "success," if not tactically, then spiritually.

Conclusion

Ultimately, there are two ways one can measure the level of danger presented by a terrorist threat: the number and frequency of attacks, or the death toll and property damage those attacks exact. To use the former metric, one must conclude that political ideology is the more dangerous threat to the United States. However, it is the contention of this essay that the latter metric is the more accurate one to use in assessing the level of danger, and here religious terrorism, particularly radical Islamist terrorism, continues to pose the more dangerous threat to the United States (Ritchie et al. 2013). No other constellation of terrorist groups has achieved greater success in a shorter period of time in terms of undermining the American people's sense of safety and influencing government policy than the combined efforts of Al-Qaeda and the Islamic State. No other groups continue to work as diligently and creatively to build on those achievements.

References

Jones, Seth and Catrina Doxsee. 2020. "The Escalating Terrorism Problem in the United States." Center for Strategic and International Studies, June 17. Accessed July 24, 2021. https://www.csis.org/analysis/escalating -terrorism-problem-united-states.

Ranstorp, Magnus. 1996. "Terrorism in the Name of Religion." *Journal of International Affairs* 50, no. 1: 41–62.

Ritchie, Hannah, Joe Hasell, Cameron Appel, and Max Roser. 2013. "Terrorism." *Our World in Data*, July 28. Accessed July 24, 2021. https://ourworldindata.org/terrorism.

Romano, David, Stephen Rowe, and Robert Phelps. 2019. "Correlates of Terror: Trends in Types of Terrorist Groups and Fatalities Inflicted." Edited by Greg Simons. *Cogent Social Sciences* 5, no. 1: 1584957. https://doi.org/10.1080 /23311886.2019.1584957.

Saiya, Nilay and Anthony Scime. 2015. "Explaining Religious Terrorism: A Data-Mined Analysis." *Conflict Management and Peace Science* 32, no. 5: 487–512.

Shahzad, Syed Saleem. 2007. "Takfirism: A Messianic Ideology." *Le Monde Diplomatique*, July 1. https://mondediplo.com /2007/07/03takfirism.

"Takfir." n.d. *Oxford Islamic Studies Online.* Accessed July 26, 2021. http://www.oxfordislamicstudies.com/article/opr /t125/e2319.

Wibisono, Susilo, Winnifred R. Louis, and Jolanda Jetten. 2019. "A Multidimensional Analysis of Religious Extremism." *Frontiers in Psychology.* https://doi.org/10.3389 /fpsyg.2019.02560.

Wright, Lawrence. 2007. *The Looming Tower: Al-Qaeda and the Road to 9/11.* New York: Vintage Books.

Tim Milosch *writes on international relations, political philosophy, and American foreign policy in the Middle East. He teaches*

courses in world politics, foreign policy and diplomacy, and politi-
cal economy at Biola University in La Mirada, California. He
writes and speaks on politics at www.TimTalksPolitics.com.

Middle East Terrorism: An Old Dance to a New Song?
Kevin Petit

The terrorist attack of 9/11 changed the global security environment. Nationally, it introduced a vulnerability unconsidered by
Main Street, USA. The "open society" upon which Americans
had long prided themselves suddenly seemed a liability. The
attacks launched new debates about security as a public good,
domestic surveillance versus privacy concerns, and fiscal deficit
trade-offs. Internationally, NATO invoked Article 5 on collective security in response to the September 11 terrorist attacks
on America. NATO coalitions led by the United States subsequently toppled illiberal regimes in Afghanistan and Iraq. With
al Qaeda neutralized and the Islamic State of Iraq and Syria
(ISIS) decimated, American officials face a puzzle. Is Middle
Eastern terrorism still a national security concern?

Terrorism in the Middle East is still a security concern
for its threat to the U.S. homeland. Terrorism is becoming
increasingly decentralized and more technologically advanced.
This does not necessarily equate to more large-scale 9/11-
type attacks. It does suggest, however, that the United States
remains vulnerable due to increased global interconnectivity
and the streamlining of the radicalization process. Dissatisfied
with socioeconomic conditions in the Middle East, Arab youth
are signaling exodus to Western states outfitted with immigration systems that may reject or accept them. If prohibited
from emigrating, some youth become aggrieved. Conversely, if
youth who allowed to emigrate struggle in their new circumstances, they maybe also become aggrieved. Youths mired in
these mindsets can become vulnerable to technology-assisted
radicalization processes. Thus, the three necessary conditions

for Middle Eastern terrorism to persist in the West are access, grievance, and the radicalization process.

Terrorism is a form of asymmetric warfare waged by the weak against the strong. It is designed to coerce behavior or achieve a political aim by violent threats or acts against innocent people (Kilcullen 2010; Caldwell and Williams 2016). Terrorism seeks an audience beyond its immediate victims (Stern 2000; O'Neill 2005; Hoffman 2017). This is a departure from past "wanton and senseless violence" theories when the political message was ambiguous or hidden. Even Unabomber Ted Kaczynski, a recluse cut off from society, penned a 35,000-word manifesto to emote his grievances to the outside world.

The mechanism of Middle Eastern terrorism threatening the developed Western countries begins with access. Access is defined as a terrorist perpetrator, or a proxy, with physical or virtual penetration of the target society. For terrorists to conduct physical attacks inside a country they have to obtain a presence there, whether by entering the country themselves or radicalizing someone who is already there. The large migrations out of the region to Western states as a result of revolution and war provides opportunities for ISIS-affiliated individuals to do that directly, or for nonaffiliates to become radicalized once in-country.

The 2008–2010 Arab Youth Poll showed 200 million Arabs under the age of 30 desired to live under a democracy (John 2020). This was a harbinger of the Arab Spring that began in 2011. Unfortunately, the democratic wave did not unfold as hoped. A decade later and frustrated that the Arab Spring did not bring structural change, the same survey found that 60 percent of surveyed Arab youth yearned to migrate from the Middle East. The virtual penetration of a society that targets disaffected youths of all origin for radicalization is even easier for terrorist groups like ISIS to carry out. Thus, developed nations face a conundrum: Arab youth will be permitted entry or they will not. Both offer difficulty and can influence the second step of the process: grievance.

Grievances come in many forms but may be simplified into two: personal and political. Personal grievances are perceptions that individuals have been personally wronged. Political grievances are beliefs that a government or political actor has committed an injustice (Smith 2018). If an Arab youth seeking to emigrate is not permitted entry, he or she may become aggrieved, blaming an isolationist, xenophobic policy. Conversely, if the asylum seeker gains entry but does not realize prosperity commiserate with expectations, then different grievances can form. The scholarly literature is clear that grievances are not behind all terrorist attacks, but they are credited in 80% of the "lone wolf" attacks in the United States (Smith 2018).

The perception of being wronged invokes the right to demand positive outcomes. Feelings of injustice are often employed by people to act more selfishly. Political grievers, in turn, direct anger, rage, and antagonism toward society (Koomen and van der Pligt 2016). This mindset is the vulnerability that facilitates the radicalization process.

The final stage is radicalization. Radicalization occurs when an individual changes from a nonviolent belief system to one that actively advocates or uses violence for societal or political change. In the 21st century, the internet has made radicalization accessible to multitudes. First, aggrieved people can readily find others who share their frustration and viewpoint. The internet solves the coordination problem by match-making two or more individuals who cooperate for a common outcome. Joining a group of like-minded individuals fosters a sense of belonging and community.

Second, physical isolation coupled with virtual social communities helps block out alternate viewpoints. Here, aggrieved people stay comfortably angry in their information bubble.

Third, the internet offers many ways to dehumanize others and encourage violence. Scholars agree that the internet is a significant factor in radicalization, specifically of Arab youth, for recruitment and increased involvement of terrorism (Kruglanski et al. 2007).

Internet radicalization is not a problem unique to the Middle East, but it does have precedence. The internet has lubricated the gears of Middle East terrorism from Damascus to Islamabad, and Ankara to Sana'a. Specifically, the Islamic State of Iraq and ash-Sham (ISIS), al Qaeda (AQ), or other designated foreign terrorist organizations allied with these two groups account for the most deadly terrorist attacks inside the United States. ISIS and AQ have inspired a plethora of violence. From 2013 to 2016, ISIS/AQ-inspired attacks in Boston, Garland (TX), Chattanooga, San Bernardino, and Orlando combined to kill 72 and wound 343. This is to say nothing of similar attacks in Europe.

Finally, Middle Eastern terrorism may become a great power competitor tactic. Fatigued from decades of conflict in the Middle East, the United States is drawing down its military presence in the region. U.S. disengagement opens opportunities for other states, including rising hegemons, to fill the vacuum. Power shifts are happening as China, Russia, and Iran maneuver for influence while they fulfill their regional and global aims. As with the Cold War, greedy and revisionist states are likely to clamor for power below the threshold of declared war, engaging in cyber, propaganda, and political attacks against the United States and their other rivals. Russia has already engaged in cognitive sabotage by fake news and truth decay in the United States' 2016 elections (Rich 2018).

With a free hand in the Middle East, these adversaries are free to orchestrate state-sponsored, unconventional warfare campaigns using proxies. These proxies, which often seek out disaffected and politically powerless Arab youth to grow their ranks, may be witting or unwitting agents. States grooming emigres can bolster expectations about equality, opportunity, wealth, and liberty. Once on the ground the reality may not match the expectation, making the youth vulnerable to radicalization.

Terrorism is a tactic by the weak to challenge the strong. Congruent with power imbalance, terrorists seek vulnerability and exploit weakness. In the age of globalization, terrorism as a violent political tactic has become decentralized, networked, and technologically advanced. Thus, the theorized mechanism of radicalization is a threat to the United States. Simultaneously, the Middle East is becoming demographically younger every year, with millions who yearn to migrate for better education and opportunity for themselves and their families.

The West's open society, advancement of fairness and equality, and care for individual human rights, however, also presents a vulnerability for hostile actors to try and exploit once their agents have access. These factors together suggest terrorism in the Middle East will remain a concern for the United States and other countries even decades after 9/11.

References

Caldwell, Dan and Robert E. Williams Jr. 2016. *Seeking Security in an Insecure World*. Lanham: Rowman & Littlefield.

Hoffman, Bruce. 2017. *Inside Terrorism*. New York: Columbia University Press.

John, Sunil. 2020. "2020 Arab Youth Survey: A Voice for Change." Accessed May 18, 2021. http://www .arabyouthsurvey.com/whitepaper.html.

Kilcullen, David. 2010. *Counterinsurgency*. New York: Oxford University Press.

Koomen, Willem and Joop van der Pligt. 2016. *The Psychology of Radicalization and Terrorism*. New York: Routledge.

Kruglanski, Arie W., Martha Crenshaw, Jerrold M. Post, and Jeff Victoroff. 2007. "What Should This Fight Be Called?: Metaphors of Counterterrorism and their Implications." *Psychological Science in the Public Interest* 8, no. 3: 97–113.

O'Neill, Bard. 2005. *Insurgency and Terrorism: From Revolution to Apocalypse*. Sterling: Potomac Books.

Rich, Michael D. 2018. *Truth Decay: An Initial Exploration of the Diminishing Role of Facts and Analysis in American Public Life*. Santa Monica: Rand Corporation.

Smith, Alison G. 2018. "How Radicalization to Terrorism
Occurs in the United States: What Research Sponsored
by the National Institute of Justice Tells Us." National
Institute of Justice NCJ 250171. Accessed May 18, 2021.
https://permanent.fdlp.gov/gpo110219/250171.pdf.

Stern, Jessica. 2000. *The Ultimate Terrorists.* Cambridge:
Harvard University Press.

*Kevin Petit is a former U.S. Army officer with multiple deploy-
ments to Iraq and Afghanistan. He teaches asymmetric warfare in
the National Intelligence University in Washington, D.C.*

Surging Militant Islamist Violence in Africa Shifts Locus of International Terrorism
Candace Cook

Terrorism is on the rise, driven by militant Islamist groups pro-
liferating across West, East, and Southeastern Africa. In 2020,
there were 4,958 violent events by militant Islamist groups
across the continent—a 43% spike from the year before (Africa
Center for Strategic Studies 2021b). This follows a decade of
nearly uninterrupted growth in violent events (Africa Center
2020a). Violence is spiking in parts of the Sahel and the Lake
Chad Basin region, while al Shabaab activity in the Horn of
Africa increased 33% over the past year (Africa Center 2021b).
Sub-Saharan Africa holds seven of the ten countries with the
largest increase in terrorism in 2020 (Institute for Economics
& Peace 2020). This sharp rise in violent extremism shifts the
locus of international terrorism to Africa and poses significant
regional and international security concerns.

While many militant Islamist groups in Africa have links
to Al Qaeda or the Islamic State, each group has emerged and
evolved from local concerns shaped by their social, political,
and economic environments (Østebø 2012). Repressive and
corrupt governments with exclusionary politics fuel socioeconomic grievances and ethnic marginalization, leading to

increased risks that populations will turn to violent extremism (United States Agency for International Development 2009). Heavy-handed counterterrorism responses from government security forces coupled with failures to protect local communities spur recruitment into militant Islamist groups. Many of these fragile states grapple with explosive population growth. This exacerbates land and resource tensions, while leaving unemployed youth vulnerable to extremist ideologies (Sakor 2020).

In the Horn region, al Shabaab is the continent's most sophisticated and enduring militant Islamist group. After its creation in 2006, it initially focused on waging an insurgency against the Somali government, but in the past decade it expanded its operational reach to neighboring Kenya and Uganda. Al Shabaab continues to control wide swathes of territory in southern Somalia (Office of the Director of National Intelligence 2021). According to the commander of American Special Operations forces in Africa, al Shabaab has become "the largest, wealthiest and most violent Al Qaeda-associated group in the world" (Schmitt and Savage 2021).

Boko Haram in northeast Nigeria began as a rural-based insurgency in 2013 but has evolved into a regional terrorist threat extending to Cameroon, Chad, and Niger (Mahmood and Ani 2018). Internal rivalries and leadership disputes resulted in the creation of the Boko Haram offshoot, Islamic State in West Africa (ISWA) in 2016. Violent attacks by both groups continue to rise as battles escalate with state security forces and aligned militias (Africa Center 2021b).

In the Sahel, the expansion of militant Islamist groups emanated from the political instability that followed the 2012 Tuareg rebellion in Mali, and the subsequent overthrow of the government in that state. Militant Islamist violence in the region doubled every year from 2015 to 2019, spreading beyond northern and central Mali to Burkina Faso and Niger (Le Roux 2019). There is now concern that the historically peaceful and stable countries of coastal West Africa are vulnerable to this violent expansion. To the west, the number of attacks near the Mali–Senegal border doubled in 2020 (United Nations Security Council 2021), and to the south, the Cote d'Ivoire–Burkina Faso border saw increases in violence (Assanvo 2021).

In northern Mozambique, a local conflict fueled by economic and political exclusion—and further compounded by resentment over forced resettlement from lands with valuable deposits of rubies and natural gas—grew into an insurgency (Pirio, Pitelli, and Adam 2019). Fears are mounting that this could become the next frontier for militant Islamist activity on the continent, prompting southern African states to deploy a standby force in hopes to halt regional expansion (Reuters 2021).

Terrorism in Africa is becoming deadlier as well. Violent extremist groups exploit existing intercommunal tensions to stoke further violence among local populations. This has weakened the social fabric between village communities, which allows armed groups to establish protection rackets and other forms of coercive behavior (Ammour 2020). Moreover, militant Islamist groups across Africa are increasingly tapping into transnational criminal networks, which provide high-reward, low-risk ways to make a profit through smuggling, human trafficking, and other black-market activities (Africa Center 2017). A 2012 gold boom in the Sahel, for instance, opened up a new source of funding for violent extremists in Mali, Burkina Faso, and Niger as armed groups took control of informal mining sites (International Crisis Group 2019).

International efforts using a militaristic approach to halt terrorism in Africa are failing. The year 2020 was the deadliest by militant Islamists in the Sahel (Africa Center 2020b), while 1.2 million have been displaced in Burkina Faso as a result of violent extremism originating in Mali (Africa Center 2021c). The insurgency in Mozambique has tripled those displaced in the past year (Africa Center 2021c).

Furthermore, conflict continues to be the primary driver of acute food crises in Africa (Africa Center 2021a). In West

Africa, 23.6 million people are projected to face severe food insecurity amid the rising displacement from conflict (Africa Center 2021c). Moreover, the escalation of militant Islamist violence widens instability beyond Africa's borders. Militant Islamist groups in Africa have sought to threaten U.S. and Western interests in the region, and have demonstrated the capacity to conduct high-profile attacks across the continent. Further, they have actively targeted U.S. and regional forces (Schmitt and Dahir 2020).

A recent UN report warned the COVID-19 pandemic gave al Qaeda and Islamic State–linked groups the opportunity to further undermine governments in conflict zones, with these groups potentially staging a spate of preplanned attacks once pandemic restrictions on movement are lifted (Burke 2021). If governance is not addressed as part of the solution, violent extremism in Africa will continue to expand and intensify, as it has in the past decade.

References

Africa Center for Strategic Studies. 2021a. *Food Insecurity Crisis Mounting in Africa.* Infographic. https://africacenter. org/spotlight/food-insecurity-crisis-mounting-africa/.

Africa Center for Strategic Studies. 2021b. *Spike in Militant Islamist Violence in Africa Underscores Shifting Security Landscape.* Infographic. https://africacenter.org/spotlight /spike-militant-islamist-violence-africa-shifting-security -landscape/.

Africa Center for Strategic Studies. 2021c. *32 Million Africans Forcibly Displaced by Conflict and Repression.* Infographic. https://africacenter.org/spotlight/32-million-africans -forcibly-displaced-by-conflict-and-repression/.

Africa Center for Strategic Studies. 2020a. *African Militant Islamist Groups Set Record for Violent Activity.* Infographic. https://africacenter.org/spotlight/african-militant-islamist -groups-new-record-violent-activity/.

Africa Center for Strategic Studies. 2020b. *Islamic State in the Greater Sahara Expanding Its Threat and Reach in the Sahel.* Infographic. https://africacenter.org/spotlight/islamic-state -in-the-greater-sahara-expanding-its-threat-and-reach-in -the-sahel/.

Africa Center for Strategic Studies. 2017. *The Illicit Superhighway: Transnational Organized Crime in Africa.* Infographic. https://africacenter.org/spotlight/the-illicit -superhighway-transnational-organized-crime-in-africa/.

Ammour, Laurence-Aïda. 2020. *How Violent Extremist Groups Exploit Intercommunal Conflicts in the Sahel.* Africa Center for Strategic Studies Spotlight. https://africacenter .org/spotlight/how-violent-extremist-groups-exploit -intercommunal-conflicts-in-the-sahel/.

Assanvo, William. 2021. "Terrorism in Côte d'Ivoire Is No Longer Just an External Threat." Institute for Security Studies, June 15. https://issafrica.org/iss-today/terrorism -in-cote-divoire-is-no-longer-just-an-external-threat.

Burke, Jason. 2021. "Islamic Extremists Planning 'Rash of Attacks' After Covid Curbs Lifted, Says UN." *Guardian,* February 5, 2021. https://www.theguardian.com/world/2021 /feb/05/islamic-extremists-planning-rash-of-attacks-after -covid-curbs-lifted-says-un.

Institute for Economics & Peace. 2020. *Global Terrorism Index 2020: Measuring the Impact of Terrorism,* November. https://www.visionofhumanity.org/wp-content/uploads /2020/11/GTI-2020-web-2.pdf.

International Crisis Group. 2019. *Getting a Grip on Central Sahel's Gold Rush.* Report No. 282. https://www .crisisgroup.org/africa/sahel/burkina-faso/282-reprendre -en-main-la-ruee-vers-lor-au-sahel-central.

Le Roux, Pauline. 2019. *Responding to the Rise in Violent Extremism in the Sahel.* Africa Security Brief No. 36. Washington, D.C.: Africa Center for Strategic Studies.

https://africacenter.org/publication/responding-rise
-violent-extremism-sahel/.

Mahmood, Omar S, and Ndubuisi Christian Ani. 2018.
Factional Dynamics within Boko Haram. Institute for
Security Studies. https://issafrica.s3.amazonaws.com/site
/uploads/2018-07-06-research-report-2.pdf.

Office of the Director of National Intelligence. 2021.
Annual Threat Assessment of the US Intelligence Community.
Washington, D.C.: Office of the Director of National
Intelligence. https://www.dni.gov/files/ODNI/documents
/assessments/ATA-2021-Unclassified-Report.pdf.

Østebø, Terje. 2012. *Islamic Militancy in Africa.* Africa
Security Brief No. 23. Washington, D.C.: Africa Center for
Strategic Studies. https://africacenter.org/publication
/islamic-militancy-in-africa/.

Pirio, Gregory, Robert Pittelli, and Yussuf Adam. 2019. *The
Many Drivers Enabling Violent Extremism in Northern
Mozambique.* Africa Center for Strategic Studies Spotlight.
https://africacenter.org/spotlight/the-many-drivers
-enabling-violent-extremism-in-northern-mozambique/.

Reuters. 2021. "African Nations to Send Troops to Tackle
Mozambique Insurgency." *Reuters*, June 23, 2021. https://
www.reuters.com/world/africa/african-nations-send-troops
-tackle-mozambique-insurgency-2021-06-23/.

Sakor, Bintu Zahara. 2020. *Is Demography a Threat to Peace
and Security in the Sahel?* Dakar-Ponty, Senegal: Peace
Research Institute Oslo (PRIO) and the United Nations
Population Fund (UNFPA). https://wcaro.unfpa.org/sites
/default/files/pub-pdf/en_-_is_demography_a_threat_to
_peace_and_security_in_the_sahel.pdf.

Schmitt, Eric, and Charlie Savage. 2021. "Pentagon Weighs
Proposal to Send Dozens of Troops Back to Somalia."
New York Times, June 15, 2021. https://www.nytimes.
com/2021/06/15/us/politics/pentagon-troops

-somalia.html?action=click&module=Top%20Stories
&pgtype=Homepage.

Schmitt, Eric, and Abdi Latif Dahir. 2020. "Al Qaeda Branch
in Somalia Threatens Americans in East Africa—and Even
the U.S." *New York Times,* March 21, 2020. https://www
.nytimes.com/2020/03/21/world/africa/al-qaeda-somalia
-shabab.html.

United Nations Security Council. 2021. *Twenty-seventh report
of the Analytical Support and Sanctions Monitoring Team
submitted pursuant to resolution 2368 (2017) concerning
ISIL (Da'esh), Al-Qaida and associated individuals and
entities.* New York, NY: UN Headquarters. https://undocs
.org/S/2021/68.

United States Agency for International Development. 2009.
Guide to Drivers of Violent Extremism. https://pdf.usaid.gov
/pdf_docs/Pnadt978.pdf.

Candace Cook *is a research associate at the Africa Center for Strategic Studies in Washington, D.C. She holds an M.A. in national security studies with a concentration in African security from CSU San Bernardino.*

The views expressed in this article are those of the author and do not reflect the official policy or position of the Africa Center for Strategic Studies, the National Defense University, the Department of Defense, or the U.S. government.

4 Profiles

al Qaeda

Origins and Early Years

Al Qaeda ("the Base") is a transnational Salafi-Jihadist terrorist group that is infamous for carrying out the terrorist attacks on the United States on September 11, 2001. The organization still exists, but in a much degraded and more fragmented form compared to before the 9/11 attacks.

In April 1978 the Communist People's Democratic Party of Afghanistan (PDPA) launched the Saur Revolution to overthrow dictator Mohammed Daoud Khan. Starting by Christmas 1979, Soviet military forces invaded Afghanistan to prop up the fledgling PDPA communist government, whose policies had led to violence against and dissatisfaction among Afghans. When the country's many ethnic minorities organized in armed rebellion against the government, the nation fell into civil war.

Al Qaeda was established in 1988 by Abdullah Azzam, Osama bin Laden, and Ayman al-Zawahiri. Azzam was known as the "Father of Modern Jihad" and spearheaded the effort of

---

Civil liberties are one of the more contentious areas in domestic policy debates of the terrorism issue. Governments seek increased powers of surveillance to prevent attacks while civil liberties groups seek to protect and preserve a right to privacy. Determining the appropriate balance between the transparency needed for democratic governance and the secrecy necessary for security is a constant battle in polities. Here a demonstrator shows support for Edward Snowden after he disclosed the existence of secret surveillance programs. (Mike K./Dreamstime.com)

Arab Muslim foreign fighters to travel to Afghanistan to participate in the war against the Soviets. Osama bin Laden was the
wealthy son of a Yemeni construction magnate who had significant business contracts with the Saudi royal family. Zawahiri
was the leader of Egyptian Islamic Jihad, which had experience
in carrying out terrorist acts owing to its operational practices
against the Egyptian government in the 1980s.

With the Soviet War in Afghanistan wrapping up, these
leaders sought to create a network of militants to take jihad
back to their home countries to operate against their own governments, which they viewed as corrupt and un-Islamic. Al
Qaeda's worldview is that an axis of Christian crusaders and
Jews actively conspire to subjugate Muslims and control Arab-
led governments in the region with puppet dictators. The goal
of the organization is to destroy Western powers and create
a global Islamic caliphate that governs both religiously and
politically.

Azzam was killed in a car bombing in Peshawar, Pakistan, in
1989. By the early 1990s al Qaeda and Egyptian Islamic Jihad
officially merged, with Osama bin Laden holding the leadership
position but Egyptian militants holding most deputy and mid-
level roles in the organization. Over the course of its history,
al Qaeda's leadership moved between different host countries.

Osama bin Laden was kicked out of his birthplace, the
Kingdom of Saudi Arabia, after condemning the Saudi royals for basing U.S. forces during and after the Persian Gulf
War. For bin Laden the presence of "crusaders" in the holiest
lands in Islam was unacceptable and un-Islamic. Bin Laden
called for the Saudi King Fahd to use al Qaeda and recruit a
force of Mujahadeen ("holy warriors") to fight against Saddam
Hussein's Iraqi forces. He saw the king's rejection of his proposal as confirming the dominance of the West and the cor-
ruption of the monarchy since King Fahd trusted in "crusader"
forces instead of Islamic ones.

In the mid-1990s Osama bin Laden moved to Sudan at
the invitation of that nation's government. In 1994 Osama

bin Laden lost his Saudi passport after sustaining his criticism of the royal family. He was also disowned by the rest of his family. Bin Laden's stay in Sudan was short-lived, and in 1996 the Sudanese government declared him unwelcome. He moved to Afghanistan, where he came under the protection of the Taliban. In exchange for allowing al Qaeda to set up its operations in Afghanistan, the Taliban received paramilitary training from the terrorist group. In 1996 Osama bin Laden also announced his declaration of holy war against the United States. At this point the organization altered its methods from paramilitary training of militants to focus on large, high-profile terrorist attacks.

Following bin Laden's declaration, Al Qaeda directed and sponsored attacks such as the 1998 East Africa embassy bombings. The organization also attempted to bomb the Los Angeles International Airport on New Year's Eve of 1999, but the plot was foiled by a customs inspector. This was followed by a successful attack on the U.S.S. *Cole* warship at Aden harbor in Yemen in 2000. The organization then directed and financed the September 11 attacks, leading the U.S. government to declare a global war on terrorism.

Al Qaeda went on the defensive after 9/11 as U.S. military forces working with the Northern Alliance militarily removed the Taliban government from its control of the country. Al Qaeda militants fought in mountain hideouts in the east of Afghanistan, but Osama bin Laden ultimately escaped the dragnet and made his way to Pakistan.

Adopting the Franchise Model in the War on Terror

In the following years al Qaeda branched out by effectively licensing a series of regional franchises. Groups of Salafi-Jihadist militants operating in their home regions pledged loyalty to Osama bin Laden and took the name of al Qaeda as a stamp on their existing organizations. For them there was a certain legitimacy within jihadist circles for being tied to the brand that had committed the 9/11 attacks. Osama bin Laden and the other al Qaeda leadership were able to claim global influence by accepting these pledges. Often the leaders of these franchises were foreign fighters who had returned to their home countries from waging jihad against the Soviets in Afghanistan in the 1980s. In practice these groups had a great deal of autonomy, and although they were pledged to bin Laden, in some cases these leaders ignored his exhortations even as they shared information and resources.

In October 2004 the group Tawhid wal-Jihad, under the leadership of Abu Musab al-Zarqawi, officially became al Qaeda in Iraq. Zarqawi already had loose ties to al Qaeda but gained increasing influence during the Iraq War. This group became a major player in the Sunni insurgency against the government of Iraq and U.S. forces in the aftermath of the coalition invasion that deposed Saddam Hussein in 2003. In addition to attacks on security forces, it engaged in terrorism against Shi'a Arabs in attempts to foment a civil war in Iraq between Sunni and Shi'a. Zarqawi was killed in a U.S. airstrike in 2006, but the group persisted. After his death it changed its name to the Islamic State and effectively broke from al Qaeda.

In Algeria, the Islamic Armed Group (GIA) that had arisen from the Islamist faction in that country's civil war itself split into separate factions. One of these agreed with the ideology of the GIA but was concerned that the indiscriminate killings were tactically problematic and sapping the group of support. This faction took the name Salafist Group for Preaching and Combat (GSPC). In 2006 this faction pledged loyalty to Osama bin Laden and became al Qaeda in the Islamic Maghreb (AQIM). In addition to terrorist attacks, the group regularly carries out kidnap for ransom operations as well as engages in smuggling throughout West Africa. It is unique among al Qaeda franchises for how many acts are focused on criminal financing relative to the number of outright terror attacks. AQIM also regularly undergoes various splits and "remergers" with certain militant leaders, indicating a somewhat loose organizational structure.

One of the earliest affiliates of al Qaeda is the Abu Sayyaf group. Militants in this group hailed from the Moro National Liberation Front (MNLF) in the Philippines. They met with Osama bin Laden in Afghanistan during the war against the Soviets and upon returning to the Philippines initiated attacks against that government in the 1990s. In the 2000s the group expanded its operations to carry out kidnaping for ransom while also engaging in terrorism, such as the 2004 bombing of a Filipino ferry that killed 116. The group increasingly turned to more criminal activity and has been less active in its operations today. Despite origins with al Qaeda the leadership pledged loyalty to the Islamic State in 2014.

The group al Qaeda in the Arabian Peninsula (AQAP) did not officially pledge loyalty, but rather grew out of the union of existing networks of al Qaeda elements in Saudi Arabia and Yemen in 2009. Today the group is mostly based out of Yemen. In terms of foreign terrorism, this is one of the most active franchises. It was responsible for a series of plots such as inspiring the 2009 Fort Hood shootings and planning the Christmas underwear bombing attempt of an American airliner that same year.

An American and Yemeni citizen, Anwar al-Awlaki, was a popular propagandist for Salafi-Jihadists and a member of the group. He was killed in a U.S. drone strike in 2011; that same year also saw the Yemeni government collapse as part of the Arab uprisings. AQAP also sponsored the January 2015 attacks against the *Charlie Hebdo* offices in Paris. In 2014 the Iranian-backed Shi'a Houthi movement captured the Yemeni capital of Sanaa. AQAP took a more defensive stance given the civil war dynamics, and in 2015 the group's leadership sustained a series of decapitation strikes that have limited its ability to conduct attacks abroad.

The Somali group Harakat al-Shabaab al-Mujahadeen (HSM, "The Movement of Youthful Holy Warriors), frequently called al Shabaab, pledged loyalty to al Qaeda in 2012. The group emerged in the 2000s as a Salafi-Jihadist faction of the Islamic

Courts Union, an Islamist movement that created a judicial system to fill the void in governance left by warlord era of the 1990s. The al Shabaab faction effectively launched an internal coup to overtake the movement and was bolstered in its recruitment efforts after the 2006 intervention of Ethiopian forces.

The Transitional Somali Government invited Ethiopian forces to intervene in order to help it combat al Shabaab, but al Shabaab appealed to Somali nationals in the diaspora to join the fight against the Ethiopian "crusaders." The group has long engaged as an insurgency against the Federal Government of Somalia and the forces of the African Union Mission in Somalia (AMISOM) sponsored by many East African countries who have sent forces, but it supplements this guerilla activity with high-casualty terrorist attacks. Its leader Ahmed Godane was killed in a drone strike in 2014, but the group persists. It has a developed institutional apparatus with both paramilitary combatants as well as its own intelligence and secret police force. Despite this institutional organization of the group and its Salafi-Jihadist ideology, it is subject to clan politics and factionalism in Somalia.

The year 2012 also saw a break-away faction of the Nigerian terrorist group Boko Haram work with AQIM, although it had never officially pledged loyalty until January 2022. This Ansaru group, led by Khalid al-Barnawi (the son of Boko Haram's founder), challenged leader Abubakr Shekau because it disagreed with his intentional targeting of noncombatants. Al-Barnawi was arrested by Nigerian forces in 2016 and has since fallen into obscurity. Shekau and the rest of Boko Haram saw a further split in 2015 when another rival, former spokesman Musab al-Barnawi, split from the group to create the Islamic State West Africa Province (ISWAP). This faction killed Shekau in 2021.

Rivalry with the Islamic State and Decline

Al Qaeda's more recent attempts involving affiliates have been more mixed. Ayman al-Zawahiri announced the creation of al Qaeda in the Indian Subcontinent (AQIS) in 2014. This was a new development as up to this point most franchises had started on their own initiative and later pledged to al Qaeda. In the case of AQIS it was announced by the central al Qaeda leadership. Despite this its leader was killed in 2019 in Afghanistan. Overall, it has been largely overshadowed by the Islamic State Khorasan Province. In Syria, the al Qaeda–linked Nusra Front merged with other groups to form Hayat Tahrir al Sham (Assembly for the Liberation of the Levant) in 2017. This group has not pledged loyalty to al Qaeda following the merger, and analysts are mixed as to whether it maintains close ties with al Qaeda central or is an independent entity. Al Qaeda leader al-Zawahiri claimed that the split and merger was undertaken without his permission.

Most recently al Qaeda has faced a series of challenges to its legitimacy within Salafi-Jihadist circles. The 2011 killing of leader Osama bin Laden at a safe house in Abottabad, Pakistan, by U.S. special forces on the orders of President Obama was a major blow to the organization. The compound in which bin Laden had been hiding was in the same town as the Pakistani Military Academy, raising suspicions about the extent to which elements in the government of Pakistan facilitated his movement. Pakistan's Inter-Services Intelligence had a relationship with the Taliban and al Qaeda elements previously and regularly uses jihadist militants as part of its foreign policy.

The killing and burial at sea of bin Laden by American forces did not destroy the group outright but has created space for rivals to move in. al-Zawahiri officially stepped into the leadership role but did not enjoy the same charisma and inspiration that Osama bin Laden provided in Salafi-Jihadist circles. His leadership was short-lived: He was killed in a drone strike by U.S. forces in Afghanistan in July 2022, and the group has failed to announce a successor following his death.

The emergence of the Islamic State in establishing a caliphate in the summer of 2014 within territories in Syria and Iraq caused al Qaeda to take a backseat. This move was a significant popularity blow to al Qaeda. In the subsequent years many former franchises have effectively jumped ship and pledged loyalty to the Islamic State.

Bibliography

Center for Strategic and International Studies. 2018. "Hay'at Tahrir al-Sham (HTS)." Transnational Threats Project, Terrorism Backgrounder. https://www.csis.org/programs /transnational-threats-project/past-projects/terrorism -backgrounders/hayat-tahrir-al-sham.

Lebovich, Andrew. 2019. "Al-Qaeda in the Islamic Maghreb (AQIM)." Mapping Armed Groups in Mali and the Sahel. European Council on Foreign Relations. https://ecfr.eu /special/sahel_mapping/aqim.

Mapping Militant Organizations. 2018. "Al Qaeda in the Indian Subcontinent." Center for International Security and Cooperation, Freeman Spogli Institute, Stanford University. Last modified July 2018. https://cisac.fsi .stanford.edu/mappingmilitants/profiles/al-qaeda -indian-subcontinent-aqis.

Mapping Militant Organizations. 2020. "Al Qaeda in the Arabian Peninsula." Center for International Security and Cooperation, Freeman Spogli Institute, Stanford University. Last modified February 2020. https://cisac.fsi .stanford.edu/mappingmilitants/profiles/al-qaeda -arabian-peninsula.

Mir, Asfandyar. 2022. "The Latest on al-Qaida after al-Zawahiri: 3 Things You Need to Know." *The Olive Branch*, United States Institute of Peace, August 9. https://www .usip.org/blog/2022/08/latest-al-qaida-after-al-zawahiri -3-things-you-need-know.

Sirrs, Owen. 2018. *Pakistan's Inter-Services Intelligence Directorate: Covert Action and Internal Operations.* New York: Routledge.

Edward Snowden (1983–)

Edward Snowden was an employee of Booz Allen Hamilton who was contracted to the National Security Agency (NSA) in May 2013, when he disclosed covert U.S. government surveillance programs to journalists and subsequently fled the United States. He now lives in Russia, where he cannot be extradited. Snowden is a controversial figure who, depending on one's views, is heralded as either a traitor to the United States or a patriotic whistleblower for exposing secret government surveillance activity on millions of Americans.

Background

Snowden came from a family with a history of federal service. His father was an officer in the U.S. Coast Guard, and his mother was a clerk for a U.S. District Court judge. He missed part of his high school after contracting mononucleosis but later took and passed the General Educational Development (GED) test in lieu of graduating. In May 2004 he enlisted in the U.S. Army and attempted to become a special forces candidate. He was disqualified and discharged from the service in September after sustaining a leg injury during training. He next worked as a security guard for a language research center at the University of Maryland that had ties to the U.S. government. He next became an employee with the Central Intelligence Agency (CIA) due to his computer skills but resigned after three years to work for Dell as a contractor to the CIA. Government officials assert that at this time Snowden began downloading most of the classified material that he later released to journalists.

Disclosing Government Programs

Snowden claims that a major decision point for him was the March 13, 2013, testimony of the Director of National Intelligence James Clapper to the Senate Select Committee on Intelligence. During the testimony Clapper was asked if the National

Security Agency collects data on millions of Americans, to which Clapper replied "No, sir . . . not wittingly." Snowden contends that after seeing Clapper lie in his appearance before Congress he decided to resign from his position with Dell and take a new one with Booz Allen Hamilton in order to specifically gain access to NSA data.

Shortly before the disclosures went public in May 2013, Snowden traveled to Hong Kong and gave a television interview about the programs. While there he made statements critical of the United States in support of the Chinese government and sought amnesty in various European countries. These governments denied his requests, but in June his asylum claim was accepted by the government of Russia. He now resides there to avoid prosecution by the U.S. government since Russia does not have an extradition treaty with the United States.

Impact on the Privacy Debate

Officials from various government intelligence agencies assert that Snowden took tens of thousands if not millions of top-secret documents. Journalist Glenn Greenwald states that Snowden gave approximately 10,000 documents to his team in May 2013. Initial reporting focused on the disclosure of two global surveillance programs: one that tracks internet content and another that tracks users' metadata. Snowden argued that the programs were a massive intrusion on privacy and an overreach of government authority.

Civil libertarians consider the bulk data collection to have been an "unreasonable search" in violation of the Fourth Amendment conducted on a mass scale, given that the warrants cited were claimed to be blanket and not specific to individuals. Conversely, government officials counter that the programs were legal since Foreign Intelligence Surveillance Courts (FISC) signed off on warrants for the collection of domestic content, and that the precedent of case law derived from the 1979 *Smith v. Maryland* Supreme Court decision meant that no warrants were required for the collection of metadata (data about data rather than the content itself).

Government officials insist that Snowden has done incalculable damage to U.S. national security by disclosing sensitive sources and methods that altered the behavior of terrorist actors to avoid detection and tracking. Civil libertarians assert that he is a whistleblower who did the country a service by disclosing the existence of illegal programs that infringe upon citizens' rights against unreasonable search and seizure.

Bibliography

Frontline. 2014. "United States of Secrets." Public Broadcasting Service, May 13 and May 20. https://www.pbs.org/wgbh /frontline/documentary/united-states-of-secrets/.

Smith v. Maryland, 442 U.S. 735 (1979). *Thomson Reuters*. Accessed February 3, 2023. https://caselaw.findlaw.com /us-supreme-court/442/735.html.

U.S. House of Representatives Permanent Select Committee on Intelligence. 2016. *Review of the Unauthorized Disclosures of Former National Security Agency Contractor Edward Snowden* (Unclassified). H. Rept. 114–891. Washington, D.C.: U.S. Government Publishing Office, September 15. https://irp.fas.org/congress/2016_rpt /hpsci-snowden.pdf.

Federal Bureau of Investigation (FBI)

The Federal Bureau of Investigation (FBI) is the primary federal law enforcement agency in the United States and has domestic counterterrorism as one of its core missions today. Today such activities are carried out in the National Security Division of the Bureau, which is divided into a Counterintelligence Division, a Counterterrorism Division, a Weapons of Mass Destruction Directorate, and other offices.

Background

The FBI is housed in the U.S. Department of Justice and began as the Bureau of Investigation in 1908 due to the Justice Department's desire to have its own agency that was not dependent on the Treasury Department's Secret Service. The primary rationale for the bureau began with the desire to investigate crimes related to interstate commerce, and its first investigations tracked human trafficking related to prostitution.

In 1924 the bureau came under the directorship of J. Edgar Hoover, who remained in that position until his death in 1972. In 1935 the agency's name was changed to the current title of Federal Bureau of Investigation, and throughout the 1920s and 1930s much of its activity was directed to combating mafia bosses who thrived during the Prohibition era, as well as outlaw gangsters who regularly robbed banks and fled across state lines. It was at this time that the bureau's agents gained the aura associated with being crime-fighting government men ("G-Men") who killed or arrested a number of these criminal figures. Notable takedowns by the FBI included George Kelly Barnes, John Dillinger, and Al Karpis. The FBI never relinquished this mission and continues to prosecute organized crime elements well into the contemporary era, with notable takedowns of mafia organizations like the Gambino crime family in the 1980s.

Counterintelligence

Heading into the 1940s the bureau shifted a great deal of its focus to national security and assumed the duties of conducting counterintelligence, or activities undertaken to catch spies and their enablers from foreign nations. Counterintelligence is effectively the defense in matters of espionage and focuses on preventing hostile actors from obtaining one's secrets or engaging in sabotage. Heading into World War II FBI agents focused their efforts on individuals tied to Germany, Japan, and the Soviet Union. In the immediate run up to the war the FBI identified Germany spy Frederick Duquesne as the leader of a wider ring and ultimately brought his U.S.-based network down. This was due to the cooperation of one of the German agents in the spy ring, who defected to the United States and worked with the bureau to accumulate evidence against the 33 members of the ring.

Counterintelligence efforts further extended to seeking Soviet spies operating in the United States in the early Cold War period. One of the most significant cases were the arrests of Julius and Ethel Rosenberg, a married communist couple who were instrumental in obtaining and transferring U.S. military secrets to the Soviet Union. This history of the bureau showcases how it was a seemingly natural fit for the organization to handle governmental counterterrorism tasks given its past national security counterespionage investigations as well as its many field offices distributed throughout the United States.

Director Hoover helped turn the bureau into a major player in American security, but the legacy of his leadership was contentious. The successes on the national security front were matched by an uninterrupted directorship for nearly five decades, and he amassed considerable personal and bureaucratic power. During his tenure as director he was at odds at various times with many government figures—including presidents—and his leadership was also marred by numerous violations of the law with respect to civil liberties.

Counterintelligence operations during the Cold War were not just focused on individuals tied to nation-states such as the Soviet Union. Many illegal domestic operations were undertaken as part of the Counterintelligence Program (COINTELPRO) that targeted the Ku Klux Klan and various communist and New Left groups such as the Communist Party of the United States, the Black Panthers, the American Indian Movement, and women's rights groups that included figures in the civil rights movement and antiwar movement of the 1960s. The bulk of these illegal overreaches of governmental power were unearthed in congressional investigations and hearings in the 1970s led by Senator

Frank Church of Idaho and Representative Otis Pike of New York. These bodies ultimately became the standing Senate Select Committee on Intelligence (SSCI) and the House Permanent Select Committee on Intelligence (HPSCI) that today conduct oversight of the U.S. Intelligence Community.

Counterterrorism

With respect to counterterrorism, in 1982 the FBI assumed a lead domestic role for this mission in the United States. It created the Hostage Rescue Team (HRT) as a specialized SWAT-style unit in preparation for the 1984 Los Angeles Summer Olympic Games. The catalyst for this effort was the poor response by German authorities to a Black September terrorist attack at the 1972 Munich games. The HRT persists today as a premier special response team that is reported to regularly train with elite Defense Department units in the Joint Special Operations Command (JSOC). Despite this expertise the conduct of the bureau and other government agencies was challenged and questioned in several high-profile incidents in the 1990s. The deadly outcomes of sieges by the FBI and other federal authorities at Ruby Ridge in 1992 and Waco in 1993 spurred a dramatic increase in antigovernment sentiment, especially among the far right.

Since the 9/11 attacks the bureau accelerated its move into a counterterrorism portfolio and is the lead agency in using the provisions of the Patriot Act and its legacy statutes. Today the bureau has extensive laboratory infrastructure to aid in investigations, be it the forensic analysis of DNA, ballistics, or explosives. The more recent additions to the bureau's forensic portfolio include detection of radioactive, biological, or chemical weapons of mass destruction as well as cyber capabilities.

Bibliography

Blatvinis, Raymond J. 2007. *The Origins of FBI Counter-Intelligence*. Lawrence: University Press of Kansas.

Davis, James Kirkpatrick. 1992. *Spying on America: The FBI's Domestic Counter-Intelligence Program.* Westport: Praeger.

Laub, Zachary. 2017. "The FBI's Role in National Security." Council on Foreign Relations, Backgrounder. June 21, 2017. https://www.cfr.org/backgrounder/fbis-role -national-security.

Longstreth, Samuel. 2022. "FBI Hostage Rescue Team (HRT): Domestic Delta." Grey Dynamics, December 27. https://greydynamics.com/fbi-hostage-rescue-team-hrt -domestic-delta/.

Foreign Intelligence Surveillance Court (FISC)

The Foreign Intelligence Surveillance Court (FISC) is a federal court established by the Foreign Intelligence Surveillance Act (FISA) of 1978. The purpose of the body is to provide oversight over the government in conducting surveillance on foreign individuals suspected of spying against the United States or seeking to engage in acts of terrorism.

Structure of FISC

The U.S. Constitution has little to say about the composition of the judicial branch in Article III compared to the executive and legislative branches in Articles I and II, but it specifies that Congress may create a federal court system under the direction of a single federal Supreme Court. This system has since taken form as a series of 94 federal district courts where decisions may be appealed under 13 appellate courts, themselves presided over by the Supreme Court.

There are other federal courts created by Congress for various purposes, such as the martial courts for members of the military and courts for international trade issues. FISC is one such court. It was created based on the recommendation of the Church Committee after its hearings on government abuses in the 1970s.

The court is located in Washington, D.C., and its 11 judges are drawn from the 94 district courts around the country who are appointed by the chief justice of the Supreme Court. Each judge serves for a term of seven years and may not serve on the FISC again after their term expires. Should the government be denied a surveillance warrant, it can appeal the decision to the Foreign Intelligence Surveillance Court of Review, which is composed of three judges drawn from the district or appellate courts. Should the case be heard and denied at this level, the government can then petition the Supreme Court to hear its appeal.

FISA Process for Counterintelligence

The purpose of the court is to ensure that foreign spies operating in the United States are caught while ensuring that government powers are not abused. Foreign spies could cause great harm to U.S. security and interests through their actions, and investigations of this nature are deemed highly sensitive. If court cases were held in the open then defenders could require that the sources and means used to obtain information in the case against them be disclosed and thus made public. This would jeopardize the ability of government security agencies to carry out surveillance on other threats.

Consequently, the court operates in an *ex parte* manner such that the subjects of surveillance are not a party to the court's proceedings and remain unaware of any proceedings initiated against them. Only the government executive branch agencies seeking surveillance and the judicial branch courts reviewing the warrants are parties. The proceedings in the court are not made public, and all court officials and staffers must hold special clearances to access the information.

The FISA legislation permits government authorities to physically search and electronically surveil an individual for up to one year without approval by FISC so long as the information deals with foreign intelligence matters and does not include a U.S. person. The government may seek a warrant from FISC if they can provide probable cause that the individual is an agent of a foreign power and specify specific areas to be surveilled. Moreover, the government agencies must ensure that they take measures to limit the acquisition of information about U.S. persons, although they could review communications between the subject of the surveillance and American persons. Surveillance of American persons may be conducted so long as the courts authorize warrants for 90-day intervals.

Congressional Oversight

Oversight duties related to the executive branch are facilitated primarily through warrants that FISC issues; however, there is also an oversight role for Congress. The Senate Select Committee on Intelligence (SSCI) and the House Permanent Select Committee (HSPCI) by law must receive reports about requests from the attorney general. In this manner all branches of government participate in the process, with the executive branch carrying out surveillance requests and activities, the courts issuing warrants approving surveillance, and Congress also overseeing warrant requests through reporting requirements. Based on government data of requests for electronic surveillance, there have been 299 government requests denied by FISC; however, only 12 total denials were prior to 2015. There have been over 2,000 cases of warrant requests being modified before being accepted, but most surveillance warrants are granted by FISC, and these number over 42,000.

Adding Counterterrorism to FISA

Under provisions of the 2001 Patriot Act, the Foreign Intelligence Surveillance Act was amended to include terrorism in addition to espionage as a grounds for surveillance. Terrorism by most definitions is conducted by non-state groups, and so the 2001 revision also removed the requirement stipulating backing by a foreign government as applied to espionage cases.

Role in Privacy Debate

The main controversy surrounding FISC is with respect to the retention and searching of Americans' data as part of national security surveillance activities. Disclosures indicated that a warrant had been issued to a large telecommunications provider for daily cell phone records of all of its customers. The records were not the actual voice or messaging content but rather data about such communications such as type, direction, duration, and location of such communications. Nonetheless, these warrants were requested in a blanket manner rather than specifically outlining specific individuals of surveillance. The government asserted that such metadata was not content and thus legal to obtain, but the Ninth Circuit Court of Appeals in 2020 determined that the data collection was illegal via the decision in the 2020 *United States v. Moalin* case.

Bibliography

Aftergood, Steven. 2022. "Foreign Intelligence Surveillance Act." Department of Justice Annual Reports to Congress ("107 Reports"). Federation of American Scientists. Updated April 29. https://irp.fas.org/agency/doj/fisa/index.html#rept.

Goitein, Elizabeth and Faiza Patel. 2015. *What Went Wrong with the FISA Court.* Brennan Center for Justice. New York University School of Law, March 18. https://www.brennancenter.org/media/140/download.

Liu, Edward C. 2021. *Origins and Impact of the Foreign Intelligence Surveillance Act (FISA) Provisions that Expired on March 15, 2020.* CRS Report no. R40138. Washington, D.C.: Congressional Research Service, March 31. https://crsreports.congress.gov/product/pdf/R/R40138/24.

Ott, Marvin C. 2019. "Intelligence Oversight in Congress: Perilous Times." Foreign Policy Research Institute, National Security Program, April 17. https://www.fpri.org/article/2019/04/intelligence-oversight-in-congress-perilous-times/.

Rosenbach, Eric and Aki J. Peritz. 2009. "Congressional Oversight of the Intelligence Community." Belfer Center for Science and International Affairs, Harvard Kennedy School of Government, July. https://www.belfercenter.org /publication/congressional-oversight-intelligence-community.

United States v. Moalin, No. 13–50572 (United States Court of Appeals for the Ninth Circuit, November 10, 2016). https://cdn.ca9.uscourts.gov/datastore/opinions/2020/09 /02/13-50572.pdf.

George W. Bush (1946–)

George W. Bush (born July 6, 1946) was the 43rd president of the United States, whose legacy is defined by his administration's responses to the terrorist attacks on September 11, 2001, that killed nearly 3,000 Americans. In the aftermath of that stunning attack, President Bush's administration elevated terrorism from a peripheral challenge to a grave national security threat that justified significant federal policy changes and energies.

The War on Terrorism

President Bush entered office with a foreign policy platform skeptical of nation-building and a defense policy geared toward a technology-driven transformation of military forces to prepare for the next generation's challenges by nation-states. Less than a year into office, however, the September 11 attacks by al Qaeda against targets in New York and Washington, D.C., led to a reorientation of policy in what President Bush first called a "War on Terrorism" and what was later called the "Global War on Terrorism." The reorientation encompassed three main policy shifts pertaining to the use of force abroad, the expansion of domestic surveillance and law enforcement powers, and nation-building.

Aggressive International Counterterrorism

First, Bush directed American foreign and military actions toward a sustained campaign against al Qaeda and its affiliates in the Middle East, Africa, and Asia. Because the adversary was a violent non-state actor, policies of preemption were adopted under the logic that terrorists who had used suicide attacks could not be deterred the way that a nation-state could. This preemption meant that the U.S. government forces would go on the offensive to seek out terrorists in efforts to eliminate them before they could launch attacks, and that continued pressure would help prevent them from being able to plan large-scale attacks like 9/11. This military action was congressionally authorized not as a war declaration, given the absence of a nation-state opponent, but rather under an expansive Authorization to Use Military Force (AUMF) in 2001.

Military efforts initially focused on al Qaeda in Afghanistan as well as their Taliban allies. The campaign was broadened from pursing non-state terrorist groups to include regime change for states that had previously used weapons of mass destruction, and the U.S. government invaded Iraq in March 2003 to remove Iraqi dictator Saddam Hussein. Concurrently the AUMF also authorized actions against al Qaeda insurgents and terrorist affiliates around the world such as Abu Sayyaf Group in the Philippines, al Qaeda in the Arabian Peninsula in Yemen, al Shabaab in Somalia, al Qaeda in the Islamic Maghreb (AQIM) in Algeria, al Qaeda in Iraq (AQI), and the Taliban in Afghanistan and Pakistan.

The global reach of these efforts led to new legal and policy challenges, such as what to do with captured militants and terrorists termed "enemy combatants" who were not fighting as nationals in a state's military but were also not citizens of the United States. The administration settled on moving these detainees to the military base at Guantanamo Bay, Cuba, given the legal gray area.

Expanding Domestic Security Powers

Second, President Bush backed a comprehensive reorganization and expansion of the federal government. He supported the 2001 USA PATRIOT Act, which domestically grave greater surveillance and arrest powers to federal law enforcement agencies in the name of fighting terrorism and preventing future attacks. His administration also championed a new cabinet-level federal department, which Congress created with the 2002 Homeland Security Act. This Department of Homeland Security (DHS) constituted a reorganization effort aimed at centralizing existing government agencies with portfolios in border and coastal policing, customs and immigration, transportation security, critical infrastructure protection, and emergency preparedness. In short, the DHS reorganization was seen as a shield to complement the sword of actions under the AUMF.

Finally, President Bush backed the Intelligence Reform and Terrorism Prevention Act of 2004, which created the Office of the Director of National Intelligence (ODNI) to nominally oversee U.S. intelligence efforts. The act also replaced the director of the Central Intelligence Agency (CIA) with the position of director of national intelligence as the chief intelligence advisor to the president. The logic was to try and foster a greater culture of cooperation and communication within the federal government's many intelligence agencies to better share relevant information to identify and prevent future attacks.

Embracing Nation-Building

Third, the policy approach adopted a substantially broader understanding of counterterrorism to include efforts at nation-building. In addition to seeking the destruction of al Qaeda elements, Bush's administration prioritized the economic and political development of affected states under the logic that leaving them with failed or failing governance would enable terrorist groups to operate from their territory. Al Qaeda had done just this in Afghanistan under the Taliban. The logic assumed that turning economically and politically developing states into democracies would make them inherently more peaceful through integration with other democratic governments.

The ultimate record of U.S. counterterrorism efforts due to the moves of the Bush administration remains controversial. The aggressive pursuit of al Qaeda and its franchises put them on the defensive; however, the war in Iraq attracted numerous foreign fighters from around the region along with the propagation of similar Salafi-Jihadist militant groups.

Bibliography

Bush, George W. 2002. *The National Security Strategy of the United States of America*. September 17. https://nssarchive .us/wp-content/uploads/2020/04/2002.pdf.

Dobbins, James, Michele A. Poole, Austin Long, and Benjamin Runkle. 2008. *After the War: Nation-Building from FDR to George W. Bush*. Rand Corporation Monograph 716. Santa Monica: Rand. https://www.rand .org/pubs/monographs/MG716.html.

Leffler, Melvyn P. 2011. "9/11 in Retrospect: George W. Bush's Grand Strategy, Reconsidered." *Foreign Affairs* 90, no. 5 (September/October): 33–44.

Masters, Jonathan. 2022. "Guantanamo Bay: 20 Years of Counterterrorism and Controversy." Council on Foreign Relations, September 9. https://www.cfr.org/article /guantanamo-bay-twenty-years-counterterrorism-and -controversy.

Hamas

The Islamic Resistance Movement (Harakat al-Muqawama al-Islamiya, commonly known as Hamas) is an organization in the Palestinian territories that concurrently operates as a terrorist group, insurgent group, and political party. It seeks to create an Islamic government in control of Israel and the Palestinian territories. In the 1990s and early 2000s it engaged in a campaign of suicide terror attacks against Israeli targets. It presently maintains control over the Gaza Strip after a 2006 split with its rival group Fatah, which controls the West Bank.

Background

Hamas was founded in 1987 by Ahmed Yassin as a part of the Muslim Brotherhood movement that itself started in neighboring Egypt. The brotherhood argues that "Islam is the solution" to political and social problems and as an Islamist group looks to enact *sharia* (Islamic law) in the societies where it operates. The group was formally created as part of the First *Intifada* ("uprising") of Palestinians against Israeli control of the West Bank and the Gaza Strip in 1988. Israel acquired the West Bank from Jordan and Gaza from Egypt after the 1967 Six Day War, in which Israel fought against military forces from the Arab governments of Egypt, Iraq, Jordan, Saudi Arabia, and Syria. In the decades following the war, Israeli military forces continued to occupy the territories, and Palestinian militants under the Palestinian Liberation Organization (PLO) fought a concerted campaign to create a secular Palestinian state out of the territories of Israel, the West Bank, and Gaza. Hamas rose as an Islamist counter to the secular PLO.

Although the Muslim Brotherhood and Hamas are both Islamist of a Sunni orientation, they are not Salafi-Jihadist. Its 1988 charter declares it to be a part of the Muslim Brotherhood movement and dedicated to jihad against the Israeli government until an Islamic Palestinian state is created; it also contains anti-Semitic remarks and calls for the destruction of the state of Israel. In 2017 the group revised its charter to remove its connection to the Muslim Brotherhood as well as to argue that it is anti-Zionist instead of anti-Semitic. Anti-Zionism opposes a Jewish state such as Israel, whereas anti-Semitism is hostility and prejudice against ethnic Jews regardless of citizenship.

Adoption of Suicide Attacks

Hamas opposed the Oslo Accords in 1993 that outlined the Israeli–Palestinian peace process between the Israeli government and the Palestinian Liberation Organization under Fatah head Yasir Arafat. Starting in April 1993 Hamas conducted suicide terror attacks in an effort to derail this process. Through the year 2016 the group conducted 64 such attacks on its own and numerous others in conjunction with other Palestinian militant groups. Of these, 44 took place during the Second Intifada that began in September 2000 and ended in February 2005.

Most targets of these attacks were Israeli public buses, malls, and restaurants. Founder Ahmed Yassin sanctioned such attacks and survived an Israeli airstrike that targeted him in 2003 before Israel forces succeeded in killing him in a 2004 gunship strike. In 2005 the Israeli government unilaterally withdrew its forces and settlers from the Gaza Strip under the direction of Prime Minister Ariel Sharon. The Palestinian National Authority (PNA) then proceeded with elections in 2006, in which Hamas defeated Fatah for control of the PNA. Fatah had dominated the PLO/PNA since its inception and failed to relinquish its control of the West Bank. Hamas, in turn, seized the authority's institutions in Gaza. This situation remained in place as of the close of 2022.

Change in Attack Profile

Largely in response to the intifada, the government of Israel bolstered work on its walled security barrier between Israeli territory and the West Bank. Some portions of this barrier cross into the U.N.-recognized territory of the West Bank. Since the erection of the Israeli security barrier, the group's level of ground-based attacks has dropped significantly. Instead, it relies on various short-range, unguided rocket attacks against Israeli cities. Despite being a Sunni group, Hamas receives financial and military assistance from the Islamic Republic of Iran.

Bibliography

Jefferis, Jennifer. 2016. *Hamas: Terrorism, Governance, and its Future in Middle East Politics.* Santa Barbara: ABC-CLIO.

Laub, Zachary and Kali Robinson. 2021. "What Is Hamas?" *Council on Foreign Relations Backgrounder*, August 17. https://www.cfr.org/backgrounder/what-hamas.

Moghadam, Assaf. 2003. "Palestinian Suicide Terrorism in the Second Intifada: Motivations and Organizational Aspects." *Studies in Conflict & Terrorism* 26, no. 2: 65–92.

Schanzer, Jonathan. 2008. *Hamas vs. Fatah: The Struggle for Palestine.* New York: Palgrave Macmillan.

Hezbollah

Hezbollah ("Party of God") is a Shi'a Arab terrorist organization, insurgent group, and political party in Lebanon. It has its origins as the first successful export of the ideology of the 1979 Islamic Revolution of Iran to the Arab world.

Lebanon's Ethnic Makeup

Lebanon is a highly heterogenous society with a government that guarantees political representation along ethnoreligious lines. The country is broadly composed of Arab Christians and Muslims but with various sects. Among the leading groups based on population are Maronite Christians, Sunni Muslims, and Shi'a Muslims. Both before and after French colonial control, the country's Maronite Christians held important positions in government and society, and to a lesser extent Sunni Muslims had important economic clout in the urban areas. Lebanon's Shi'a Arabs were previously part of the feudal *za'im* ("boss") system that was dominant in that country; however, the Shi'a inhabited the poorer rural areas in the east and south.

Hezbollah's Origins

In 1974 a Shi'a Arab political figure named Musa al-Sadr led a "Movement of the Dispossessed" that asserted Shi'a identity against these elites. As the country headed toward civil war, the movement coalesced into a political party and militia named Amal (Afwaj al-Muqawama al-Lubnaniyah; "Lebanese Resistance Groups"; also the Arabic word for hope). Musa al-Sadr disappeared in 1978 after traveling to Libya.

In the 1980s Hezbollah grew out of this movement as an Islamist faction. The group derives its religious inspiration from Khomeini's ideology and associated teachings based out of Qom, Iran, rather than schools affiliated with Arab Shi'a that operate from Najaf, Iraq. In its 1985 manifesto the group described itself as a resistance force against Israel and vowed to seek the destruction of that country.

Hezbollah is effectively a proxy force of the Iranian government, which supplies it with regular funding and material support. Elements of the group also work with Iran's Islamic Revolutionary Guard Corps, Quds Force. Elements of the group with Iranian backing conducted the bombing of U.S. Marines and French paratroopers in 1983. In the 1990s the group also carried out a series of international terrorist attacks against Jewish targets in cooperation with Iran's Quds Force. Among its best-known operatives was Imad Mugniyeh.

Insurgency Against Israel

Throughout the 1990s the group waged a stout guerilla campaign against Israeli forces in the south of Lebanon, and in 2000 the group claimed victory after Israel announced its withdrawal from that area. Hezbollah, however, refused to abide by the 1990 Ta'if agreement that ended the Lebanese Civil War and required that all militias remove their arms. Despite securing Israel's removal from Lebanese territory the group maintained its weaponry. In the summer of 2006, Israel went to war with the group after Hezbollah operatives attacked an

Israeli military patrol and kidnaped two Israeli soldiers. Israeli forces relied on air strikes and a limited ground incursion using reservists. Despite Israel's limited military advances into Lebanon, Hezbollah was not destroyed and so claimed to have successfully resisted.

Regional Expansion as an Iranian Extension

Today Hezbollah plays an integral role as a conduit between the Islamic Republic of Iran and Arab Shi'a groups in Syria, Iraq, and Yemen. In the Iraq War it took a leading role in training Iraqi and Syrian fighters to do battle with U.S. forces in the 2000s. In the early phases of the Syrian Civil War it fought directly on behalf of the Syrian government, an ally of Iran. There it took a crucial but controversial role in preserving Syrian President Bashar al-Assad's grip on the country by fighting against Sunni rebels. Hezbollah operatives later fought against Islamic State militants in Iraq after that group's rise in 2014.

Bibliography

Bergman, Ronin. 2015. "The Hezbollah Connection." *New York Times Magazine*, February 10. https://www .nytimes.com/2015/02/15/magazine/the-hezbollah -connection.html.

Biddle, Stephen and Jeffrey A. Friedman. 2008. *The 2006 Lebanon Campaign and the Future of Warfare: Implications for Army and Defense Policy*. Strategic Studies Institute Monograph, U.S. Army War College. Carlisle: Army War College Press.

Jahanbani, Nakissa and Suzanne Weedon Levy. 2022. *Iran Entangled: Iran and Hezbollah's Support to Proxies Operating in Syria*. Combating Terrorism Center at West Point Military Academy, April. https://ctc.usma.edu/wp-content /uploads/2022/04/Iran-Entangled.pdf.

Levitt, Matthew and David Schenker. 2008. "Who Was
    Imad Mugniyeh?" Washington Institute for Near East
    Policy, *Policywatch 1340*, February 14. https://www
    .washingtoninstitute.org/policy-analysis/who-was-imad
    -mughniyeh.
Norton, Augustus Richard. 2018. *Hezbollah: A Short History.*
    Princeton: Princeton University Press.

Illich Ramirez Sanchez (1949–)

Ilich Ramirez Sanchez (born October 12, 1949), commonly
known as Carlos the Jackal, is a Venezuelan national known
for having conducted a series of terrorist attacks in the 1970s
and early 1980s. Named after the Soviet leader Vladimir Ilich
Lenin, he was raised in a Marxist household and later became
a member of the Marxist Popular Front for the Liberation of
Palestine (PFLP).

Sanchez exemplified the idea of a transnational terrorist by
working with different international groups to conduct attacks
against a variety of targets in different countries and by regularly seeking haven in sympathizer states during his operational years. He is currently serving consecutive life sentences
in France for attacks he committed there in 1974, 1982, and
1983. Over the course of his career, he led or participated in
13 attacks in Europe that killed 18 people and wounded scores
more. Most of these attacks targeted Jewish and French targets,
and he frequently struck elements of the transportation sector
such as aircraft and rail lines.

The OPEC Attack

The most famous Carlos the Jackal attack came in 1975, when
he attacked the meeting of the Organization of Petroleum-
Exporting Countries (OPEC) in Vienna, Austria. OPEC is a
cartel of the world's leading oil manufacturers who fixed production quotas to maintain price levels, and Arab producers
such as Saudi Arabia and Iran are among its most powerful

members. Carlos and five other German and Arab terrorists killed a policeman and took 63 OPEC representatives hostage at the conference in Vienna. They demanded that the Austrian government broadcast their political messages and arrange for an aircraft to fly them to Algeria in exchange for the release of some hostages.

Sanchez' ambition in the raid was to kill the oil ministers for Saudi Arabia and Iran, but he ultimately released them in exchange for safe passage. There is widespread speculation that Arab governments paid a ransom for the release of these ministers. Because Sanchez failed to achieve the objectives of the PFLP, he was kicked out of the group.

A "Broker" of Terrorism

Sanchez was perhaps the most well-connected terrorist in the second half of the 20th century. Over the span of his career he maintained links with the Palestinian George Habash of the Popular Front for the Liberation of Palestine (PFLP), members of the Japanese Red Army, the Soviet Union by way of East Germany's Stasi intelligence service, and Muammar Ghaddafi of Libya. At one point Sanchez was given his own headquarters in East Berlin to carry out attacks against targets in Germany and France. During the early 1980s, he operated out of Hungary. When he was later denied the use of that territory, he took refuge in Damascus, Syria, in 1985. He stayed there until his banishment from the country in 1991 after the Gulf War. Sanchez then made his way to Sudan, where he was ultimately captured in 1994 and extradited to France to stand trial for his earlier crimes. He remains incarcerated there and claims to have converted to Islam while still retaining his revolutionary beliefs.

Bibliography

Bacon, Tricia. 2018. *Why Terrorist Groups Form International Alliances*. Philadelphia: University of Pennsylvania Press.

Follain, John. 2011. *Jackal: The Complete Story of the Legendary Terrorist, Carlos the Jackal.* New York: Arcade.

Islamic State

The Islamic State is a Salafi-Jihadist group that evolved from al Qaeda in Iraq. It was initially called the Islamic State of Iraq and Syria (ISIS). The group took control of the western Iraqi cities of Fallujah and Ramadi in 2013. Capitalizing on the anarchy of the Syrian Civil War, the group acquired territory in the northeast of Syria. It made the city of Raqqa its de facto capital after capturing it from al Qaeda elements in January 2014. Staging forces from these territories, it expanded into northern Iraq in June, defeating Iraqi military forces and capturing the northern cities of Mosul, Tikrit, and Sinjar. The swift defeat of the Iraqi military enabled the group to capture millions in U.S.-supplied military equipment that it then put into service for further conquests.

The group carried out numerous atrocities in the areas it conquered, particularly in northern Iraq, where it engaged in ethnic cleansing against Yazidis at Sinjar. The operational characteristics of the Islamic State include its reliance on prison breaks to release incarcerated allies, the use of suicide bombers in conjunction with conventional attacks, and its heavy use of propaganda to attract foreign fighters and inspire lone wolf attacks in Western countries.

From Regional to Global Aspirations

In June 2014 its leader, Abu Bakr al-Baghdadi, announced that the name of the organization had changed to the Islamic State and declared himself the caliph. He did so at the al-Nuri Mosque in Mosul in a carefully scripted appearance that mimicked the appearance and practices of Muhammad according to hadith (a collection of sayings from the prophet Muhammad that are central to the Islamic faith). This spectacle sent the message that the caliphate had been reborn and was to be global in scope. Following this move various Salafi-Jihadist groups pledged loyalty to the new entity, and Islamic State propaganda made heavy mention of how the group intended to unite Muslims by tearing down the artificial national barriers imposed across the region by the secret 1916 Sykes-Picot agreement, which divided the old Ottoman Empire into sections controlled by Great Britain and France.

From Global Stature to Regional Expansions

Islamic State branches now include the Caucasus Emirate in Chechnya, which maintained links with jihadists since 2009 despite not having formally pledged loyalty to bin Laden. In 2014 its senior leaders defected to the Islamic State and it moved to Syria to fuse with al-Baghdadi's caliphate directly. These Chechen militants were among the most tactically capable fighters in the organization's ranks.

Moving from the Caucasus to Egypt, the Islamic State Sinai Province officially left its al Qaeda orientation to pledge allegiance to al-Baghdadi in 2014. It continues to sustain an insurgency against the government of Egypt as well as terrorist attacks like the downing of a Russian passenger plane over Sinai. Elsewhere in Africa the group made notable gains. In 2015 a faction of Boko Haram split to create the Islamic State West Africa Province. In May 2021 this faction defeated the main Boko Haram grouping and killed its longtime leader Abubakr Shekau to become the paramount Salafi-Jihadist group in West Africa.

In al Qaeda and the Taliban's home theater of Afghanistan, another faction pledged allegiance to the group. The Islamic State Khorasan Province was created in 2015 as a splinter from the Taliban in the east of Afghanistan. Soon after its founding the group launched suicide terror bombings in Afghanistan and Pakistan. Some mid-level leaders from Syria relocated to this sector before the caliphate's fall. Its initial leader and the subsequent three replacements were all killed in U.S. airstrikes, yet the group continues to sustain operational capabilities. It is best known for the terror attack at the Kabul International Airport during the evacuation of the United States from Afghanistan in August 2021.

Demise and Recent Developments

Despite its rapid proliferation regionally and globally in 2014, the Islamic State core was short-lived. Forces from the United States worked with local Kurds and Iraqis to fight against the Islamic State. The Russian government worked with Syria, Iran, and Iraqi Shi'a militias to do so as well. Using airstrikes and ground forces, these efforts rolled back the Islamic State's territorial gains and captured Raqqa in October 2017. At this point the remaining Islamic State leadership fled to other parts of northern Syria near the Turkish border under the control of Sunni rebels. There Abu Bakr al-Baghdadi was killed in a 2019 commando raid by the U.S. special operations troops, as was his immediate successor three years later.

As of 2023 the core leadership of the Islamic State seems in disarray; however, the group endures in the form of its franchises and has even seen expansion. The most recent iteration is the Islamic State Central African Province that was formed in 2017 and is active in Mozambique as an element in the conflict in Cabo Delgado. The group remains a threat to other nations because of the sponsorship and inspiration it provides to violent militants around the world outside of Iraq and Syria. Islamic State terrorists account for attacks in the United States, France, Indonesia, Belgium, the United Kingdom, Austria, Spain, Iran, Egypt, Pakistan, the Philippines, and Sri Lanka.

Bibliography

Doxsee, Catrina and Jared Thompson. 2021. "Examining Extremism: Islamic State Khorasan Province (ISKP)."

Center for Strategic and International Studies, Transnatioanl Threats Project, September 8. https://www.csis.org/blogs/examining-extremism/examining-extremism-islamic-state-khorasan-province-iskp.

Mapping Militant Organizations. 2021. "The Islamic State." Center for International Security and Cooperation, Freeman Spogli Institute, Stanford University. Last modified April 2021. https://cisac.fsi.stanford.edu/mappingmilitants/profiles/islamic-state.

McCants, William. 2015. "The Believer: How an Introvert with a Passion for Religion and Soccer Became Abu Bakr al Baghdadi, Leader of the Islamic State." Brookings Institution, September 1. http://csweb.brookings.edu/content/research/essays/2015/thebeliever.html.

Sturdee, Nick and Mairbek Vatchagaev. 2020. "ISIS in the North Caucasus." Newlines Institute for Strategy and Policy, October 26. https://newlinesinstitute.org/isis/isis-in-the-north-caucasus/.

Warner, Jason, Ryan Cummings, Héni Nsaibia and Ryan O'Farrell. 2022. *The Islamic State in Africa: The Emergence, Evolution, and Future of the Next Jihadist Battlefront.* Oxford: Oxford University Press.

Weiss, Michael and Hassan Hassan. 2020. *ISIS: Inside the Army of Terror.* New York: Regan Arts.

The Wilson Center. 2019. "Timeline: The Rise, Spread, and Fall of the Islamic State." Middle East Programs, October 28. https://www.wilsoncenter.org/article/timeline-the-rise-spread-and-fall-the-islamic-state.

Narodnaya Volya

Narodnaya Volya ("People's Freedom") was a Russian leftist terrorist group that operated between 1879 and 1887 and was dedicated to overthrowing the Tsarist monarchy. It adhered to the concept of "propaganda by the deed," where a vanguard of revolutionaries was inspired to spark a wider class-based revolution by killing the leaders who they saw as perpetuating that system. In this political theory, the bourgeois class sat atop a house of cards that only needed a spark of direct action to be brought down.

Narodnaya Volya targeted the leadership of the Russian Empire in hopes of generating a broad-based peasant revolution against the Tsar's rule. Operationally the group maintained a high level of secrecy and was directed by an executive committee. Tactically it implemented attacks using a cell structure. Its most infamous attack was the successful assassination of Tsar Alexander II in 1881. This and other assassinations inspired similar actions by anarchists in Europe and the United States in the succeeding decades. The group also popularized the use of dynamite as a tool of political assassination. Altogether its methods set the stage for revolutionary terrorism that would appear in the industrial age.

Bibliography

Seth, Ronald. 1966. *The Russian Terrorists: The Story of the Narodniki*. London: Barrie & Rockliff.

Yarmolinsky, Avrahm. 2014. *Road to Revolution: A Century of Russian Radicalism*. Princeton: Princeton University Press.

Rand Paul (1963–)

Rand Paul (born January 7, 1963) represents the Commonwealth of Kentucky as the junior senator and has done so since January 3, 2011. He is a noted civil libertarian Republican party member. As a civil libertarian Senator Paul's position is generally such that the fears of government abuse of power are more worrisome than the damage that can be inflicted by foreign threats. Senator Paul's political positions strongly revolve around the rights of individuals and states versus those of the federal government. In counterterrorism policy debates he is an opponent of indefinite detention, the general use of targeted killings, government surveillance of U.S. citizens, and the militarization of policing in the United States.

Opposition to Indefinite Detention

One example of Senator Paul's civil liberties concerns is the policy of indefinite detention. This is when a government holds an individual in custody without an expiration date on the detention or fulfilling a process to bring that individual to trial. In June 2017 he introduced legislation to end indefinite detention that he sees as authorized by the 2001 Authorization to Use Military Force (AUMF) passed after the 9/11 attacks. He argued that current law under section 2021 of the AUMF permits wartime rules of allowing the detention of those engaging in hostilities against the United States, including Americans. Senator Paul stated that he has no issue with capturing and sending non-American enemy combatants who have taken arms against U.S. forces captured to the Guantanamo Bay Naval Base for detention, so long as they are judged in military tribunals and are not detained indefinitely.

Filibuster over Targeted Killings

Among the most publicized cases of Senator Paul's activism were his filibusters over the 2013 confirmation of John Brennan as director of the Central Intelligence Agency, and in 2015 over the reauthorization of the Patriot Act. A filibuster is an intentional delay of a vote on legislation that is allowed due to U.S. Senate procedural rules. In a talking filibuster a senator may speak on the floor for an unlimited amount of time so long as they remain in the chamber and do not yield the floor. A speaker may recognize a fellow senator in the chamber to ask a question, and allies may in turn take some of the speaking burden from the main speaker when called upon. However, this still requires the main speaker to be present on the floor. For the wider body to proceed to a vote and end debate, the body must invoke cloture. Cloture requires a three-fifths majority of at least 60 senators, and in practice this means that the common simple majority of one party having at least 51 senators is not enough to end the filibuster.

In the March 2013 case Senator Paul lasted nearly 13 hours on the Senate floor before allowing the vote of John Brennan's nomination to lead the CIA to proceed. At the heart of his filibuster was clarification regarding the legality of the authority. Senator Paul had written to Attorney General Eric Holder asking if the president of the United States could order the killing of an American citizens on American soil with a drone strike without trial, and Holder's response was that the U.S. government had no intention of doing so. Senator Paul was unsatisfied with the response. Following the filibuster attempt Attorney General Holder wrote an additional letter explicitly stating that the president does not have the authority to use a weaponized drone to kill an American not engaged in combat on American soil.

At the heart of the issue was the case of Anwar al-Awlaki, an American citizen who became a major figure in the al Qaeda affiliated group al Qaeda in the Arabian Peninsula (AQAP) and engaged in correspondence with Muslims to engage in attacks against the U.S. homeland, such as in Fort Hood in November 2009. Al-Awlaki was killed in a drone strike in September 2011, and civil libertarians were troubled over the example it established because he was a U.S. citizen who had not been given due process and a trial. Prior to his nomination Director Brennan was President Obama's counterterrorism advisor and an architect of the policy to significantly expand drone strikes in East Africa, the Middle East, and South/Central Asia. Part of the duties included reorganizing management of the kill list of drone targets to centralize operation from the White House.

Filibuster over Domestic Surveillance

In May 2015, one month after announcing his presidential run, Senator Paul attempted a filibuster for 10 hours and 31 minutes over reauthorization of section 215 of the Patriot Act. This section authorized the bulk collection of data. The provisions in section 215 expired shortly afterward but were partially restored with the passage of the USA FREEDOM Act. That bill included language that prevents the U.S. government from directly collecting bulk data of Americans; however, the government can still obtain custody of users' metadata sourced from private telephone and internet companies.

Relatedly, Senator Paul considers Edward Snowden to be a whistleblower for disclosing information about U.S. intelligence programs to the media, and in 2020 called for him to be pardoned. In May 2013 Snowden revealed the existence of classified mass surveillance programs with part of Snowden's unauthorized disclosures including the bulk collection of U.S. citizens' metadata, or data about data. Senator Paul holds the perspective that the Fourth Amendment's language prohibits the U.S. government doing so as it constitutes an "illegal search and seizure" without a warrant specifically naming the individual to be searched.

Opposition to the Militarization of Policing

In addition to civil liberties concerns in the areas of indefinite detention, targeted killings, and domestic surveillance, Senator Paul has sponsored legislation against the militarization of policework. These bills focus on ending federal policies such as the Defense Department's 1033 program, where excess U.S. military material such as armored vehicles, rifles, magazines, ammunition, and other kit are transferred to law enforcement agencies. Civil libertarians like Senator Paul see this equipment flow as encouraging law enforcement to see the policed as enemies rather than members of communities.

Bibliography

Balko, Radley. 2014. *Rise of the Warrior Cop: The Militarization of America's Police Forces*. New York: Public Affairs.

Gee, Harvey. 2015. "National Insecurity: The National Defense Authorization Act, the Indefinite Detention of American Citizens, and a Call for Heightened Judicial Scrutiny." *University of Illinois Chicago Law Review* 49, no. 1: 69–99.

Lauter, David and Timothy M. Phelps. 2014. "Memo Justifying Drone Killings of American Al Qaeda Leader Is Released." *Los Angeles Times*, July 23. https://www.latimes .com/nation/nationnow/la-na-nn-drone-memo-awlaki -20140623-story.html.

Liu, Jodie. 2015. "So What Does the USA Freedom Act Do Anyway?" *Lawfare, FISA*, June 3. https://www.lawfareblog .com/so-what-does-usa-freedom-act-do-anyway.

Theodore Kaczynski (1942–2023)

Theodore Kaczynski (born May 22, 1942; died June 10, 2023) was a university professor of mathematics and an American domestic terrorist known as the Unabomber (an acronym for UNiversity and Airline BOMbing based on his earliest targets). Kaczynski mailed bombs targeting symbols of technology such as engineering, computer science, and genetics professors along with computer stores. He was heavily influenced by French anarchist philosopher Jacques Ellul's book *The Technological Society*, which asserted that technological advances were corrupting and enslaving humanity to serve technology rather than be served by it. Kaczynski's political aim in his bombing campaign was to collapse industrial society and revert to one marked by preindustrial organization and environmental preservation. He eluded law enforcement for 18 years before his arrest in 1996.

Background

Kaczynski grew up in a working-class home in Chicago, Illinois. As an infant he spent a prolonged period in isolation under medical care for a series of unexplained rashes. During this period, he had minimal contact with his parents, and family members later said the experience scarred him emotionally. By all accounts Kaczynski was a child genius. His IQ score when in middle school was 167, and in high school he participated in a range of extracurricular activities including the marching band and the mathematics, German, and biology clubs. Kaczynski attended Harvard on a scholarship at age 16 and earned his bachelor of arts degree in mathematics four years later. In his second year at Harvard University, Kaczynski was a participant in psychological studies that involved verbally abusive attacks targeting his ego for the purposes of studying Kaczynski's reactions.

In 1962 Kaczynski was accepted to the University of Michigan for graduate studies, where he earned a doctoral degree in mathematics in five years. He accepted a tenure track position in mathematics at University of California, Berkeley upon graduation. After just two years he resigned from his position and moved back home to live with his parents in Illinois.

In 1971 he built a cabin in a remote part of Montana where he lived for most of the next 25 years without access to water or power. He survived by working odd jobs and securing financial assistance from his family. Kaczynski also built traps around his property and set fire to buildings under construction near his cabin.

Terrorist Bombing Campaign

Kaczynski's first four targets were in Illinois, an area that he was familiar with, and featured basic bomb designs. In 1978 he mailed his first bomb to an engineering professor at Northwestern University. Suspicious of the parcel, the professor turned it over to the police, and an officer was injured upon opening it. A second package bomb sent to Northwestern a year later wounded a graduate student when it exploded. This third attempt was planted on an American Airlines flight from Chicago to Washington, D.C. The device's timer did not function as intended, and the bomb did not detonate with full power, thus allowing the crew to make an emergency landing.

Kaczynski's fourth target was the president of United Airlines, Percy Wood. The bomb sent to Wood was directed to his home in Lake Forest, Illinois. This began a trend in some of his bombings where Kaczynski selected targets with names that had a reference to woods or nature. He also embedded parts of trees in his bomb designs, such as the use of splinters as shrapnel.

A fifth bomb mailed in 1981 targeting an engineering professor in Utah named Leroy Wood Bearnson was defused by authorities. The next attack was against a computer scientist named Patrick Fischer at Vanderbilt that wounded the department secretary who opened the parcel. Subsequent bombs were sent to various industries and universities.

As the terrorist's bomb designs advanced, so did their lethality. A computer store owner became the first fatality from one of his bombs in 1985, and his final two bombs also killed the recipients of the packages. His last attack in April 1995 killed a lumber industry lobbyist in Sacramento. Altogether he sent 16 bombs that killed three, injured another 23, and created fear around the country.

Arrest

In 1995 Kaczynski sent a 35,000-word typewritten manifesto to print media outlets with a demand that they publish the work or else he would continue with his bombing campaign. After extensive deliberation, Attorney General Janet Reno approved publication of the work in the hope some readers could help identify the author.

After publication of the manifesto, Kaczynski's brother identified similarities in writing style to that of his troubled brother. He contacted a private investigator to follow up on Ted's whereabouts. He then provided writing samples from various letters he had received over the years, allowing the FBI to conduct linguistic analysis that concluded Ted Kaczynski was the author of the manifesto. The operation to arrest Ted Kaczynski was rushed after the FBI learned that someone had leaked the identity of his brother to CBS News, which intended to broadcast the story the following day. Kaczynski was arrested on April 3, 1996. He was later convicted for the three murders and the use of mailing bombs. Kaczynski was found dead in his prison cell in June 2023 at age 81. He had developed late-stage cancer and early reports suggest he took his own life.

Bibliography

Chase, Alston. 2004. *A Mind for Murder: The Education of the Unabomber and the Origins of Modern Terrorism*. New York: W.W. Norton & Company.

Federal Bureau of Investigation. 2023. "The Unabomber." FBI History. Accessed February 3. https://www.fbi.gov /history/famous-cases/unabomber.

McFadden, Robert D. 1996. "Prisoner of Rage: From a Child of Promise to the Unabom Suspect." *The New York Times*, May 26. https://www.nytimes.com/1996/05/26/us /prisoner-of-rage-a-special-report-from-a-child-of-promise -to-the-unabom-suspect.html.

Timothy McVeigh (1968–2001)

Timothy McVeigh holds the distinction of being the deadliest domestic terrorist in U.S. history for his bombing of the Oklahoma City Federal building in 1995. He was executed by the U.S. government in June 2001 via lethal injection after receiving the death sentence for his crimes.

Background

Born on April 23, 1968, McVeigh was raised in upstate New York. His parents divorced when he was 10 years old, and he enlisted in the U.S. Army after graduating high school. While in the Army he became a gunner on the Bradley armored fighting vehicle and served in Operation Desert Storm during the Persian Gulf War in 1991. McVeigh held white supremacist views and read literature depicting a violent revolution against the federal government that would end in a race war and the death of all non-whites. After the war he attempted to join U.S. Army Special Forces but did not make the cut. He left military service with an honorable discharge later that year.

As a civilian McVeigh was aimless and unhappy in life. He was dissatisfied with his work as a security guard along with his lack of success in relationships. He became addicted to gambling and went bankrupt as a result of unpaid debts. In 1993 he moved to Texas, where his hatred for the government became further entrenched. He worked at gun shows where he sold survival gear and distributed antigovernment literature during this period.

Radicalization

McVeigh was particularly furious at the federal law enforcement actions in Ruby Ridge, Idaho. In 1992 federal agents prepared to arrest survivalist Randy Weaver on illegal weapons charges. Armed agents in camouflage scouting on the property were detected by the family dog, who alerted the Weavers. When the dog and family members stumbled on the scouting party, a firefight ensued that resulted in the death of Weaver's son Sammy, who was later found to have been shot in the back. U.S. Marshal William Degan was also killed in the encounter. In the subsequent siege an FBI sniper shot and wounded Randy but also hit his wife Vicki, killing her while she held the couple's infant daughter. In particular, McVeigh called for retribution against the FBI sniper whose name and address he supplied to individuals at gun shows.

While living in Texas McVeigh also went to Waco to protest federal law enforcement actions during the siege involving David Koresh and the Branch Davidians. After a brief stay in Arizona, McVeigh moved to a rural farm in Michigan to stay with Terry Nichols, a fellow military veteran he had met while in the Army. The two men saw the televised conclusion of the Waco siege, in which 49 adults and 27 children perished as the Branch Davidian compound burned to the ground. McVeigh and Nichols became determined to attack the U.S. government for revenge over the Waco siege. The two men experimented with explosive devices as they worked various gun shows across Michigan. The passage of the 1994 Federal Assault Weapons Ban further enraged McVeigh, who saw it both as an unconstitutional attempt by the government to disarm citizens and a threat to his livelihood on the gun show circuit.

Planning and Executing the Oklahoma City Bombing

McVeigh first considered an assassination campaign against government officials but rejected that approach after considering the extensive security barriers of such a plan. He and Nichols subsequently decided to bomb a large federal building because it would have high visibility. They moved to Kansas and began assembling and storing the vast quantities of fertilizer needed to construct a bomb. They also stole various explosives from commercial mining sites to help act as the fuse. McVeigh then rented a Ryder truck and loaded the finished bomb into it. He selected the date of April 19, 1995, for the attack to coincide with the second anniversary of the end of the Waco siege as well as the anniversary of the American Revolution's battles at Lexington and Concord.

On April 19 McVeigh parked the explosives-laden vehicle outside the Alfred P. Murrah Federal Building, started the time fuse, and fled the scene on foot to a waiting getaway vehicle. McVeigh was arrested on the highway leaving Oklahoma after he was stopped by police for a missing a vehicle registration tag.

Back in Oklahoma City, the explosion registered the power of two and a half tons of dynamite. It demolished the front of the building and collapsed multiple floors above ground level, killing 168 people inside. Included in the death count were 19 children, most of whom were in the on-site daycare.

Despite McVeigh's attack being a clear case of terrorism by targeting noncombatants, he justified the attack claiming that the facility was part of the "command and control" of the enemy. He maintained that he was acting as a soldier fighting in a war. One result of the bombing was the measures that the U.S. government implemented to better protect facilities by installing barriers to prevent vehicle traffic from getting too close to structures.

McVeigh was charged with the murder of eight federal agents, plotting to use a weapon of mass destruction, and destroying a federal structure. On June 11, 2001, he was executed for his crimes at the federal prison at Terre Haute, Indiana.

Bibliography

Federal Bureau of Investigation. 1995. "Oklahoma City Bombing Case Files." *FBI Records: The Vault.* https://vault.fbi.gov/OKBOMB/OKBOMB%20Part%2001%20of%2001/view.

Linder, Douglas O. 2023. "The Oklahoma Bombing Conspirators." *Famous Trials.* Accessed February 3, 2023. https://www.famous-trials.com/oklacity/713-conspirators.

Stickney, Brandon M. 1996. *All-American Monster: The Unauthorized Biography of Timothy McVeigh.* Amherst: Prometheus.

U.S. Special Operations Command (SOCOM)

Special Operations Command (SOCOM) is the primary element of the U.S. government tasked with unconventional warfare and counterterrorism. It is part of the Department of Defense and is one of its 11 unified combatant commands (COCOMs), of which six are geographically based and the remaining five, including SOCOM, are based on function.

Background

SOCOM and all other combatant commands were born out of reforms from the 1986 Defense Reorganization Act informally known as "Goldwater-Nichols" after its chief sponsors in Congress, Senator Barry Goldwater of Arizona and Representative

Bill Nichols of Alabama. These congressmen drafted the legislation in response to Operation Urgent Fury, the U.S. invasion of Grenada in 1983. Overall, the invasion was a success; however, after-action performance reviews identified numerous interoperability failures between the different armed services. For example, Navy SEALs (Sea, Air, and Land) on the ground during the invasion were unable to directly contact an Air Force gunship for support.

The legislation created the unified combatant commands to streamline the chain of command in having all services answer to one senior officer regardless of the service they belonged to. It also created incentives for the services to work more closely together toward a culture of jointness, such as requiring rotations in a service different from one's own for promotion.

Combat Elements

SOCOM oversees commando elements from all military services that includes but is not limited to U.S. Army Special Forces (Green Berets), U.S. Naval Special Warfare SEALs, and Marine Raiders of Marine Forces Special Operations Command (MARSOC). SOCOM also includes units such as the U.S. Army's 160th Special Operations Aviation Regiment (SOAR, the "Night Stalkers") and the U.S. Air Force Special Operations Group. These latter elements typically aid with the insertion into and recovery of SOCOM forces from their areas of operations, while Air Force Special Operations entail combat elements including so-called "combat controllers" who embed with the previously mentioned units and can call in precision air strikes.

There are many areas of overlap; however, the units within SOCOM specialize in certain duties based on their service history and focus. For instance, Navy SEALs prepare for unconventional warfare in the maritime environment whereas Army special forces obtain language and cultural training to specialize in training and fighting with allied indigenous forces using guerilla warfare tactics.

The Best of the Best

Notably, one component of SOCOM called the Joint Special Operations Command (JSOC) includes "tier one" units that are known to be the best in their field and work closely together. These units are typically tasked with the most challenging covert operations directly ordered by the president and include the Army's Special Forces Operational Detachment Delta (SFOD-D; "Delta Force," also known as the Combat Applications Group CAG), the Navy's Special Warfare Development Group (DEVGRU, formerly Seal Team Six), and the Air Force's 24th Special Tactics Squadron. One might think of these tier-one units as their respective service's "all-star" teams that draw upon the best talent available in their special operations units.

Elements of JSOC were involved in Operation Neptune Spear, the secret military operation that killed Osama bin Laden in his compound in Abbottabad, Pakistan on May 2, 2011. Subsequent actions undertaken by JSOC elements included killing Islamic State Deputy Commander Abu Ala al-Afri in a gunfight after he refused to surrender, along with raids that killed Islamic State leader Abu Bakr al-Baghdadi in October 2019 and his successor Abu Ibrahim al-Hashimi al-Quraishi in February 2022. Each of these leaders was in Syria, and the latter two killed themselves using suicide explosives after engaging in combat with JSOC forces.

Bibliography

Feickert, Andrew. 2022. *U.S. Special Operations Forces (SOF): Background and Issues for Congress.* CRS Report no. RS21048. Washington, D.C.: Congressional Research Service, May 11. https://crsreports.congress.gov/product /pdf/RS/RS21048.

Hamre, John J. 2016. "Reflections: Looking Back at the Need for Goldwater-Nichols." Center for Strategic and

International Studies, January 27. https://www.csis.org
/analysis/reflections-looking-back-need-goldwater-nichols.

Smith, Jordan. 2022. "JSOC: America's Joint Special
Operations Command." *Grey Dynamics,* October 14.
https://greydynamics.com/jsoc-americas-joint-special
-operations-command/.

5 Data and Documents

Data

Killed and Wounded by Terrorist Attacks (1970–2020)

Table 5.1 outlines the annual number of individuals killed and wounded in terrorist attacks. The data is aggregated from terrorist incidents outlined in the Global Terrorism Database, but in order to maintain focus on terrorism it excludes cases of military, police, or other militant groups as targets. Those cases may be seen as having more to do with insurgency. Overall, the total number of casualties due to terror attacks saw marked increases after the War on Terrorism.

Table 5.1 Killed and Wounded by Terrorist Attacks (1970–2020)

Year	Killed	Wounded
1970	140	144
1971	84	56
1972	357	346
1973	233	472
1974	434	821

(continued)

The most devastating terrorist attack in history remains al Qaeda's strikes against the United States on September 11, 2001. Most of the nearly 3,000 killed and 25,000 wounded were at the World Trade Center site in New York City. Here is a view from New Jersey looking across the Hudson River to lower Manhattan with lights illuminating where the Twin Towers once stood. The site now hosts the One World Trade Center complex. (Daleinus/Dreamstime.com)

Table 5.1 (*continued*)

Year	Killed	Wounded
1975	347	603
1976	451	632
1977	331	472
1978	1088	1335
1979	1301	1904
1980	2144	2897
1981	1925	2171
1982	2211	2746
1983	3003	2418
1984	4855	3809
1985	3059	3724
1986	3059	4552
1987	3645	3987
1988	4172	4960
1989	4654	3491
1990	4138	4094
1991	4293	4583
1992	5824	7630
1994	5646	6088
1995	4144	12035
1996	5431	8959
1997	9145	7528
1998	3485	7456
1999	2449	4379
2000	3067	4118
2001	6533	26841
2002	3587	5904
2003	2245	5583
2004	3981	8931
2005	3983	8792

Table 5.1   (continued)

Year	Killed	Wounded
2006	7078	12017
2007	8780	16685
2008	6756	15454
2009	7653	17429
2010	5811	12837
2011	5777	10931
2012	6997	14412
2013	11964	24691
2014	24360	25485
2015	20775	28872
2016	19012	27344
2017	12919	15488
2018	11009	11226
2019	8831	10087
2020	9537	7032

Data Source: Study of Terrorism and Responses to Terrorism (START), University of Maryland (2023). The Global Terrorism Database. https://www.start.umd.edu /gtd/access/

Killed and Wounded by Suicide Terrorist Attacks (1974–2017)

Table 5.2 outlines the annual number of individuals killed and wounded in suicide terrorist attacks. The data is aggregated from the Suicide Attack Network Dataset, but to maintain focus on terrorism it excludes suicide attacks against military, police, or other militant groups as targets. Only cases of non-combatant, civilian targets are included as alternate cases are more akin to insurgency. As with the data for combined terrorist attacks, the specific subset of suicide terrorism grew significantly after the onset of the War on Terrorism.

Table 5.2 Killed and Wounded by Suicide Terrorist Attacks (1974–2017)

Year	Killed	Wounded	Suicide Attacks
1974	18	20	3
1975	0	0	0
1976	0	0	0
1977	0	0	0
1978	0	0	0
1979	0	0	0
1980	0	0	0
1981	61	100	1
1982	0	0	1
1983	69	172	2
1984	38	70	2
1985	32	46	9
1986	7	12	2
1987	12	144	3
1990	0	3	1
1991	87	230	3
1992	29	242	1
1993	33	139	10
1994	204	498	7
1995	179	510	19
1996	287	1777	15
1997	44	546	8
1998	277	5226	12
1999	42	227	11
2000	141	400	22
2001	3014	3669	58
2002	661	2656	66
2003	704	3137	73
2004	1615	4501	112

Table 5.2   (continued)

Year	Killed	Wounded	Suicide Attacks
2005	2666	5622	248
2006	1968	4269	207
2007	4906	8953	304
2008	2527	5656	254
2009	2449	6733	229
2010	2247	5069	211
2011	1478	2960	141
2012	1454	2971	158
2013	2466	5619	232
2014	2226	4665	291
2015	3406	6716	360
2016	3270	6017	312
2017	3324	5844	334

Data Source: Acosta, Benjamin. Suicide Attack Network Dataset. 2018. https://www.revolutionarymilitant.org/sand

Number and Types of Terror Attacks (1970–2020)

Table 5.3 outlines the annual number of attacks based on categories of the leading types of terrorist attacks. These categories include armed assaults such as mass shootings, the specific targeting of individuals through assassinations, bombings, and direct attacks on facilities. The data is aggregated from terrorist incidents outlined in the Global Terrorism Database, but in order to maintain focus on terrorism it excludes cases of military, police, or other militant groups as targets. Those cases may be seen as having more to do with insurgency. The data demonstrates that bombings are the most common form of terrorist attack, followed by armed assaults. By comparison assassinations and attacks on infrastructure are less frequent.

Table 5.3 Number and Types of Terror Attacks (1970–2020)

Year	Armed Assault	Assassination	Bombing	Facility Attack
1970	29	16	248	137
1971	26	18	190	69
1972	15	181	146	15
1973	46	96	112	25
1974	34	107	236	40
1975	52	123	320	57
1976	85	137	347	105
1977	185	94	577	169
1978	136	160	533	158
1979	271	364	921	181
1980	322	448	897	160
1981	263	280	922	135
1982	270	253	984	141
1983	220	230	961	133
1984	324	318	1490	148
1985	192	197	1183	129
1986	251	264	1249	129
1987	383	350	1230	118
1988	386	623	1333	138
1989	478	767	1441	236
1990	440	616	1454	174
1991	491	550	1695	336
1992	632	791	1445	449
1994	488	605	952	181
1995	540	558	619	285
1996	476	376	1006	195
1997	653	387	921	132
1998	172	24	409	57
1999	259	55	511	109
2000	351	87	714	104
2001	423	118	632	117

Table 5.3   (continued)

Year	Armed Assault	Assassination	Bombing	Facility Attack
2002	261	67	544	46
2003	181	73	495	79
2004	158	88	439	28
2005	288	171	706	46
2006	510	128	1061	100
2007	507	113	1199	97
2008	850	156	2194	269
2009	906	162	2290	321
2010	856	209	2132	277
2011	940	194	2092	223
2012	839	354	3015	273
2013	1188	653	4106	489
2014	1749	649	5629	706
2015	1511	706	5235	657
2016	1344	653	5127	645
2017	1058	679	3469	692
2018	1252	661	2369	615
2019	1042	572	1986	574
2020	1034	464	1660	608

Data Source: Study of Terrorism and Responses to Terrorism (START), University of Maryland. 2023. *The Global Terrorism Database*. https://www.start.umd.edu /gtd/access/

Types of Terrorist Group and Degree of Success Achieved (1866–2014)

Table 5.4 shows data from the Revolutionary and Militant Organizations (REVMOD) dataset. The data was formatted to focus specifically on groups that use terrorism. Readers should understand that this data does not refer *solely* to terrorist groups, as several militant organizations included in the table use terrorism in conjunction with insurgency or other forms of violence. These cross-tabulations account for 337 organizations between 1866 to 2014 and examine their relative level of success at achieving their goals based on the type of group. Readers should understand that a number of organizations may share mixed traits, and so the author coded mixed cases into specific categories based on which form they most closely and exclusively met. For instance, although Hamas calls for a Palestinian state and could be seen as nationalist, it specifically seeks an Islamic government and so was coded as religious. Similarly, although the Irish Republican Army is leftwing in orientation, it was coded as predominantly nationalist for its desire to bring Northern Ireland into the broader Republic of Ireland. Readers can contest this framework and are invited to review the source data for themselves. Based on this scheme the data indicates that nearly 87% of all militant groups that in some way use terrorism fail to achieve any of their goals, and that only 5% of all groups achieve a form of complete success. Of these the groups with a nationalist orientation are relatively the most successful, whereas religious groups are the least.

Table 5.4 Types of Terrorist Group and Degree of Success Achieved (1866–2014)

Success vs. Type	Nationalist	Leftwing	Rightwing	Religious	Total
No success	97	89	24	83	293
	25.7%	23.6%	6.4%	22.0%	86.9%
Partial success	11	5	4	6	26
	33.3%	15.2%	12.1%	18.2%	7.7%
Complete success	9	3	4	2	18
	31.0%	10.3%	13.8%	6.9%	5.3%
Total	117	97	32	91	337
	34.7%	28.8%	9.5%	27.0%	100.0%

Data Source: Acosta, Benjamin. "Reconceptualizing Resistance Organizations and Outcomes: Introducing the Revolutionary and Militant Organizations dataset (REVMOD)," Journal of Peace Research, 56, no. 5 (2019): 724–734. https://www .revolutionarymilitant.org

Rebel Leader Cause of Death (1964–2012)

Table 5.5 shows an excerpt of data from the 2021 release of the Rebel Organization Leaders Database (ROLE). Readers should understand that this coverage does not refer *solely* to terrorist group leaders, as several rebels use terrorism in conjunction with other violent and nonviolent forms of political activity. The table provides a breakdown of the cause of death for 179 rebel leaders over a 48-year period. Looking at single categories, the majority of rebel leaders die from disease or natural causes, which would include incarceration; however, in the aggregate over 55% of leaders died in a violent manner.

Table 5.5 Rebel Leader Cause of Death (1964–2012)

Rebel Leader Cause of Death	Number	Percent
Disease or natural causes	80	44.7%
Killed in action	25	14.0%
Assassinated by government	30	16.8%
Assassinated by external state	14	7.8%
Assassinated by rival group	11	6.2%
Executed	7	3.9%
Fratricide	3	1.7%
Accident	6	3.4%
Suicide	2	1.1%
Homicide	1	0.6%
Total	179	100

Data Source: Acosta, Benjamin; Huang, Reyko; and Daniel Silverman. "Introducing ROLE: A Database of Rebel Leader Attributes in Armed Conflict." *Journal of Peace Research*. Online first. https://www.rebelleaders.org

DOCUMENTS

Action as Propaganda (1885)

Johann Most, writing in his publication Freheit *("Freedom"), outlines a popular sentiment within the anarchist movement that*

terrorist actions must serve as a means of propaganda to further the movement's aims. He discounts nonviolent methods as well as those who advocate institutional paths to change in the established political process.

We have said a hundred times or more that when modern revolutionaries carry out actions, what is important is not solely these actions themselves but also the propagandistic effect they are able to achieve. Hence, we preach not only action in and for itself, but also action as propaganda. It is a phenomenally simple matter, yet over and over again we meet people, even people close to the center of our party, who either do not, or do not wish, to understand. We have recently had a clear enough illustration of this over the Lieske affair . . . So our question is this: what is the purpose of the anarchists' threats—an eye for an eye, a tooth for a tooth—if they are not followed up by action? Or are perhaps the 'law and order' rabble, all of them blackguards extraordinary, to be done away in a dark corner so that no one knows the why and the wherefore of what happened? It would be a form of action, certainly, but not action as propaganda. The great thing about anarchist vengeance is that is proclaims loud and clear for everyone to hear, that: this man or that man must die for this and this reason; and that at the first opportunity which presents itself for the realization of such a threat, the rascal in question is really and truly dispatched to the other world. And this is indeed what happened with Alexander Romanov, with Messenzoff, with Sudeikin, with Bloch and Hlubeck, with Rumpff and others. Once such an action has been carried out, the important thing is that the world learns of it from the revolutionaries, so that everyone knows what the position is. The overwhelming impression this makes is shown by how the reactionaries have repeatedly tried to hush up revolutionary actions that have taken place, or present them in a different light. This has often been possible in Russia, especially, because of the conditions governing the press there. In order to achieve the desired success in the fullest measure, immediately after the action has been carried out, especially in the town where it took place, posters should be put up setting out the reasons for the action in such a way as to draw from them the best possible benefit. And in those cases where this was not done, the reason was simply that it proved inadvisable to involve the number of participants that would have been required; or that there was a lack of money. It was all the more natural in these cases for the anarchist press to glorify and explicate the deeds at every opportunity. For it to have adopted an attitude of indifference toward such actions, or even to have denied them, would have been perfectly idiotic treachery. 'Freiheit' has always pursued this policy. It is nothing more than insipid, sallow envy which makes those demagogues who are continually mocking us with cries of 'Carry on, then, carry on' condemn this aspect of our behavior, among others, whenever they can, as a crime. This miserable tribe is well aware that no action carried out by anarchists can have its proper propagandist effect if those organs whose responsibility it is neither give suitable prominence to such actions, nor make it palatable to the people. It is this, above all, which puts the reactionaries in a rage.

Source: Most, Johann. 1885. "Action as Propaganda." *Freiheit*, July 25. Accessed March 25, 2022. http://dwardmac.pitzer .edu/Anarchist_Archives/bright/most/actionprop.html.

Jihad Against Jews and Crusaders (1998)

This statement by al Qaeda's senior leadership constitutes a self-declared fatwa, *or Islamic religious ruling. Notably none of the authors possessed legitimacy as religious scholars to issue such a ruling, and the document features selective religious citations from different Islamic contexts.*

The document serves as a specific example of a religious ideology being used as a justification for terrorism. This one relies on an interpretation of defensive jihad *("holy struggle") as an individual duty of all Muslims, a sentiment popular within Salafi-Jihadist circles. The authors demand that all Muslims take up arms against U.S. and Israeli interests, who they see as evil powers working in unison to destroy and divide Muslims. Salafi-Jihadists such as these authors challenge the idea of the state-based international system and see interstate conflicts involving Arab governments as conspiracies.*

The authors especially single out the presence of invited American forces in the Kingdom of Saudi Arabia during the 1990s as a grievance, as well as Israeli governance over Jerusalem and the Palestinian territories. They characterize terrorism as a religious duty by exhorting Muslims to target civilians in addition to military assets. This document was published in February 1998, six months before the East Africa embassy bombings in August that killed 224 and wounded thousands. The overwhelming majority of those killed or injured in the attacks were Kenyan and Tanzanian, not American.

Praise be to Allah, who revealed the Book, controls the clouds, defeats factionalism, and says in His Book: "But when the forbidden months are past, then fight and slay the pagans wherever ye find them, seize them, beleaguer them, and lie in wait for them in every stratagem (of war)"; and peace be upon our Prophet, Muhammad Bin-'Abdallah, who said: I have been sent with the sword between my hands to ensure that no one but Allah is worshipped, Allah who put my livelihood under the shadow of my spear and who inflicts humiliation and scorn on those who disobey my orders.

The Arabian Peninsula has never—since Allah made it flat, created its desert, and encircled it with seas—been stormed by any forces like the crusader armies spreading in it like locusts, eating its riches and wiping out its plantations. All this is happening at a time in which nations are attacking Muslims like people fighting over a plate of food. In the light of the grave situation and the lack of support, we and you are obliged to discuss current events, and we should all agree on how to settle the matter.

No one argues today about three facts that are known to everyone; we will list them, in order to remind everyone:

First, for over seven years the United States has been occupying the lands of Islam in the holiest of places, the Arabian Peninsula, plundering its riches, dictating to its rulers, humiliating its people, terrorizing its neighbors, and turning its bases in the Peninsula into a spearhead through which to fight the neighboring Muslim peoples.

If some people have in the past argued about the fact of the occupation, all the people of the Peninsula have now acknowledged it. The best proof of this is the Americans' continuing aggression against the Iraqi people using the Peninsula as a staging post, even though all its rulers are against their territories being used to that end, but they are helpless.

Second, despite the great devastation inflicted on the Iraqi people by the crusader-Zionist alliance, and despite the huge number of those killed, which has exceeded 1 million . . . despite all this, the Americans are once against trying to repeat the horrific massacres, as though they are not content with the protracted blockade imposed after the ferocious war or the fragmentation and devastation.

So here they come to annihilate what is left of this people and to humiliate their Muslim neighbors.

Third, if the Americans' aims behind these wars are religious and economic, the aim is also to serve the Jews' petty state and divert attention from its occupation of Jerusalem and murder of Muslims there. The best proof of this is their eagerness to destroy Iraq, the strongest neighboring Arab state, and their endeavor to fragment all the states of the region such as Iraq, Saudi Arabia, Egypt, and Sudan into paper statelets and through their disunion and weakness to guarantee Israel's survival and the continuation of the brutal crusade occupation of the Peninsula.

All these crimes and sins committed by the Americans are a clear declaration of war on Allah, his messenger, and Muslims. And ulema have throughout Islamic history unanimously agreed that the jihad is an individual duty if the enemy destroys the Muslim countries. This was revealed by Imam Bin-Qadamah in 'Al- Mughni,' Imam al-Kisa'i in 'Al-Bada'i,' al-Qurtubi in his interpretation, and the shaykh of al-Islam in his books, where he said: 'As for the fighting to repulse [an enemy], it is aimed at defending sanctity and religion, and it is a duty as agreed [by the ulema]. Nothing is more sacred than belief except repulsing an enemy who is attacking religion and life.'

On that basis, and in compliance with Allah's order, we issue the following fatwa to all Muslims:

The ruling to kill the Americans and their allies—civilians and military—is an individual duty for every Muslim who can do it in any country in which it is possible to do it, in order to liberate the al-Aqsa Mosque and the holy mosque [Mecca] from their grip, and in order for their armies to move out of all the lands of Islam, defeated and unable to threaten any Muslim. This is in accordance with the words of Almighty Allah, "and fight the pagans all together as they fight you all together," and "fight them until there is no more tumult or oppression, and there prevail justice and faith in Allah."

This is in addition to the words of Almighty Allah: "And why should ye not fight in the cause of Allah and of those who, being weak, are ill-treated (and oppressed)?—women and children, whose cry is: 'Our Lord, rescue us from this town, whose people are oppressors; and raise for us from thee one who will help!'"

We—with Allah's help—call on every Muslim who believes in Allah and wishes to be rewarded to comply with Allah's order to kill the Americans and plunder their money wherever and whenever they find it. We also call on Muslim ulema, leaders, youths, and soldiers to launch the raid on Satan's U.S. troops and the devil's supporters allying with them, and to displace those who are behind them so that they may learn a lesson.

Almighty Allah said: "O ye who believe, give your response to Allah and His Apostle, when He calleth you to that which will give you life. And know that Allah cometh between a man and his heart, and that it is He to whom ye shall all be gathered."

Almighty Allah also says: "O ye who believe, what is the matter with you, that when ye are asked to go forth in the cause of Allah, ye cling so heavily to the earth! Do ye prefer the life of this world to the hereafter? But little is the comfort of this life, as compared with the hereafter. Unless ye go forth, He will punish you with a grievous penalty, and put others in your place; but Him ye would not harm in the least. For Allah hath power over all things."

Almighty Allah also says: "So lose no heart, nor fall into despair. For ye must gain mastery if ye are true in faith."

Source: Bin Laden, Osama, al-Zawahiri, Ayman, Taha, Ahmed Refai, Hamza, Mir, and Fazlur Rahman. 1998. "Jihad Against Jews and Crusaders," World Islamic Front Statement, *Al-Quds al-Arabi*, February 23. Accessed March 26, 2022. https://irp.fas.org/world/para/docs/980223-fatwa.htm.

The 9/11 Commission Report (2004)

This excerpt from the 9/11 Commission Report outlines the internal decision-making within the U.S. government regarding attempts to kill Osama bin Laden following the 1998 East Africa embassy attacks. This account explains part of the deliberations following the August 1998 cruise missile strikes at Al Qaeda camps in Afghanistan and chronicles the complexities and risks of the option.

Kandahar, May 1999

It was in Kandahar that perhaps the last, and most likely the best, opportunity arose for targeting Bin Ladin with cruise missiles before 9/11. In May 1999, CIA assets in Afghanistan reported on Bin Ladin's location in and around Kandahar over the course of five days and nights. The reporting was very detailed and came from several sources. If this intelligence was not "actionable," working-level officials said at the time and today, it was hard for them to imagine how any intelligence on Bin Ladin in Afghanistan would meet the standard. Communications were good, and the cruise missiles were ready. "This was in our strike zone," a senior military officer said. "It was a fat pitch, a home run." He expected the missiles to fly. When the decision came back that they should stand down, not shoot, the officer said, "we all just slumped." He told us he knew of no one at the Pentagon or the CIA who thought it was a bad gamble. Bin Ladin "should have been a dead man" that night, he said.[173]

Working-level CIA officials agreed. While there was a conflicting intelligence report about Bin Ladin's whereabouts, the experts discounted it. At the time, CIA working-level officials were told by their managers that the strikes were not ordered because the military doubted the intelligence and worried about collateral damage. Replying to a frustrated colleague in the field, the Bin Ladin unit chief wrote: "having a chance to get [Bin Ladin] three times in 36 hours and foregoing the chance each time has made me a bit angry. . . . [T]he DCI finds himself alone at the table, with the other princip[als] basically saying 'we'll go along with your decision Mr. Director,' and implicitly saying that the Agency will hang alone if the attack doesn't get Bin Ladin."[174] But the military officer quoted earlier recalled that the Pentagon had been willing to act. He told us that Clarke informed him and others that Tenet assessed the chance of the intelligence being accurate as 50–50. This officer believed that Tenet's assessment was the key to the decision.[175]

Tenet told us he does not remember any details about this episode, except that the intelligence came from a single uncorroborated source and that there was a risk of collateral damage. The story is further complicated by Tenet's absence from the critical principals meeting on this strike (he was apparently out of town); his deputy, John Gordon, was representing the CIA.

Gordon recalled having presented the intelligence in a positive light, with appropriate caveats, but stating that this intelligence was about as good as it could get.[176]

Berger remembered only that in all such cases, the call had been Tenet's. Berger felt sure that Tenet was eager to get Bin Ladin. In his view, Tenet did his job responsibly. "George would call and say, 'We just don't have it,'" Berger said.[177]

The decision not to strike in May 1999 may now seem hard to understand. In fairness, we note two points: First, in December 1998, the principals' wariness about ordering a strike appears to have been vindicated: Bin Ladin left his room unexpectedly, and if a strike had been ordered he would not have been hit. Second, the administration, and the CIA in particular, was in the midst of intense scrutiny and criticism in May 1999 because faulty intelligence had just led the United States to mistakenly bomb the Chinese embassy in Belgrade during the NATO war against Serbia. This episode may have made officials more cautious than might otherwise have been the case.[178]

From May 1999 until September 2001, policymakers did not again actively consider a missile strike against Bin Ladin.[179] The principals did give some further consideration in 1999 to more general strikes, reviving Clarke's "Delenda" notion of hitting camps and infrastructure to disrupt al Qaeda's organization. In the first months of 1999, the Joint Staff had developed broader target lists to undertake a "focused campaign" against the infrastructure of Bin Ladin's network and to hit Taliban government sites as well. General Shelton told us that the Taliban targets were "easier" to hit and more substantial.[180]

Part of the context for considering broader strikes in the summer of 1999 was renewed worry about Bin Ladin's ambitions to acquire weapons of mass destruction. In May and June, the U.S. government received a flurry of ominous reports, including more information about chemical weapons training or development at the Derunta camp and possible attempts to amass nuclear material at Herat.[181]

By late June, U.S. and other intelligence services had concluded that al Qaeda was in pre-attack mode, perhaps again involving Abu Hafs the Mauritanian. On June 25, at Clarke's request, Berger convened the Small Group in his office to discuss the alert, Bin Ladin's WMD programs, and his location. "Should we pre-empt by attacking UBL facilities?" Clarke urged Berger to ask his colleagues.[182]

In his handwritten notes on the meeting paper, Berger jotted down the presence of 7 to 11 families in the Tarnak Farms facility, which could mean 60–65 casualties. Berger noted the possible "slight impact" on Bin Ladin and added, "if he responds, we're blamed."[183] The NSC staff raised the option of waiting until after a terrorist attack, and then retaliating, including possible strikes on the Taliban. But Clarke observed that Bin Ladin would probably empty his camps after an attack.[184]

The military route seemed to have reached a dead end. In December 1999, Clarke urged Berger to ask the principals to ask themselves: "Why have there been no real options lately for direct US military action?"[185]. There are no notes recording whether the question was discussed or, if it was, how it was answered.

Reports of possible attacks by Bin Ladin kept coming in throughout 1999. They included a threat to blow up the FBI building in Washington, D.C. In September, the CSG reviewed a possible threat to a flight out of Los Angeles or New York.[186] These warnings came amid dozens of others that flooded in.

With military and diplomatic options practically exhausted by the summer of 1999, the U.S. government seemed to be back where it had been in the summer of 1998—relying on the CIA to find some other option.

References

173. John Maher III interview (Apr. 22, 2004). For an account of the reporting from this period written by Mike, see CIA memo, Jeff to Tenet, "Tracking Usama Bin Ladin,

14–20 May 1999," May 21, 1999. Mike's account was also used to prepare the DCI for a May 25, 1999, Principals Committee meeting. CIA briefing materials, "Background Information: Evaluating the Quality of Intelligence on Bin Ladin (UBL) in Qandahar, 13–20 May, 1999," undated (probably May 25, 1999).

174. CIA email, Mike to Schroen, "Re: Your Note," May 17, 1999.

175. John Maher III interview (Apr. 22, 2004).

176. George Tenet interview (Jan. 22, 2004); John Gordon interview (May 13, 2004).

177. Samuel Berger interview (Jan. 14, 2004).

178. The May 1999 intelligence on Bin Ladin's location in Kandahar came as criticism of the CIA over the recent bombing of the Chinese embassy in Belgrade was at its peak. The DCI later testified that this bombing was the result of a CIA mistake. Testimony of George Tenet before the House Permanent Select Committee on Intelligence, July 22, 1999. On Bin Ladin's whereabouts during the December 1998 episode, see John Maher III interview (Apr. 22, 2004).

179. Cruise missiles were readied for another possible strike in early July 1999. But none of the officials we have interviewed recalled that an opportunity arose at that time justifying the consideration of a strike. See, e.g., John Maher III interview (Apr. 22, 2004).

180. Hugh Shelton interview (Feb. 5, 2004); DOD briefing materials, UBL JCS Focused Campaign, undated.

181. NSC memo, Benjamin to Berger and Steinberg, Apr. 29, 1999; NSC email, Clarke to Berger, May 26, 1999.

182. NSC memo, Clarke to Berger, June 24, 1999. For Clarke's request to Berger to convene the Small Group, see NSC memo, Clarke to Berger, Analysis/Options re UBL, Jun. 13, 1999. See also NSC email, Storey to Berger and Clarke, June 24, 1999.

183. Berger notes on NSC memo, Clarke to Berger, June 24, 1999.

184. NSC memo, Clarke to Berger, June 24, 1999.

185. NSC memo, Clarke to Berger, UBL review for Dec. 3, 1999, Small Group meeting, Dec. 2, 1999.

186. NSC memo, CSG agenda, Sept. 24, 1999.

Source: National Commission on Terrorist Attacks. 2004. "Responses to Al Qaeda's Initial Assaults." In *The 9/11 Commission Report: Final Report of the National Commission on Terrorist Attacks Upon the United States*, 140–141, July 22. Accessed June 20, 2022. https://www.govinfo.gov/content /pkg/GPO-911REPORT/pdf/GPO-911REPORT.pdf.

Speech on Military Commissions to Try Suspected Terrorists (2006)

This 2006 speech from President George W. Bush followed the Hamdan v. Rumsfeld *ruling, which determined that U.S. military commissions of captured militants were unconstitutional because they had not been authorized by Congress. In the speech President Bush calls for Congress to pass legislation authorizing the tribunals and announces that detainees who had been in CIA custody for years were being transferred to the detention camp at Guantanamo Bay, Cuba. He maintains that the interrogation and treatment of detainees by Central Intelligence Agency and Department of Defense personnel was lawful and necessary.*

. . . After the 9/11 attacks, our coalition launched operations across the world to remove terrorist safe havens, and capture or kill terrorist operatives and leaders. Working with our allies, we've captured and detained thousands of terrorists and enemy fighters in Afghanistan, in Iraq, and other fronts of this war on terror. These enemy—these are enemy combatants, who were waging war on our nation. We have a right under the laws of war, and we have an obligation to the American people, to detain these enemies and stop them from rejoining the battle.

Most of the enemy combatants we capture are held in Afghanistan or in Iraq, where they're questioned by our military personnel. Many are released after questioning, or turned over to local authorities—if we determine that they do not pose a continuing threat and no longer have significant intelligence value. Others remain in American custody near the battlefield, to ensure that they don't return to the fight.

In some cases, we determine that individuals we have captured pose a significant threat, or may have intelligence that we and our allies need to have to prevent new attacks. Many are al Qaeda operatives or Taliban fighters trying to conceal their identities, and they withhold information that could save American lives. In these cases, it has been necessary to move these individuals to an environment where they can be held secretly [*sic*], questioned by experts, and—when appropriate—prosecuted for terrorist acts.

Some of these individuals are taken to the United States Naval Base at Guantanamo Bay, Cuba. It's important for Americans and others across the world to understand the kind of people held at Guantanamo. These aren't common criminals, or bystanders accidentally swept up on the battlefield—we have in place a rigorous process to ensure those held at Guantanamo Bay belong at Guantanamo. Those held at Guantanamo include suspected bomb makers, terrorist trainers, recruiters and facilitators, and potential suicide bombers. They are in our custody so they cannot murder our people. One detainee held at Guantanamo told a questioner questioning him—he said this: "I'll never forget your face. I will kill you, your brothers, your mother, and sisters."

In addition to the terrorists held at Guantanamo, a small number of suspected terrorist leaders and operatives captured during the war have been held and questioned outside the United States, in a separate program operated by the Central Intelligence Agency. This group includes individuals believed to be the key architects of the September the 11th attacks, and attacks on the USS Cole, an operative involved in the bombings of our embassies in Kenya and Tanzania, and individuals involved in other attacks that have taken the lives of innocent civilians across the world. These are dangerous men with unparalleled knowledge about terrorist networks and their plans for new attacks. The security of our nation and the lives of our citizens depend on our ability to learn what these terrorists know. . . .

Within months of September the 11th, 2001, we captured a man known as Abu Zubaydah. We believe that Zubaydah was a senior terrorist leader and a trusted associate of Osama bin Laden. Our intelligence community believes he had run a terrorist camp in Afghanistan where some of the 9/11 hijackers trained, and that he helped smuggle al Qaeda leaders out of Afghanistan after coalition forces arrived to liberate that country. Zubaydah was severely wounded during the firefight that brought him into custody—and he survived only because of the medical care arranged by the CIA.

After he recovered, Zubaydah was defiant and evasive. He declared his hatred of America. During questioning, he at first disclosed what he thought was nominal information—and then stopped all cooperation. Well, in fact, the "nominal" information he gave us turned out to be quite important. For example, Zubaydah disclosed Khalid Sheikh Mohammed— or KSM—was the mastermind behind the 9/11 attacks, and used the alias "Muktar." This was a vital piece of the puzzle that helped our intelligence community pursue KSM. Abu Zubaydah also provided information that helped stop a terrorist attack being planned for inside the United States—an attack about which we had no previous information. Zubaydah told us that al Qaeda operatives were planning to launch an attack in the U.S., and provided physical descriptions of the operatives and information on their general location. Based on the information he provided, the operatives were detained—one while traveling to the United States.

We knew that Zubaydah had more information that could save innocent lives, but he stopped talking. As his questioning proceeded, it became clear that he had received training on how to resist interrogation. And so the CIA used an alternative set of procedures. These procedures were designed to be safe, to comply with our laws, our Constitution, and our treaty obligations. The Department of Justice reviewed the authorized methods extensively and determined them to be lawful. I cannot describe the specific methods used—I think you understand why—if I did, it would help the terrorists learn how to resist questioning, and to keep information from us that we need to prevent new attacks on our country. But I can say the procedures were tough, and they were safe, and lawful, and necessary.

Zubaydah was questioned using these procedures, and soon he began to provide information on key al Qaeda operatives, including information that helped us find and capture more of those responsible for the attacks on September the 11th . . .

The information we get from these detainees is corroborated by intelligence, and we've received—that we've received from other sources—and together this intelligence has helped us connect the dots and stop attacks before they occur. Information from the terrorists questioned in this program helped unravel plots and terrorist cells in Europe and in other places. It's helped our allies protect their people from deadly enemies. This program has been, and remains, one of the most vital tools in our war against the terrorists. It is invaluable to America and to our allies. Were it not for this program, our intelligence community believes that al Qaeda and its allies would have succeeded in launching another attack against the American homeland. By giving us information about terrorist plans we could not get anywhere else, this program has saved innocent lives.

This program has been subject to multiple legal reviews by the Department of Justice and CIA lawyers; they've determined it complied with our laws. This program has received strict oversight by the CIA's Inspector General. A small number of key leaders from both political parties on Capitol Hill were

briefed about this program. All those involved in the questioning of the terrorists are carefully chosen and they're screened
from a pool of experienced CIA officers. Those selected to conduct the most sensitive questioning had to complete more than
250 additional hours of specialized training before they are
allowed to have contact with a captured terrorist . . .

The CIA program has detained only a limited number of
terrorists at any given time—and once we've determined that
the terrorists held by the CIA have little or no additional intelligence value, many of them have been returned to their home
countries for prosecution or detention by their governments.
Others have been accused of terrible crimes against the American people, and we have a duty to bring those responsible for
these crimes to justice. So we intend to prosecute these men, as
appropriate, for their crimes.

Soon after the war on terror began, I authorized a system of
military commissions to try foreign terrorists accused of war
crimes. Military commissions have been used by Presidents
from George Washington to Franklin Roosevelt to prosecute
war criminals, because the rules for trying enemy combatants
in a time of conflict must be different from those for trying
common criminals or members of our own military. One of the
first suspected terrorists to be put on trial by military commission was one of Osama bin Laden's bodyguards—a man named
Hamdan. His lawyers challenged the legality of the military
commission system. It took more than two years for this case
to make its way through the courts. The Court of Appeals for
the District of Columbia Circuit upheld the military commissions we had designed, but this past June, the Supreme Court
overturned that decision. The Supreme Court determined
that military commissions are an appropriate venue for trying
terrorists, but ruled that military commissions needed to be
explicitly authorized by the United States Congress.

So today, I'm sending Congress legislation to specifically
authorize the creation of military commissions to try terrorists
for war crimes . . .

We're now approaching the five-year anniversary of the 9/11 attacks—and the families of those murdered that day have waited patiently for justice. Some of the families are with us today—they should have to wait no longer. So I'm announcing today that Khalid Sheikh Mohammed, Abu Zubaydah, Ramzi bin al-Shibh, and 11 other terrorists in CIA custody have been transferred to the United States Naval Base at Guantanamo Bay. They are being held in the custody of the Department of Defense. As soon as Congress acts to authorize the military commissions I have proposed, the men our intelligence officials believe orchestrated the deaths of nearly 3,000 Americans on September the 11th, 2001, can face justice . . .

These men will be held in a high-security facility at Guantanamo. The International Committee of the Red Cross is being advised of their detention, and will have the opportunity to meet with them. Those charged with crimes will be given access to attorneys who will help them prepare their defense—and they will be presumed innocent. While at Guantanamo, they will have access to the same food, clothing, medical care, and opportunities for worship as other detainees. They will be questioned subject to the new U.S. Army Field Manual, which the Department of Defense is issuing today. And they will continue to be treated with the humanity that they denied others.

As we move forward with the prosecutions, we will continue to urge nations across the world to take back their nationals at Guantanamo who will not be prosecuted by our military commissions. America has no interest in being the world's jailer. But one of the reasons we have not been able to close Guantanamo is that many countries have refused to take back their nationals held at the facility. Other countries have not provided adequate assurances that their nationals will not be mistreated—or they will not return to the battlefield, as more than a dozen people released from Guantanamo already have. We will continue working to transfer individuals held at Guantanamo, and ask other countries to work with us in this process. And we will move toward the day when we can eventually close the detention facility at Guantanamo Bay.

I know Americans have heard conflicting information about Guantanamo. Let me give you some facts. Of the thousands of terrorists captured across the world, only about 770 have ever been sent to Guantanamo. Of these, about 315 have been returned to other countries so far—and about 455 remain in our custody. They are provided the same quality of medical care as the American service members who guard them. The International Committee of the Red Cross has the opportunity to meet privately with all who are held there. The facility has been visited by government officials from more than 30 countries, and delegations from international organizations, as well. After the Organization for Security and Cooperation in Europe came to visit, one of its delegation members called Guantanamo "a model prison" where people are treated better than in prisons in his own country. Our troops can take great pride in the work they do at Guantanamo Bay—and so can the American people.

As we prosecute suspected terrorist leaders and operatives who have now been transferred to Guantanamo, we'll continue searching for those who have stepped forward to take their places. This nation is going to stay on the offense to protect the American people. We will continue to bring the world's most dangerous terrorists to justice—and we will continue working to collect the vital intelligence we need to protect our country. The current transfers mean that there are now no terrorists in the CIA program. But as more high-ranking terrorists are captured, the need to obtain intelligence from them will remain critical—and having a CIA program for questioning terrorists will continue to be crucial to getting life-saving information . . .

Source: Bush, George W. 2006. "Speech on Military Commissions to Try Suspected Terrorists." Transcript of speech delivered at the White House, Washington, DC, September 6. Accessed June 28, 2022. https://georgewbush-whitehouse .archives.gov/news/releases/2006/09/20060906-3.html.

Coercive Interrogation Techniques: Do They Work, Are They Reliable, and What Did the FBI Know About Them? (2008)

This congressional testimony by a former FBI agent outlines the "rapport"-based approach to interrogations as a counter to controversial "enhanced" interrogation techniques based on coercion that were initially used by the Central Intelligence Agency and Department of Defense. The agent advances the case that methods based on rapport yield more information and of a greater quality than information obtained under duress.

. . . It is my belief, based on a 27-year career as a special agent and interviews with hundreds of subjects in custodial settings, including members of al Qaeda, that the use of coercive interrogation techniques is not effective. The alternative approach, sometimes referred to as "rapport building," is more effective, efficient, and reliable. Scientists, psychiatrists, psychologists, law enforcement and intelligence agents, all of whom have studied both approaches, have come to the same conclusion. The CIA's own training manual advises its agents that heavy-handed techniques can impair a subject's ability to accurately recall information and, at worst, produce apathy and complete withdrawal.

I have personally used the rapport-building approach successfully with al Qaeda members and other terrorists who were detained by U.S. authorities. The information elicited led to numerous indictments, successful prosecutions, and actionable intelligence which was then disseminated to the CIA and the NSA and others. This approach, which the FBI practices, is effective, lawful, and consistent with the principles of due process. And in addition to its intelligence-gathering potential, it can do nothing but improve our image in the eyes of the world community.

A skilled interrogator, using elicitation techniques and understanding the end game, will serve the public's safety and our national security. The ultimate outcomes might be gathering evidence to support a prosecution or obtaining actionable intelligence to prevent a terrorist attack. I accept the argument that coercion will obtain a certain kind of information. I do not, however, accept the argument that sleep deprivation, sensory deprivation, head slapping, isolation, temperature extremes, stress positions, waterboarding, and the like will produce accurate information. An interrogation using rapport building obtains more reliable information and changes the relationship between the interrogator and the subject. Once a bond is formed between the two, the latter takes the investigator on a journey of discovery and sheds light on the darkest, most closely held secrets of an organization like al Qaeda. U.S. intelligence and law enforcement agents seldom get the chance to interrogate al Qaeda subject matter experts like Khalid Sheikh Mohammed, Ramzi Bin Al-Shib, Jamal Ahmed Al-Fadel, L'houssaine Kertchtou, Ali Abelseoud Mohamed, and Ibhn Sheikh Al-Libi, and these opportunities are too precious to waste. I am convinced by my experience that the rapport-building approach is the way to go in these circumstances.

As the conversion from antagonist to ally takes hold within the process and the recalcitrant subject begins to cooperate, the interrogator assumes the role of caretaker. He or she can then shape the conversation, listen intently for inconsistencies, and, finally, save untold man-hours chasing after false leads.

Critics of rapport building often say that the enemy we face today—the radical Islamist who is ready and willing to die for Allah—requires a more aggressive approach. They frame the debate by injecting the ticking bomb scenario. They suggest that there is no time to break bread with these killers. In fact, there are those who believe that the 9/11 attacks occurred because we treated terrorism as a law enforcement issue. This was not the case. In the months before the attacks, the "chatter" suggested that "something big" was imminent, but neither the law enforcement nor the intelligence community had an agent who knew what al Qaeda intended to do on that fateful day.

The rapport-building approach used on an al Qaeda operative might have helped to address this frightening and dangerous reality.

I participated in many interviews with suspected al Qaeda members where actionable, reliable information was obtained. It was used in the successful prosecutions of al Qaeda operatives who murdered American citizens. The image of a former al Qaeda operative testifying under oath in district court and repudiating bin Laden and al Qaeda and its ideology of hate sent a powerful message to citizens of America and the world. Showcasing that message had an immediate impact. It highlighted the fact that bin Laden and al Qaeda are vulnerable, and it effectively answered those who believe in his omnipotence, America's weakness, and the hypocrisy of her leaders.

Bin Laden and his advisors often refer to U.S. intelligence and law enforcement agents as "blood" people. They mean simply this: We, according to bin Laden, use torture to extract information. Bin Laden has theorized that the most loyal al Qaeda sympathizer will break within 72 hours and give up operational information. Therefore, he has kept operational details about impending attacks strictly compartmentalized. In other words, those in the know or with a need to know were limited to a few trusted followers. My experiences and those of my former FBI colleagues would certainly support this conclusion.

The majority of jihadists detained post-9/11 were clueless when it came to al Qaeda's operational plans, and I do not believe many of the detainees posed a direct threat to the U.S. or were confidants of bin Laden or Ayman Zawahiri. A heavy-handed approach with these detainees was unlikely to generate any useful intelligence, and it served to validate bin Laden's take on America and our intelligence-gathering propensities.

Of course, obtaining reliable information from jihadist foot soldiers in Afghanistan and Iraq is vital to protect our troops, who are in harm's way. But even on the battlefield and under exigent circumstances, rapport building is more effective in gaining information for force protection in my opinion.

Enhanced and coercive interrogation techniques are ineffective even under extreme circumstances. Senator, I have spoken to a number of FBI agents who were seconded to Gitmo as interrogators. In confidence, they told me the vast majority of detainees questioned under these stressful conditions were of little or no value as sources of useful intelligence.

Information is power, and the lack of reliable human intelligence assets, who are capable of telling us what al Qaeda is up to, is the greatest challenge facing U.S. law enforcement and the intelligence community. Technological assets, like signals intelligence, targeted wiretapping, and computer exploitation have preempted some terrorist attacks, and we are all grateful for that. I submit, however, that the most effective countermeasure to the threat posed by al Qaeda and like-minded groups is and always will be the apostate who chooses to cooperate and, if you will pardon the expression, "spills the beans." Gaining the cooperation of an al Qaeda member is a formidable task, but it is not impossible. I have witnessed al Qaeda members who pledged "bayat" to bin Laden cross the threshold and cooperate with the FBI because they were treated humanely, understood what due process was about, and were literally seduced by our legal system, as strange as that may sound.

I am reminded of a conversation I had with an aide to bin Laden. He told me al Qaeda believes in the "sleeping dog" theory. The sheik is very patient, and the brothers will wait for as long as it takes for the dog to nod off before they attack. I believe we cannot relax our vigilance in the hope that bin Laden will forget.

There are three questions I would like this Committee to ponder. Has the use of coercive interrogation techniques lessened al Qaeda's thirst for revenge against the U.S.? Have these methods helped to recruit a new generation of jihadist martyrs? Has the use of coercive interrogation produced the reliable information its proponents claim for it? I would suggest that the answers are no, yes, and no.

Based on my experience in talking to al Qaeda members, I am persuaded that revenge, in the form of a catastrophic attack on the homeland, is coming, that a new generation of jihadist martyrs, motivated in part by the images from Abu Ghraib, is, as we speak, planning to kill Americans and that nothing gleaned from the use of coercive interrogation techniques will be of any significant use in forestalling this calamitous eventuality.

Torture degrades our image abroad and complicates our working relationships with foreign law enforcement and intelligence agencies. If I were the director of marketing for al Qaeda and intent on replenishing the ranks of jihadists, I know what my first piece of marketing collateral would be. It would be a blast e-mail with an attachment. The attachment would contain a picture of Private England pointing at the stacked, naked bodies of the detainees at Abu Ghraib. This picture screams out for revenge, and the day of reckoning will come. The consequences of coercive intelligence gathering will not evaporate with time.

I am hopeful that this Committee will use its oversight responsibility judiciously and try to move the debate in the direction of the prohibition of coercive interrogation techniques. This debate is a crucial one, and I know each member of the Committee understands that. The decisions you make will have a far-reaching impact on our national security.

Proponents of the ticking bomb scenario seek to forestall discussions on interrogation techniques by ratcheting up the intensity of the debate to panic mode. There simply is no time to talk with a terrorist who might have information about an impending attack. Lives are at stake and the clock is ticking, so it just makes sense to do whatever it takes to get the information. Experienced interrogators do not buy this scenario. They know that a committed terrorist caught in this conundrum will seek to throw his interrogator off the track or use it to his propaganda advantage. "Go ahead and kill me, God is great." Neither the ticking bomb scenario nor the idea of a torture warrant makes sense to me. To the best of my recollection, the first time I learned that coercive interrogation techniques were being used on detainees was in November 2001 at Bagram Air Base in Afghanistan. One case I am personally aware of involved Ibhn Sheikh Al-Libi, the emir of an al Qaeda training camp in Afghanistan. The FBI agents on the scene were prepared to accord Al-Libi the due process rights he might expect as an American citizen. The agents concluded after questioning that he would be a high-value and cooperative source of information as well as a potential witness in the trials of Richard Reid and Zacarias Moussaoui. Before the agents could proceed, a robust debate ensued between the FBI and the CIA. The CIA prevailed, and Al-Libi was rendered to parts unknown, possibly Egypt. I do not know the exact nature of the information his interrogation produced, but it is common knowledge that he has since recanted all that he said. I feel that a very significant opportunity to utilize the rapport-building approach was missed.

Without compromising delicate investigations, I can tell you that the FBI has amassed a considerable amount of reliable information on al Qaeda using rapport building. I will not attempt a full recounting in the interest of brevity, but here are a few salient examples.

I personally learned that al Qaeda tried unsuccessfully to obtain fissionable material in 1993 and that they experimented with chemical and biological agents. I also became aware of how they selected targets and conducted surveillance on them. And I learned of their intentions to use airplanes as weapons before this became a deadly reality. These interrogations also yielded information about al Qaeda's finances, recruiting methods, the location of camps, the links between al Qaeda and Hezbollah, bin Laden's security detail, and the identities of other al Qaeda members who were subsequently indicted in absentia and remain on the FBI's most wanted list. I am convinced of the efficacy of rapport-building interrogation techniques by these and other experiences.

Senator and gentlemen of the Committee, let me say that my heart tells me that torture and all forms of excessive coercion are inhumane and un-American, and my experience tells me that they just don't work . . .

Source: Cloonan, John E. 2008. "Coercive Interrogation Techniques: Do they Work, Are They Reliable, and What Did the FBI Know About Them?" Testimony to U.S. Senate Committee on the Judiciary Hearing, 110th Cong. 2nd sess., June 10. Accessed June 28, 2022. https://www.govinfo.gov/content/pkg/CHRG-110shrg53740/html/CHRG-110shrg53740.htm.

Veto Message from the President—S.2040 (2016)

This veto statement by President Obama outlines his rationale for opposing the Justice Against Sponsors of Terrorism Act (JASTA) passed by Congress. The act enables U.S. nationals to file civil lawsuits against foreign governments. Prior to the act, federal law did not allow courts to do so if the governments were not designated as state sponsors of terrorism. The act was driven by families of the victims of the 9/11 attacks who sought to file suit against the Kingdom of Saudi Arabia for members of that government having provided assistance to the 9/11 hijackers.

President Obama argued that removing sovereign immunity would threaten the relationship that the U.S. government has with other governments and impede the kind of cooperation needed to prevent attacks. President Obama's veto was subsequently overridden by Congress and JASTA became law.

TO THE SENATE OF THE UNITED STATES:

I am returning herewith without my approval S. 2040, the "Justice Against Sponsors of Terrorism Act" (JASTA), which would, among other things, remove sovereign immunity in U.S. courts from foreign governments that are not designated state sponsors of terrorism.

I have deep sympathy for the families of the victims of the terrorist attacks of September 11, 2001 (9/11), who have suffered grievously. I also have a deep appreciation of these families' desire to pursue justice and am strongly committed to assisting them in their efforts.

Consistent with this commitment, over the past 8 years, I have directed my Administration to pursue relentlessly al Qa'ida, the terrorist group that planned the 9/11 attacks. The heroic efforts of our military and counterterrorism professionals have decimated al-Qa'ida's leadership and killed Osama bin Laden. My Administration also strongly supported, and I signed into law, legislation which ensured that those who bravely responded on that terrible day and other survivors of the attacks will be able to receive treatment for any injuries resulting from the attacks. And my Administration also directed the Intelligence Community to perform a declassification review of "Part Four of the Joint Congressional Inquiry into Intelligence Community Activities Before and After the Terrorist Attacks of September 11," so that the families of 9/11 victims and broader public can better understand the information investigators gathered following that dark day of our history.

Notwithstanding these significant efforts, I recognize that there is nothing that could ever erase the grief the 9/11 families have endured. My Administration therefore remains resolute in its commitment to assist these families in their pursuit of justice and do whatever we can to prevent another attack in the United States. Enacting JASTA into law, however, would neither protect Americans from terrorist attacks nor improve the effectiveness of our response to such attacks. As drafted, JASTA would allow private litigation against foreign governments in U.S. courts based on allegations that such foreign governments' actions abroad made them responsible for terrorism-related injuries on U.S. soil. This legislation would permit litigation against countries that have neither been designated by the executive branch as state sponsors of terrorism nor taken direct actions in the United States to carry out an attack here. The JASTA would be detrimental to U.S. national interests more broadly, which is why I am returning it without my approval.

First, JASTA threatens to reduce the effectiveness of our response to indications that a foreign government has taken steps outside our borders to provide support for terrorism, by taking such matters out of the hands of national security and foreign policy professionals and placing them in the hands of private litigants and courts.

Any indication that a foreign government played a role in a terrorist attack on U.S. soil is a matter of deep concern and merits a forceful, unified Federal Government response that considers the wide range of important and effective tools available. One of these tools is designating the foreign government in question as a state sponsor of terrorism, which carries with it a litany of repercussions, including the foreign government being stripped of its sovereign immunity before U.S. courts in certain terrorism-related cases and subjected to a range of sanctions. Given these serious consequences, state sponsor of terrorism designations are made only after national security, foreign policy, and intelligence professionals carefully review all available information to determine whether a country meets the criteria that the Congress established.

In contrast, JASTA departs from longstanding standards and practice under our Foreign Sovereign Immunities Act and threatens to strip all foreign governments of immunity from judicial process in the United States based solely upon allegations by private litigants that a foreign government's overseas conduct had some role or connection to a group or person that carried out a terrorist attack inside the United States. This would invite consequential decisions to be made based upon incomplete information and risk having different courts reaching different conclusions about the culpability of individual foreign governments and their role in terrorist activities directed against the United States—which is neither an effective nor a coordinated way for us to respond to indications that a foreign government might have been behind a terrorist attack.

Second, JASTA would upset longstanding international principles regarding sovereign immunity, putting in place rules that, if applied globally, could have serious implications for U.S. national interests. The United States has a larger international presence, by far, than any other country, and sovereign immunity principles protect our Nation and its Armed Forces, officials, and assistance professionals, from foreign court proceedings. These principles also protect U.S. Government assets from attempted seizure by private litigants abroad. Removing sovereign immunity in U.S. courts from foreign governments that are not designated as state sponsors of terrorism, based solely on allegations that such foreign governments' actions abroad had a connection to terrorism-related injuries on U.S. soil, threatens to undermine these longstanding principles that protect the United States, our forces, and our personnel.

Indeed, reciprocity plays a substantial role in foreign relations, and numerous other countries already have laws that allow for the adjustment of a foreign state's immunities based on the treatment their governments receive in the courts of the other state. Enactment of JASTA could encourage foreign governments to act reciprocally and allow their domestic courts to exercise jurisdiction over the United States or U.S. officials—including our men and women in uniform—for allegedly causing injuries overseas via U.S. support to third parties. This could lead to suits against the United States or U.S. officials for actions taken by members of an armed group that received U.S. assistance, misuse of U.S. military equipment by foreign forces, or abuses committed by police units that received U.S. training, even if the allegations at issue ultimately would be without merit. And if any of these litigants were to win judgments—based on foreign domestic laws as applied by foreign courts—they would begin to look to the assets of the U.S. Government held abroad to satisfy those judgments, with potentially serious financial consequences for the United States.

Third, JASTA threatens to create complications in our relationships with even our closest partners. If JASTA were enacted, courts could potentially consider even minimal allegations accusing U.S. allies or partners of complicity in a particular terrorist attack in the United States to be sufficient to open the door to litigation and wide-ranging discovery against a foreign country—for example, the country where an individual who later committed a terrorist act traveled from or became radicalized. A number of our allies and partners have already contacted us with serious concerns about the bill. By exposing these allies and partners to this sort of litigation in U.S. courts, JASTA threatens to limit their cooperation on key national security issues, including counterterrorism initiatives, at a crucial time when we are trying to build coalitions, not create divisions.

The 9/11 attacks were the worst act of terrorism on U.S. soil, and they were met with an unprecedented U.S. Government response. The United States has taken robust and wide-ranging actions to provide justice for the victims of the 9/11 attacks and keep Americans safe, from providing financial compensation for victims and their families to conducting worldwide counterterrorism programs to bringing criminal charges against culpable individuals. I have continued and expanded upon these efforts, both to help victims of terrorism gain justice for the loss and suffering of their loved ones and to protect the United States from future attacks. The JASTA, however, does not contribute to these goals, does not enhance the safety of Americans from terrorist attacks, and undermines core U.S. interests. For these reasons, I must veto the bill.

Source: Obama, Barack H. 2016. "Veto Message from the President—S.2040," September 23. Accessed June 28, 2022. https://obamawhitehouse.archives.gov /the-press-office/2016/09/23/veto-message-president

-s2040#:~:text=I%20am%20returning%20herewith
%20without,designated%20state%20sponsors%20of
%20terrorism.

Examining the "Metastasizing" Domestic Terrorism Threat After the Buffalo Attack (2022)

This congressional testimony about domestic terrorism threats in the United States comes from a federal prosecutor who was invited to testify at Senate hearings after a white gunman murdered 10 African Americans at a Buffalo supermarket in a racially motivated attack in June 2022.

Prosecutor Justin Herdman argues in his Senate testimony that the first line of defense in foiling terrorist attacks is the proactive efforts of communities and local law enforcement working in concert. He notes that such local partnerships focusing on the signs of an impending attack have proven more effective than only identifying affiliations with certain ideological organizations. This is because many recent would-be attackers whose efforts were foiled were not connected to organizational networks and can advance from a perceived personal grievance to violence against target communities in short order. Interestingly, he argues that such local partnerships coupled with existing federal law is sufficient to handle domestic terrorism cases.

. . . I have spent nearly twenty years of my professional career, mostly as a federal prosecutor but also in the military, in the field of counterterrorism. While I bring to bear just one perspective on the work before the Committee, I believe that my experience as a federal prosecutor in the Northern District of Ohio is of particular relevance on this subject . . .

To help illustrate the changing nature of the terrorism threat, I would point to a few cases from my district on which I either worked directly as a prosecutor or supervised as US Attorney. My early work as a federal prosecutor in the office's

National Security Unit was primarily devoted to investigating and prosecuting cases involving international terrorism, which necessarily involved individuals acting on behalf of, or inspired by, designated foreign terrorist organizations. In those matters, we worked with investigators across multiple states and across the world. Coordination with the National Security Division at the Department of Justice was essential, as we often had to carefully address issues of importance to our nation's foreign policy and intelligence communities.

By 2010 in Ohio, we had started to observe an uptick in violent extremism with no connection to international terrorism. These were often individuals who had amassed weapons and were committed to violent attacks, including cases where the perpetrators had developed a plan to attack local leaders, schools, or political institutions. In 2012, a group of five Cleveland-area young men who were self-proclaimed anarchists considered a variety of violent attacks, including the G-8 summit held in Chicago that year and the Republican National Convention in Tampa. Ultimately, they attempted to detonate an explosive device at the bottom of a support column beneath the Route 82 bridge in Brecksville, Ohio—a bridge that spans a deep crossing in the Cuyahoga Valley National Park—and their intent was to bring down the entire bridge. In 2013, I was part of the trial team that prosecuted Joshua Stafford, the only conspirator who went to trial, and I left the US Attorney's office shortly thereafter for private practice.

This background helped frame my view of the counterterrorism landscape when I was sworn in as US Attorney in August 2017. At that time, I was briefed by the Cleveland FBI on a host of ongoing terrorism threats, including a number of domestic terrorism investigations. These briefings were eye-opening, as the nature of the terrorism threat had evolved even in the few short years that I had been away from the office.

In addressing my tenure as US Attorney and the varied threat picture that we faced, I would like to start by addressing the danger posed by white supremacists, either in an organized

or individual capacity. As the testimony today will demonstrate, that threat is profound and it is pervasive. In 2019, a
white supremacist named James Reardon was arrested by federal authorities for filming himself with a Nazi-era firearm and,
over audio of multiple gunshots and screaming people in the
background, threatening a mass shooting at the Jewish Community Center of Youngstown, Ohio. Reardon's commitment
to the white supremacist cause was well-established, as he had
been present in Charlottesville at the 2017 Unite the Right
rally, and federal authorities recovered the above-referenced
firearm, an MP40 submachine gun, as well as a Hitler Youth
knife and Nazi propaganda posters from Reardon's residence.
In May 2021, Reardon pleaded guilty to two federal felony
counts: transmitting a threatening communication and possession of a firearm in furtherance of a crime of violence. In
November 2021, he received a 41 month prison sentence with
five years of post-release supervision. I am particularly proud
of this case because I am convinced that we saved lives. I also
believe that this case demonstrates the power of a vigilant
member of the community, who saw the threat posted online,
and a responsive law enforcement officer, who acted quickly
and took the threat seriously.

This is a fitting place to pause, as the Jewish community is
one with whom I worked very closely as US Attorney in order to
address the wide range of threats against Jewish houses of worship, Jewish schools, and Jewish cultural organizations. White
supremacists pose a serious and ongoing threat to our Jewish
friends and neighbors, but they are by no means the only such
threat. A case that our office prosecuted in late 2018 demonstrates the complex and serious threat picture faced by America's
Jewish communities.

Damon Joseph was a resident of Toledo, a recent convert to
Islam and a self-avowed adherent to violent jihad. Having been
inspired by online videos and materials produced by the Islamic
State of Iraq and al-Sham ("ISIS"), Joseph became increasingly
radicalized in the fall of 2018. After the attack on the Tree of

Life Synagogue in Pittsburgh, Joseph conducted surveillance of two Toledo-area synagogues and scripted a nine-point plan for inflicting mass casualties at those locations. As Joseph stated: "Jews who support the state of [I]srael are desired targets." He was arrested on December 10, 2018 and ultimately pleaded guilty to both federal terrorism and federal hate crimes charges, which as far as I am aware, was the first time a prosecution for both of these offenses had been pursued. He is currently serving a twenty year term of federal imprisonment.

I am well aware that the subject matter of today's hearing is domestic terrorism and that the Joseph case is one which, at least on initial appearance, appears to fall into the more familiar category of post-9/11 international terrorism. I raise the Joseph case, though, because I think that it amply illustrates the grave threat posed to the United States and law enforcement by a host of violent actors. The threat picture that emerged while I was US Attorney was incredibly complicated and poses a heightened danger to all residents of our communities. While white supremacy and violent jihad offers adherents a somewhat cohesive set of warped principles that ultimately forms an ideology, I saw several cases that defied easy categorization because of blended, evolving, or simply non-existent ideologies.

Elizabeth Lecron and Vincent Armstrong were a Toledo-area couple who harbored a deep fascination with the Columbine shootings. One of their acquaintances, concerned with the couple's active discussions about emulating that attack, reported them to law enforcement. During the course of the FBI investigation, the couple visited Columbine High School and, over time, this sick obsession moved into active planning for a mass casualty attack at a specific Toledo bar. Elizabeth Lecron separately attempted to acquire an explosive device for use against a gas pipeline. They were arrested in December 2018 and Lecron was ultimately convicted of attempting to provide material support to terrorism, in violation of 18 USC 2339A, in a purely domestic terrorism setting. She is currently serving a fifteen year term of federal imprisonment.

Christian Ferguson and Allen Kenna were both arrested in 2020, in separate cases. Ferguson was plotting to lie in wait for a law enforcement officer and planned to capture or kill them when they responded to a false 911 call. Ferguson was specifically interested in obtaining a response by federal law enforcement because he believed they had better quality firearms and body armor to steal after he killed them. Ferguson conducted reconnaissance in a dry run and facilitated a hoax distress call to gauge response time by law enforcement.

Kenna had well-developed plans to attack an Ohio high school with explosives and firearms. Kenna had previously been seen entering that high school after school hours, where he filmed school hallways and asked questions concerning school operations, facilities and resource officers. After searching his residence and cellphone, investigators found disturbing journal entries in which Kenna expressed his desire to attack the school, as well as research he conducted on a variety of topics related to the planned attack. Similar to Ferguson, Kenna also placed false calls to law enforcement in Kansas designed to deploy SWAT officers to a school in that state.

I have focused on these cases, but there are many more from my tenure as US Attorney that kept me up at night as a federal prosecutor, and continue to do so even though I am no longer a Justice Department official. I would offer the following observations from my nearly two decade career in counterterrorism.

First, this may go without saying, but in a world of limited resources, the most effective pro-active law enforcement actions are those directed at individuals who are actively planning, plotting, and preparing to conduct violent attacks. This means that law enforcement must be focused on conduct above all else—in essence, investigators must determine whether an individual is taking steps that would indicate an attack is contemplated or imminent. This will often, but not always, include some outward expression of intent to the subject's inner circle or online community. Law enforcement must be flexible in developing strategies that are focused on this conduct, not only because that is what the Constitution requires, but because this is proven to result in prosecutions that will most effectively and efficiently disrupt plots before they occur.

Second, and related to the first, is encouraging a vigilant public and responsive law enforcement, especially at the local level. While we did see an increase in the number of reports regarding individuals suspected of being a danger to themselves or others, these complaints were also made to federal, and not local, law enforcement. I would encourage whatever efforts this Committee might be contemplating regarding local law enforcement response to threats, including threats to vulnerable populations or law enforcement itself. A police officer who knows his or her own community, and the people within it, is an excellent first line of defense against mass casualty attacks when that officer is provided with specific, credible information about a concern. We saw this model work in the James Reardon case, among others, and I am convinced that this one area—public awareness and local law enforcement responsiveness—that can be improved and save lives.

Third, ideology is helpful in identifying individuals who possess the baseline motivation to conduct an attack, particularly against communities of color, ethnicity, or faith, but modern violent extremists often bring a blurred and incoherent belief system to their plots. This means that the political outcomes sought by these domestic terrorists will often seem unserious or fanciful, but that does not make them any less dangerous. An individual with a self-developed series of hatreds or grievances can accelerate from theory to action very quickly, and with very little prompting. For this reason, network-level and organizational cases against identified violent groups are important, but they will not capture the very serious threat posed by individual extremists who are not tethered to others by a common set of beliefs.

Fourth, close coordination with certain communities under threat is absolutely essential. The example that I raised with respect to our Ohio-based Jewish communities illustrates this essential requirement for preparedness and response. While we may not be able to identify every single group or individual extremist who would threaten a specific population, we do know that certain demographics—Jewish, but also Muslim, Latino, Asian, and Black communities—are the declared targets of domestic terrorists and extremists. I am aware of federal programs that are specifically designed to enhance security at houses of worship and I have participated in such programs with Jewish, Muslim, and Black faith communities. These efforts are fruitful and I would encourage expansion of such initiatives.

Fifth, while I am welcome discussion regarding any legislative fixes contemplated by the Committee, I think that the number and variety of cases brought by one US Attorney's office demonstrates that the current suite of federal laws is adequate to deter and disrupt domestic terrorist attacks. In my opinion, we were successful in these prosecutions because they were a priority area for our office; we worked very closely with federal, state and local partners to address the domestic terrorism threat; we maintained close ties with our community partners and frequently coordinated with them; and we had an excellent group of experienced prosecutors, agents, and officers who exercised outstanding judgment and discretion during these investigations.

Source: Herdman, Justin E. 2022. "Examining the 'Metastasizing' Domestic Terrorism Threat After the Buffalo Attack." Testimony to U.S. Senate Committee on the Judiciary Hearing. 117th Cong. 2nd sess., June 7. Accessed June 28, 2022. https://www.judiciary.senate.gov/download/testimony -herdman-2022-06-07.

6 Resources

Terrorism is inherently a political phenomenon, and due to this fact it naturally falls into the field of political science. A specific group or individual's political aims help to define the stated motivation for their behavior. However, these aims are wide-ranging and manifest in a plethora of different contexts. The politics related to specific geographic realities matter with respect to stated or defined goals, but these very political preferences are animated by notions of identity and ideology. In a strategic sense, these factors shape the preferences of groups by clarifying underlying political conflicts. In a tactical manner the types of attacks require understanding of the different means by which operatives conduct attacks and how these approaches evolve.

Accordingly, there are many different dimensions by which scholars and analysts tackle the issue of terrorism. Should analysts attempt to explain terrorism at the individual level to understand why operatives join groups, or perhaps take a more strategic and "instrumental" approach by focusing on the leadership seeking political aims? Should they better approach the topic by looking at the inner workings of terror organizations

---

Counterterrorism policies include decapitation strikes in which government forces target the leaders of foreign terrorist organizations for killing. In recent decades many such strikes have been carried out against al Qaeda-affiliated leaders using Unmanned Aerial Vehicles (UAVs) such as the MQ-1 Predator pictured here. Scholars are split on the effects that such strikes have on the survivability of terrorist groups. (Dan Van Den Broeke/Dreamstime.com)

and their qualities, such as organizational style and process? Or is it optimal to consider the transnational ecology of groups operating in a space of international relations, networking with one another to solve collective action problems? The complexity of the subject involves multiple approaches to its study.

Research on terrorism is expansive and includes works related to theories, data, and analysis. Theories outline the logic for why certain inputs are expected to cause or shape the output of terrorism as a phenomenon. Theories are often generated through observation of key cases and an application of that observed relationship to other contexts and cases. Data is important from a social science standpoint to review the soundness of a theory's logic: Do actual cases fit the predictions of theories in the sense that groups behave according to the logic of the theory? In some instances a theory may be on a firm footing in a general sense, but notable outliers "buck the trend" and warrant further study to see why those outcomes deviated from the expectations. The transdisciplinary nature is also reflected in the different research methods used to terrorism. Analysis is the critical element that ties it all together and contextualizes the information by asserting what can be expected given past patterns and trends.

Scholars in the academic world tend to be most interested in the theories and seek to better fine-tune them to understand the link between cause and effect. Relatedly but differently, analysts in the professional world tend to be more interested in the actual specifics of narrow cases: How do the narrow idiosyncrasies of a case impact how terrorism will appear in that environment, and for what purpose? Often the questions are narrowly focused because the ultimate aim is to devise a specific counterterrorism policy.

The works outlined in this chapter are starting points for those who wish to delve deeper into the many aspects related to the complexity of studying terrorism. They include works on understanding the causes and motivations of terrorists, approaches to counterterrorism, factors that are associated such as the involvement of foreign governments, and specific case studies of notable groups.

Books

Anderson, Benedict. 1983. *Imagined Communities: Reflections on the Origin and Spread of Nationalism.* **London: Verso.**

Anderson's work is a classic in the field of comparative politics and instrumental in understanding nationalism and identity. It sets out to debunk the notion that national identity is "natural." Anderson argues that social identity is fluid with the implication that political entrepreneurs can use identity for mobilization. The fundamental research question he addresses is how nationalist ideologies spread throughout the world to become such significant political movements that they define the international system today. The decolonization of the 1950s and 1960s of newly independent countries who broke from their colonizers is one example of the enduring strength of national identity.

Anderson asserts that the invention of the printing press coupled with capitalism served a critical role in enabling the literature of nationalists to expand to new audiences and accordingly create new political identity groups. The effect of unifying language and reaching distance areas with the new ideas of identity generated "imagined communities" where those who adhered to the nationalist identity rarely met other members of the novel political community but came to believe in its sacredness. The identity framework marked a break from the existing imperial or monarchical systems and enabled the size and scope of identity groups to form the basis for republican movements grander than parochial life. The work is important in asserting how powerful nationalist identity is, and the work has bearing today for debates about the role of information technology in generating new "imagined communities" along nationalist or even extra-nationalist forms of identity despite vast physical distances.

Bell, J. Bowyer. 1978. *A Time of Terror: How Democratic Societies Respond to Revolutionary Violence.* **New York: Basic.**

Bell writes about terrorism with an eye toward how liberal democratic political systems should counter it. He asserts that the threat posed by terrorists is frequently overblown compared to the damage that they do given their small size and unpopular policy goals, yet governments also recognize there also is no single policy that can quickly neutralize such a terrorist threat. The author asserts that a proper balance must be struck by governments to maintain a sufficient response lest public confidence in the government plummets, while also not engaging in overreaction that harms the liberties of citizens in the country.

Bell is concerned that the medicine can be worse than the disease, arguing for a restrained "less is more" policy by the government that tackles the political issues terrorist actors claim as their grievances. He argues for more of a law enforcement approach to countering groups instead of a militarized response and cautions against dramatic escalation by the government. For Bell a military response dramatizes the case and leads to the democratic state changing its behavior to become more authoritarian, thereby granting terror actors a win and confirming their contentions about the government's legitimacy. The work is useful for understanding the case for a more restrained but still effective counterterrorism approach that is more attentive to civil liberties.

Byman, Daniel. 2015. *Al Qaeda, the Islamic State, and the Global Jihadist Movement: What Everyone Needs to Know.* **Oxford: Oxford University Press.**

Byman provides an overview of contemporary Salafi-Jihadist movements in this accessible volume. Although al Qaeda and the Islamic State have been put on the run in recent years due to counterterrorism operations, they remain relevant as organizations that have spawned a series of franchises operating in the Middle East and Africa. Charting the history of political Islamist movements and theorists, the author identifies the centrality of Salafism in most contemporary movements, starting with al Qaeda. He succinctly outlines the organizational history of this group in the lead up to the 9/11 attacks.

The author also showcases the differences between the groups that have made them rivals, despite the fact they both seek to establish Islamic caliphates by overthrowing secular regimes in the region (the "near enemy") as well as the United States (the "far enemy"). He notes the tactical differences regarding the timing of attacks, with al Qaeda seeking to destroy the far enemy first by sponsoring attacks on the U.S. homeland before moving to regional states, whereas the Islamic State saw the near enemy of Middle East regimes as ripe for revolution in the short term.

Chaliand, Gerard and Arnaud Blin. 2007. *The History of Terrorism: From Antiquity to al Qaeda*. Berkeley: University of California Press.

Chaliand and Blin's book takes a historical look at terrorism through a set of notable cases. Their work is particularly helpful by offering cases in the precontemporary era such as the ancient Jewish zealots, the Nizari assassins of the Middle Ages, the anarchist acts of terrorism at the turn of the twentieth century, and the use of the tactic by groups of the New Left. This historical perspective is helpful as a point of departure for looking to contemporary groups and their motivations. The character of terrorism changes via the impact of social change on ideologies and the tradecraft used by groups due to technological advances. That said, a review of deeply historical cases shows how the fundamental nature of terrorism is remarkably enduring throughout the ages.

Codevilla, Angelo M. 2005. *No Victory, No Peace.* **Lanham, MD: Rowman and Littlefield.**

Codevilla asserts that political leaders who do not understand war will be unable to win if they cannot realistically chart a path that matches operational means to strategic ends. He critiques the wars of the George W. Bush administration in Afghanistan and Iraq for being divorced from linking such means to ends. Devoid of effective strategy, Codevilla charges the Bush notion of a "war on terrorism" as nonsensical in that wars are fought against nation-states and not ideas. He insists that terrorism is not something that any political power can defeat given how easy it is to undertake and how its true motivation is not any specific organization but a broader societal sentiment.

Codevilla asserts that the errors of the Bush administration were compounded by seeking to replace the destroyed Taliban and Baathist regimes with liberal democratic governments that would never succeed as envisioned. For Codevilla, the enabler of terrorism was not al Qaeda enjoying safe haven in Afghanistan so much as the nature of anti-American regimes in the Middle East.

The author details how anti-American terrorist violence by Islamist elements surged in the wake of the regime changes in Afghanistan and Iraq rather than dissipated. He provocatively argues that a true victory in war against Islamist-based anti-Americanism would require going to war with countries that he asserts are well-springs of anti-Americanism but with whom the United States maintains established relations, such as Saudi Arabia and Pakistan.

Coll, Steve. 2018. *Directorate S: The CIA and America's Secret Wars in Afghanistan and Pakistan.* **New York: Penguin.**

Coll's work is an outstanding resource for understanding U.S. counterterrorism policy in South and Central Asia following the 9/11 attacks. The work is essential reading for those who seek to understand the mechanics of how intelligence and covert action operate in counterterrorism operations overseas. In particular, Coll outlines how the Pakistani counterpart to the American CIA, the Inter-Services Intelligence (ISI) agency, pursued Pakistani national interests that at times aligned with American aims but at other times were contradictory to them. The ISI's Directorate S had the responsibility for Pakistani operations in Afghanistan and Pakistan. Coll's work highlights the complexity of political relations between governments and various non-state actors and helps reader understand the shadowy nature of such complex operations in practice are more gray than black-and-white.

Comolli, Virginia. 2017. *Boko Haram: Nigeria's Islamist Insurgency*. London: Hurst & Company.

Comolli's book is a user-friendly account of a complex example of terrorism in Africa. Boko Haram is among the deadliest terror groups on record with respect to the number of civilians killed. Comolli first grounds her analysis in the history of Islamist movements in the northeast of Nigeria to suggest that the politically driven religious sentiment behind Boko Haram's militancy is not new. She then proceeds to outline the specific circumstances that saw Mohammed Yusuf's Salafist followers turn to violence after his death in 2009 at the hands of local police forces. Abubakar Shekau's rise to replace Yusuf marked a turn toward more wanton violence targeting civilians in addition to Nigerian security forces.

Comolli outlines some key splits in the group's history but ends the book outlining the Nigerian government's counterterrorism efforts and their many failures due to internal politics and weak capacity. The failures are compounded by Boko Haram's resilience and capacity to melt into the general population in remote areas when faced with periodic Nigerian military campaigns.

Cronin, Audrey K. 2009. *How Terrorism Ends: Understanding the Decline and Demise of Terrorist Organizations.* **Princeton: Princeton University Press.**

> Cronin's book is a highly readable and important study that analyzes counterterrorism policies and other ways that terrorist groups end. Critically, she outlines the distinction between outcome goals and process goals that drive groups and supplies examples of each. Through a series of short cases in each chapter, she outlines the effects of a specific policy and chronicles the conditions by which the policy is likely or unlikely to succeed at shortening the life of a terrorist group. The policies include decapitation of the leadership whether by arrest or assassination, negotiations to facilitate a group's transition into the political process, the group successfully achieving its outcome goals, the group's implosion or marginalization, the use of repression by the state, and a group reorienting from terrorism to another tactic.
>
> She finishes with a chapter applying the conditions of each group's ending to al Qaeda, where she concludes that policies of negotiation, failure, and reorientation are the most likely to end al Qaeda. The multiple cases used in each chapter are helpful for students seeking insight into how a specific policy affected that group's pursuit of its goals and are a basis for applying her framework to new cases in the contemporary era.

Giraldo, Jeanne and Harold Trinkunas. 2007. *Terrorism Financing and State Responses: A Comparative Perspective.* **Stanford: Stanford University Press.**

> Giraldo and Trinkunas' edited work is a good introductory resource for those seeking understanding into how non-state groups like terrorist organizations finance their operations and how states have sought to halt this financing. Unlike states these groups do not have dedicated governmental bureaucracies for resource extraction the

way a national government might through taxation. The authors of the volume note both the opportunities and limitations afforded by globalization. Groups can seek to raise, hide, and move money through various connected businesses and entities; however, they also expose their resources to criminal elements who could exploit them.

Chapters by contributors consider the effects of terrorist financing through organized crime and narcotics, along with specific cases of al Qaeda and Hezbollah. There are also chapters for regional areas of Europe, East Africa, Southeast Asia, and South America. With respect to policy, the editors argue that governments face political challenges in coordinating their efforts within their many organizations as well as with foreign counterparts but that there are additional options. These include covert monitoring of financial networks, when politically viable, and working to improve public–private partnerships in this area.

Goren, Roberta. 1984. *The Soviet Union and Terrorism.* London: George Allen & Unwin.

Goren argues that the communist bloc used international terrorism as a means of waging warfare against the Western states during the Cold War. She grounds her argument in two observations. First, international terrorism was notably absent in Eastern Bloc countries during the Cold War and so seemed to only flow in one direction from the communist East to the democratic West. Second, the places in the Western world where international terrorism was used, such as West Germany or Italy, were not localities that suffered from weakness or desperation by inhabitants as is common in mental maps of why groups use the tactic. Goren finds that terrorism fits with the ideology of Marxist-Leninist thought since the 1917 Bolshevik Revolution before further outlining specific linkages between Soviet and communist-bloc intelligence services and leftwing terrorist groups. The work is especially useful as guide for evidence of global "New Left" terrorist cases during the mid to late Cold War era.

Hafez, Mohammed. 2003. *Why Muslims Rebel: Repression and Resistance in the Islamic World.* Boulder: Lynne-Rienner.

Hafez's work seeks to address why certain Islamic political groups resort to militancy versus others. He notes that poor economic factors do not account for the variation in such activity, and so next looks to the relative deprivation model of Ted Gurr. Hafez notes that this approach is also unsatisfying, because the grievances facing groups are many; however, relatively few resort to militancy as a result. He adopts a framework where a group's exclusion from the political process combined with indiscriminate repression by the state encourages radicalization. In his model a group that cannot participate in the political system by working through its institutions has no cause to see that system as legitimate, and the active, widespread repression by the state pushes groups to adopt antisystem ideologies. His primary case studies of the cases of the Islamic Group of Egypt and the Algerian Armed Islamic Group (GIA) are excellent by covering such complex cases in a condensed and accessible manner.

Hoffman, Bruce. 2017. *Inside Terrorism, Third Edition.* New York: Columbia University Press.

Hoffman's text offers a broad overview of the topic and is widely used as a textbook in upper division courses. Starting with a useful chapter contrasting definitions of the term, he moves to categorize the origins of modern terrorism and its shift to transnational forms. He then addresses contemporary topics of interest about variants including chapters on both religious and suicide terrorism.

Among his most useful and unique chapters pertain to the interaction of mass media and terrorism, where he is most interested in the effects this interplay has on public opinion. The work ends with a review of the most recent terrorism cases and projections for how the character of terrorism may evolve in the coming years. Altogether Hoffman's text is an excellent first stop for those interested in understanding more about key elements and examples of the tactic.

Kilcullen, David. 2016. *Blood Year: The Unraveling of Western Counterterrorism.* Oxford: Oxford University Press.

Dr. Kilcullen is a former Australian Army officer, academic, and policy advisor in the field of counterinsurgency. This work is a critique of U.S. foreign and defense policy in the Middle East and Afghanistan regions following the Iraq War and is a useful guide for helping understand the international politics surrounding the rise of the Islamic State in 2013. He chronicles the clash between al Qaeda and the Islamic State as the latter rose to prominence by acquiring Syrian and Iraqi territory before declaring itself the caliphate.

The author helpfully discusses the overall diplomatic and political context between nation-states in this region rather than solely focusing on the terrorism cases. He reviews the relationship between the United States and Russia over the civil wars in Libya and Syria, as well as the U.S. government's relationship with the government of Iraq in attempts to counter the Islamic State. He also brings in the U.S. government's struggle with Iran over shifts in the region. Kilcullen concludes with policy advice that governments fighting insurgents and terrorists need to maintain the political reality of the conflicts they engage in, to include prioritizing cases that pose threats to their interests, properly resourcing these efforts, and understanding that progress is measured not by battlefield terms but in what can be politically achieved in theater.

Krueger, Alan. 2007. *What Makes a Terrorist: Economics and the Roots of Terrorism.* **Princeton: Princeton University Press.**

Krueger is an economist by training, and his research approach was to statistically assess the degree by which terrorism tracks with poor socioeconomic status as measured by lower education and income. Kruger's research determined that on average terrorists were better educated and wealthier than the average individual in the areas where terrorist attacks took place. Krueger argues that terrorism is driven primarily by political rather than economic rationales. In terms of his methodology, he notably distinguishes between terrorism and civil war, even though actors in the latter can use the former as a tactic.

Laqueur, Walter. 2003. *No End to War: Terrorism in the Twenty-First Century.* **New York: Continuum Publishing.**

Laqueur adopts a historical approach to the subject of terrorism. He analyzes the notion of terrorism after 9/11 through this lens and argues that as a phenomenon it is becoming vastly more dangerous than in prior cases. He also cautions against the viability of invoking broad trends such as poverty, political oppression, or other such dynamics as stated grievances held by terrorists who themselves are a very small subset of a population.

Laqueur believes the defining trait of terrorists is their fanaticism. Laqueur's concern is that the main threat of terrorism today is not through conventional attacks, but rather through their use of unconventional weapons of mass destruction. This class of weapons includes chemical, biological, and radiological weapons. His concern is derived from the fanaticism of recent terrorists whose religious ideology drives them to seek the death of as many innocents as possible in pursuit of their aims.

For Lacquer the older model of terrorism of groups having wider participation among their population and secular-rational goals in locally defined areas has given way to those who are smaller in scale, more fanatical and universalist in their beliefs, and more indiscriminate in their attack profiles, but with increasing access to more lethal means of attack.

Levitt, Matthew. 2013. *Hezbollah: The Global Footprint of Lebanon's Party of God.* **Washington, D.C.: Georgetown University Press.**

Levitt comprehensively covers Lebanese Hezbollah ("Party of God") from its genesis as an extension of the 1979 Iranian Revolution into Lebanon. He next chronicles its rise to a terrorist organization with global reach. Hezbollah is perhaps most famous for its 1983 suicide bombings in Beirut, Lebanon, that killed over 300 U.S. and French military troops.

The book features chapters on specific Hezbollah operations in Lebanon, Europe, Argentina, Thailand, North America, the Arabian Peninsula, Israel, West Africa, and Iraq. The text is useful for those seeking insight about the group as well as the tradecraft used by transnational terrorist groups in general to conduct operations. An added insight is the essential role played by mid-level Hezbollah operative Imad Mugniyeh to facilitate many of the attacks outlined in the various chapters.

Maher, Shiraz. 2017. *Salafi-Jihadism: The History of an Idea.* **London: Penguin.**

Maher's book is essential for those doing research on Salafi-Jihadism or groups like al Qaeda or the Islamic State who adhere to that ideology. He identifies five theological concepts that interact and distinguish Salafi-Jihadists from mainstream Islamic praxis. These concepts are *jihad*, *takfir*, *al-wala wa-l-bara*, *tawhid*, and *hakimiyya*. Maher demonstrates how the concepts alone are present in mainstream in Islamic theology; however, Salafi-Jihadists interpret them in significantly more aggressive ways to try and theologically justify their violence. In the case of *jihad*, Maher argues that Salafi-Jihadists interpret the term legally to mean physically fighting against the enemies of the faith in order to promote the faith, and further see it as an obligation and not an option.

Maher argues that *takfir* ("excommunication") is a critical component of Salafi-Jihadists who believe any Muslim can declare another person to be non-Muslim. The process of *takfir* has established roots in Islamic jurisprudence, but it is involved and carefully undertaken by qualified clerics. Salafi-Jihadists, on the other hand, take it upon themselves to make the declaration as a form of conformity. *Takfir* is significant because to be outside the fold of Islam means that capital punishment can apply, and Salafi-Jihadist groups in practice regularly cite *takfir* to undertake attacks against those who otherwise profess to be Muslims.

Maher argues that Salafi-Jihadists take the term *al-wala wa-l-bara* ("to love and hate for the sake of Allah") to mean militaristically promoting what is good and rejecting what is not, requiring as much devotion to rejecting the bad as to loving the good. The term *tawhid* (oneness of Allah) factors into the names of certain Salafi-Jihadist groups, and Maher suggests that they use it to counter competing elements or loyalties to the Salafi-Jihadist understanding of Allah. Finally, *hakimiyaa* (political rule of God) is seen as a literal sovereignty of God such that government falls under His authority and laws. Maher's work is useful not only for qualifying these concepts but for showing the history and evolution of their interpretation versus mainstream thought within Islam.

Maruf, Harun and Dan Joseph. 2018. *Inside Al-Shabaab: The Secret History of Al-Qaeda's Most Powerful Ally.* Bloomington: Indiana University Press.

Maruf and Joseph compile an insider's view of leadership dynamics and clashes within the al Shabaab ("the youth") terrorist group of Somalia. First outlining the origins of the group in the Islamic Courts Union movement in the wake of the warlord era of the 1990s, the authors next demonstrate how members of the al Shabaab faction launched an internal coup to seize control of the movement. Maruf and Joseph identify how al Shabaab efforts were aided by Ethiopia's 2006 intervention that spurred many Somali expatriates to return to the country on nationalist grounds and take up arms.

The authors outline the important role played by its former uncompromising leader, Ahmed Abdi Godane, in directing terrorist and insurgent attacks against the transitional federal government of Somalia. The work provides important clan-based and personality-based political layers to those based on the Salafi-Jihadist ideology of the group. These dimensions are important for those seeking potential counterterrorism strategies based on internal division that may be applied to similar cases.

Pious, Richard M. 2006. *The War on Terrorism and the Rule of Law*. Los Angeles: Roxbury.

Pious's book is accessible and considers the leading issues related to legal concerns surrounding counterterrorism policies. He tackles controversial cases pertaining to civil liberties, government surveillance, data mining, material support, material witnesses, indefinite detention, interrogation, and military tribunals. In each chapter Pious supplies the legal grounding and policy memos and excerpts from the rulings of landmark cases that set precedents. The book further includes an index containing relevant U.S. court cases, laws and draft legislation, and executive orders pertaining to the subject matter.

Rubin, Barry and Judith C. Rubin. 2002. *Anti-American Terrorism and the Middle East: A Documentary Reader*. Oxford: Oxford University Press.

The authors compile a vast trove of primary sources related to the War on Terrorism that offer insight into the political beliefs, philosophies, and policies of leading figures and states. Included are the writings of key Islamist theorists such as Sayed Qutb, manifestos from groups such as Hezbollah, recruitment materials from terrorist groups, and speeches about terrorism from statesmen of the United States, Israeli, Pakistani, Syrian, and Iranian governments. The book also includes official government pronouncements, most-wanted lists, and legal indict-ments for attacks committed by groups. This resource is invaluable for the insight it offers by collating such a wide variety of primary source material in one volume.

Warrick, Joby. 2016. *Black Flags: The Rise of ISIS*. New York: Anchor.

Warrick reviews the beginning of the Islamic State and demonstrates how the group began as the brainchild of a Jordanian named Abu Musab al-Zarqawi. He notes how Zarqawi's own roots were secular and criminal in nature, but after his involvement in the Afghan jihad he returned to Jordan and directed his efforts to overthrow-ing the monarchy of that country. Warrick notes that after being arrested and imprisoned in 1992, Zarqawi became more radicalized and adopted the controversial Salafi-Jihadist tenet of "takfirism," in which Muslims who are not religious clerics pronounce others to be unbelievers and subject to capital punishment. Interestingly, Zarqawi was released from prison when the Jordanian monarchy passed from King Hussein to his son King Abdullah II as part of a longstanding custom of releasing prisoners from various areas around the kingdom.

Warrick further demonstrates that after Zarqawi's release, he and his band became a loose affiliate of al Qaeda but quickly branched into their own entity as al Qaeda in Iraq. His group spearheaded the Sunni resistance to the United States and the Iraqi government during the 2000s. After Zarqawi was killed by American forces in 2006, the leadership of the group eventually passed to Abu Bakr al-Baghdadi who in 2014 proclaimed an Islamic caliphate under the Islamic State of Iraq and Syria (ISIS) after an expansive military campaign that captured large swaths of territory in eastern Syria and western Iraq. As the self-proclaimed caliph al-Baghdadi undertook a number of steps to add Islamic legitimacy to his image.

Wright, Lawrence. 2007. *The Looming Tower: Al-Qaeda and the Road to 9/11*. New York: Vintage.

Using the format of a storyteller, Wright chronicles the genesis of Islamist fundamentalism from Sayed Qutb's writings and the influence that they had on Egyptian militants during the Cold War. Many of these Egyptian militants were later absorbed into al Qaeda as the group networked jihadists from the Arab world to counter the Soviet invasion of Afghanistan.

Wright critically accounts for the period following this 1980s war in Afghanistan but before September 11, 2001. He notes that certain elements in the U.S. government did not treat the terrorist threat from al Qaeda as a priority, and further demonstrates the rivalry between the Central Intelligence Agency and the Federal Bureau of Investigation in the counterterrorism mission at that time. The book is an accessible and comprehensive treatment of counterterrorism with respect to al Qaeda prior to 9/11.

Articles and Reports

Abrahms, Max. 2006. "Why Terrorism Does Not Work." *International Security*, 31, no. 2 (Fall): 42–78.

Abrahms challenges the conventional wisdom that terrorist groups target civilians for strategic purposes. Reviewing a comprehensive dataset of foreign terrorist organizations, he finds that groups who target civilians rarely achieve their political aims, and that this is irrespective of the ideology motivating the group. His research also notes that militant groups who target military targets more frequently succeed in their efforts than terrorists do. Abrahms argues that this difference is explained by the tactic regarding target selection, which distinguishes terrorist attacks from insurgent attacks.

The strategic literature assumes that terrorism is a rational tactic of coercion, but Abrahms argues that attacking civilians is antithetical to bargaining. Rather than be coerced through bargaining, he argues that civilians who bear the brunt of terror attacks pressure their government to be uncompromising. Abrahms argues that the findings are driven not so much by how terrorists attack as much as the fundamental nature of what they attack. His empirical findings also call into question the motivation of terrorist groups to engage in such attacks since they largely do not work to achieve strategic aims. This opens the discussion to consider theories that are "astrategic" and couched more in psychological logics.

Carter, David B. 2012. "A Blessing or a Curse? State Support for Terrorist Groups." *International Organization*, 66, no. 1 (Winter): 129–151.

Carter conducts an empirical study on the effects that state sponsorship of militant groups has on the survival of those groups. He looks at 648 terrorist and insurgent groups between the years of 1968 and 2006 to ensure wide geographic and time-based coverage. He first distinguishes between state sponsorship and safe haven. In the case of the former a government provides material aid to a group, whether it be funding, resources, or other tangible benefits like intelligence. In the case of safe haven a state may provide those prior elements, but it also allows the group to operate from its own territory in conducting operations. Carter finds that groups that obtain state sponsorship but not safe haven live longer than their counterparts, whereas groups that had sponsorship and a safe haven had the highest risks of failure. He also identifies that young groups that live less than six years tend to fail at higher rates than groups who survive past the ten-year mark.

Crenshaw, Martha. 1981. "The Causes of Terrorism." *Comparative Politics*, 13, no. 4 (July): 379–399.

Crenshaw approaches the subject of terrorism from an academic perspective, asking questions related to why it happens. As a social scientist her aim in this article is to shift the discourse on terrorism from historical studies that are particular to specific groups to general similarities that manifest among different cases from different times. She asserts that there is a logic of terrorism rooted in elite dissatisfaction. By this she means that terrorism is used by a very specific minority of the population that distinguishes it from the scale of mass revolution. This dissatisfaction may be rooted in exclusion from the political process or concrete grievances due to the state. Frequently such groups are spurred by a major event involving some form of governmental abuse that in turn shocks these elites into action.

Crenshaw argues that terrorism is conducted as an immediate action to pursue defined political goals that challenge the state's authority; terrorists are impatient and want to realize results or progress toward their goals now and not in the future. In the latter half of her article she migrates from systemically driven motivations to organizational concerns as well as individual psychology at work. Crenshaw notes that attacks can be used to reinforce discipline and build morale within a resistance organization, and that some part of the motivation may be due to such internal calculations. She also notes that many groups follow a model akin to religious cults where intense commitment is required of members and outside interaction with others is limited.

Crenshaw also notes the need at the individual level to distinguish between the motivations and pathologies of leaders versus that of cadres, where the former issue plans and call for attacks, but the latter execute the violence. Individual motivations may be related to guilt but can also include vengeance as a driver. Altogether the article is useful as a guide for reviewing the levels of analysis in analyzing terrorism or a specific terrorist group.

Cronin, Audrey K. 2002. "Behind the Curve: Globalization and International Terrorism." *International Security,* **27, no. 3 (Winter): 30–58.**

Cronin argues that the United States is ill-prepared to counterterrorism in the aftermath of the 9/11 attacks. She first reviews the leading types of terrorist ideology, including leftist, rightist, separatist, and religious groupings. She cites data showing how cases of terrorism have trended increasingly toward fewer but more lethal religiously inspired attacks against American targets. She argues that although religious terrorism is the dominant variant today, much of it is oriented against globalization as an umbrella for secular, democratic, market-based capitalism.

According to Cronin, traditional cultures in the Middle East are caught in transition and see the United States representing the threat of globalization as the leading economic, military, and political power in the world. Consequently, the United States and its citizens bear the ire of groups who use violence as a rejection of globalization. She then notes how globalization's qualities aid the tradecraft of those who engage in terrorism by helping groups coordinate through information technology, move freely across borders due to limited barriers, and fund their efforts through various licit and illicit forms of international commerce.

Hegghammer, Thomas. 2010. "The Rise of Muslim Foreign Fighters: Islam and the Globalization of Jihad." *International Security*, 35, no. 3 (Winter): 53–94.

Hegghammer argues that Islamist militants were a major element in conflicts in the Muslim world since the 1980s, and that a great deal of their participation was as foreign fighters. He points to cases from Palestine, Somalia, the Balkans, Chechnya, and Afghanistan, among others. As foreign fighters these militants have origins in other countries but were motivated to travel to conflict zones and take up arms as part of a jihad. Fundamentally he seeks to address why an individual would actively seek to fight another person's war.

Hegghammer reviews rival explanations for the foreign fighter dynamic before proposing his own. The first hypothesis relates to religious difference, anticipating that militants would only join conflicts along specific forms of identity such as religion or to counter a foreign invasion. A second hypothesis expected that foreign fighters would selectively choose where to go and fight based on ideology or select resources. A third theory presumed that foreign fighters were only a factor when governments allowed their nationals to leave the country to participate. Fourth, Hegghammer considered whether advances in communications technology in the 1980s accounted for the increase in the ability of foreign fighters to coordinate. Finally, he reviewed a hypothesis that a growth of the global Islamist movement manifested as more foreign fighters.

Finding each of these prior explanations implausible, Hegghammer argues that the militarization of pan-Islamist movement based in Saudi Arabia and including figures such as Abdullah Azzam accounted for the rise in foreign fighters after 1980. He distinguishes between foreign fighters entering conflicts for more basic identity and allegiance reasons akin to an Islamic patriotism, and terrorists like those who belong to al Qaeda who are more ideological in nature. Hegghammer notes that the two differ in terms of regional popularity and that their aims can be contrary at times.

Jenkins, Bryan M. 2006. "The New Age of Terrorism." In *The McGraw-Hill Homeland Security Handbook: The Definitive Guide for Law Enforcement, EMT, and All Other Security Professionals*, edited by David G. Kamien, 117–130. New York: McGraw Hill Press.

Jenkins' original argument was that terrorism is theater in that terrorists want a lot of people watching their violent actions in order to coercively communicate their cause. This chapter outlines his revision qualifying that "Many of today's terrorists want a lot of people watching and a lot of people dead" (Jenkins, 119). He contends that terrorism in the contemporary era is bloodier than it was during the Cold War and that state sponsorship is less of a factor for groups who have obtained alternate means of financing. Moreover, he argues that terrorists have changed their organizational methods to take advantage of transnational connections afforded by globalization.

Johnston, Patrick B. 2012. "Does Decapitation Work? Assessing the Effectiveness of Leadership Targeting in Counterinsurgency Campaigns." *International Security*, 36, no. 4 (Spring): 47–79.

Johnston analyzes the effects of leadership decapitation as a tactic against insurgent or terrorist groups. Although this article title refers to counterinsurgency, it does provide useful insights into counterterrorism given the similarity in approaches. He argues against the position that targeting the leader of a group has negative effects on the longevity of that group or its ability to achieve its goals. These arguments are that groups are inherently durable at the societal level, that killing or removing a leader creates a martyrdom effect that boosts the movement, and that taking out the head of an organization causes the fragmentation of that group which makes it more survivable in the long run. Johnston critiques these arguments.

Using statistical tests of 118 decapitation attempts by a government, he demonstrates that terror campaigns hit by successful leadership decapitation strikes were 25 to 30% more likely to fail following that strike. He notes that this is far from a silver bullet approach, but that the impact is nonetheless important. He cautions that decapitation policies are likely to have the greatest impact in constraining insurgent and terrorist organizations when they are coupled with an overall strategy against the group rather than used as a single option.

Jordan, Jenna. 2014. "Attacking the Leader, Missing the Mark: Why Terrorist Groups Survive Decapitation Strikes." _International Security_, 38, no. 4 (Spring): 7–38.

Jordan critiques the work of Patrick Johnston and argues that leadership decapitation has generally negative effects regarding counterterrorism efforts against al Qaeda. She argues that Johnston's data is only relevant to cases of insurgency, and that many terrorist organizations are institutionally organized such that they can survive such strikes. For Jordan the real-world use of decapitation strikes also fuels negative public opinion against the government conducting the strike on behalf of the target. In this regard the communal support a group enjoys also reinforces its durability in light of decapitation strikes.

Jordan argues that policies that pursue terrorist groups are most likely to fail despite the loss of their leadership if they are younger, smaller, and secular. Jordan argues al Qaeda will not be affected by the tactic given their bureaucratic composition as an established group with a religious ideological orientation. Methodologically she uses descriptive statistics in her work but does not conduct statistical tests of her arguments.

Kurzman, Charles. 2002. "Bin Laden and Other Thoroughly Modern Muslims." *Contexts*, 1, no. 4 (Winter): 13–20.

Kurzman argues that despite popular perception, most Islamist militants in the contemporary era have significantly modern goals and use modern methods in pursuit of them. He argues that militants such as Osama bin Laden do not actually come from religious backgrounds before claiming authority, and instead charge the religious establishments of clerics in their home countries with operating in league with the secular, autocratic, and illegitimate governments.

Kurzman further contrasts other notable cases to argue that not all Islamic fundamentalists are necessarily traditional. He emphasizes how the government of Iran as well as al Qaeda both have bureaucratic organization and processes in their operation, as well as embrace modern technology. He contrasts these organizations with groups like the Taliban who largely rely on interpersonal networks to conduct business and shun many forms of technology. Kurzman ends his article by arguing that militant Islamists are widely unpopular among most Muslims in the world.

Kydd, Andrew H. and Barbara F. Walter. 2006. "The Strategies of Terrorism." *International Security*, 31, no. 1 (Summer): 49–80.

Kydd and Walter's article is useful for explaining the leading goals and strategies considered by terrorist groups.

They begin by reviewing the five major goals sought by terrorists, which are regime change, territorial change, policy change, social control, and/or status quo maintenance. In the first case a group seeks to destroy the current government and replace it with another one. In the case of territorial change, a group seeks autonomy for its own state or to bring territory into that of another. Policy change is a more restricted goal that focuses not on wholesale governmental or state-based boundary changes but on a government halting a specific action it takes. Social control is unique from the other examples because here political violence is directed to coerce individuals in society rather than the government. The final category of status quo maintenance is when terrorists seek to preserve an existing order or government through the use of political violence.

These five goals are not mutually exclusive, and so a group may pursue more than one goal, although the overwhelming majority of groups pursue one of the first two in practice. The authors next move to the ways that groups seek to achieve these goals. Kydd and Walter argue that the strategies are based on signaling by terrorists and so are used after identifying the subject of uncertainty as well as the target of persuasion. These five strategies are attrition, intimidation, provocation, spoiling, and outbidding. Attrition strategies seek to impose long-terms costs and wear down the resistance of the state. Intimidation strategies seek to target the population of the state to give in to the terrorists' demands in exchange for a terror group halting its violence. A provocation strategy is one where the terror group seeks to get the state to overreact with its own violence as part of its response. Finally, a strategy of spoiling is meant to prevent moderate elements of one's support base from reaching a negotiated deal with the government.

The authors argue that the use of strategy is connected to the desire of the group and the intended audience of its signaling. If a group wishes to make known its desire for power, it can target the enemy government with a strategy of attrition and can target the population with a strategy of intimidation. If the group wishes to make known its resolve, it can use attrition against the government but outbidding against the population. A group that is seeking to signal its trustworthiness and credibility can adopt a strategy of spoiling for the state and provocation for the population.

Mousseau, Michael. 2002. "Market Civilization and Its Clash with Terror." *International Security,* 27, no. 3 (Winter): 5–29.

Mousseau addresses the cause of terrorism after 9/11 by arguing that it stems from a fundamental clash of culture between societies based on their level of interpersonal trust. This is unlike scholars such as Samuel Huntington who argue that the fault lines of conflict would be through the clash of various civilizations. Mousseau argues that societies fall into one of two types: clientelistic or market-based. In the first case society is organized such that trust is specific to an in-group, with individuals distrusting those in an out-group. Interaction in these societies is through reciprocal exchanges between a patron and a client, and social ties extend beyond the direct trade in goods or services. In the clientelistic system behavior is largely based on social linkages that define the in-group, such as extended family or shared ethnicity. For example, a client could offer their loyalty in exchange for the patron providing security.

Mousseau sees tribal societies as one example of this, although not an exclusive one since industrialized countries such as Italy and Greece or postindustrial regimes such as the fascist powers also exhibit clientelistic frameworks. Conversely, a market system allows for trust to be based on impersonal instruments such as contracts, with no bonds of loyalty beyond what is specified in the contract. Mousseau argues that terrorism stems from the threat that patrons in clientelistic systems face with the transition of their societies toward market-based practices. Because these actors are losing their paramount place in the arrangement, they resort to violence as a rejection of the impersonal market culture. The argument is interesting in that it seeks to account for conflict between largely developed states and terrorist groups from lesser-developed societies; however, the model sees the root of this not as inherently economic or political, but rather sociological.

Pape, Robert. 2003. "The Strategic Logic of Suicide Terrorism." *American Political Science Review*, **97, no. 3 (August): 343–361.**

Pape provides a rational choice perspective to explain the use of suicide terrorism. He argues that suicide terrorism is used by groups to specifically target democracies in order to concede territory to the terrorist group. Per his argument a group that resorts to suicide terrorism is doing so for nationalist reasons and as a form of signaling that it will take extreme measures to get its way to remove a foreign occupier. As an example, he cites the case involving the government of Israel and the terrorist group Hamas that led to Israel's withdrawal from the Gaza Strip. Pape's data covers other cases, but he does not code or review the data per attack, instead grouping it into a category of linked attacks that he terms a campaign. Moreover, he does not conduct a statistical analysis of the attack data and other measures, sticking with descriptive statistics and inference.

Post, Jerrold M. 1990. "Terrorist Psycho-Logic: Terrorist Behavior as a Product of Psychological Forces." In Walter Reich, ed., *Origins of Terrorism: Psychologies, Ideologies, Theologies, States of Mind.* **Washington, D.C.: Woodrow Wilson Center Press.**

Jerrold Post served as a psychologist with the Central Intelligence Agency where he devised psychological profiles of world leaders. After moving to academia he worked to establish a formal program in this field and in this chapter provides a psychological argument for understanding terrorist motivations. Whereas some researchers in political science see terrorists as using the tactic as a violent means to pursue a political aim, Post argues that terrorists are psychologically disposed to commit violence and join terrorist organizations in order to do so.

His argument is the opposite of the traditional political science approach in that violence is the desired end, and not a means to an end. Specifically, he argues that most terrorists do not have a mental disorder but do have personality disturbances that can increase their propensity to engage in the behavior. Post argues that unresolved identity issues can create a dynamic of splitting where the individual blames negative attributes of their self on an outside enemy while retaining their positive sense of self. Those who see themselves as unsuccessful in life, be it personally, in school, or in the work force, can displace their failure by blaming an external enemy as a coping mechanism.

Post further argues that the group dynamics of a terrorist organization reinforce this splitting in that the group offers safety through solidarity and reinforces the "bad" outside actor as the state. He adds that a group's leader must continually "use" violence to rationalize its existence, stay relevant, and keep its members happy since they ultimately are seeking this violence. In this manner the leader of a group is seen as facing pressure internally from fellow members just as much as from government security forces. Post claims his provocative argument explains why groups conduct attacks that may not be seen as strategic and also why terrorist groups may opt to continue their campaigns even when at least some of their stated goals are achievable through negotiations.

Sandler, Todd. 2003. "Collective Action and Transnational Terrorism." *The World Economy*, 26, no. 6 (June): 779–802.

As an economist Sandler approaches the study of transnational terrorism using rational choice logic in comparing the incentives facing both actors in terrorism: the non-state terrorist group and the government of the country affected. He introduces the established concept of collective action to the study of terrorism, where there are greater transaction costs associated with coordinating actions among larger, more complex organizations than smaller ones. He notes that the logic of collective action gives certain advantages to transnational groups who can pool their limited resources through networking with one another to share training, expertise, and resources. Conversely, nation-states are more complex entities made up of many different organizations and are less likely to give up their autonomy in order to cooperate on the counterterrorism front.

Sandler further argues that a substitution effect is at work when governments shore up identified vulnerabilities, such as was the case with introducing metal detectors in airports. After these machines were widely put into service, the number of skyjackings declined but other forms of terrorism such as assassination increased. Terrorist groups shift to new target sets that are not protected. Comprehensively the natural advantage in terms of organization lies with terrorist groups who can more easily solve collective action problems than the state.

Sandler also argues that while the vast expenditures associated with homeland security and counterterrorism efforts seem in excess of the actual damage caused by terrorists, there is a psychological rationale at stake that warrants paying the price. Governments must appear in control in dealing with the issue, and a minimalist approach does not provide the politically valued sense of safety that funding those apparatuses does.

Nonprint Resources

Acosta, Benjamin. 2020. "Revolutionary and Militant Organizations Dataset." Accessed February 28, 2022. https://www.revolutionarymilitant.org

Acosta constructs an original and comprehensive dataset of 537 revolutionary and militant organizations through the year 2020, which includes violent groups such as terrorists and insurgents but also includes nonviolent resistance groups. Access is free, and the dataset comes in two formats; the first is static and provides an overview of each group that aggregates the variables over its life-time, and the other is dynamic and tracks the movement of variables each year over its lifetime. Users of the dynamic data can filter the results on the "terrorism" variable to focus on only terrorist groups, or those who used the tactic in any given year. The variables include traditional measures such as the group's size, ideology, leadership, the number of attacks and deaths inflicted, target types, and birth and death dates. It also includes network data not common to other datasets, such as involvement in criminal activity, the number of ties a group has with others, state sponsors, providers of safe havens, and transitions to the political process. One of the more unique contributions of Acosta's data is the inclusion of an achievement measure that scores the group's level of success in a year compared to its stated aims. This dataset serves as a fantastic first stop in one's research to understand not just the group and its internal factors, but also how it is connected to other groups, state allies, and state adversaries in the international system. It also allows those with statistical training to assess the correlations of groups.

Acosta, Benjamin. 2018. "Suicide Attack Network Dataset." Accessed February 28, 2022. https://www.revolutionary militant.org/sand

Acosta constructs an original dataset that tracks recorded suicide attacks from 1927 until 2017. The data accounts for the date and location of each attack, whether the target was foreign or domestic, the number killed and wounded in the attack, whether the attacker's enemy is considered part of an in-group or out-group, and if the attacker was a female bomber. The latter is useful for those studying the phenomenon of gender as it relates to terrorism studies. Acosta's data is unique in its scope by accounting for all recorded cases of this specific form of attack, to include both terrorist and insurgent incidents. Users interested in the terrorism data alone can filter the results on target type to focus on those attacks. Much of this data enables researchers to test propositions about whether suicide attacks are motivated by a strategic logic of foreign occupiers, or if the motivation is broader and sociocultural in orientation. The wide scope of coverage and free access enables users to filter down to specific groups to assess their use of the tactic over time, and so is useful to add a quantitative accounting of qualitative research of a particular group.

Assayas, Olivier, director. 2010. *Carlos*. IFC Films. 5 hr., 19 min. https://www.criterionchannel.com/carlos

Assayas' critically acclaimed series about Illich Ramirez Sanchez ("Carlos the Jackal") provides insight into the dynamics of terrorist actors operating within their organizations. The work is a realistic depiction of the experiences of this high-profile transnational terrorist and is useful for understanding Cold War politics as Carlos and his operatives work with various Marxist national-liberation movements along with state sponsors such as East Germany, Libya, and the Soviet Union. Assayas' work showcases how frequently terrorist actors are enabled by other major actors in the international system to commit attacks. The film particularly highlights the roles of extremist ideological motivation and how it interacts with the personalities of individuals within such groups to inspire and motivate fellow members to commit acts of violence in the name of their antisystem cause.

Center for International Security and Cooperation. 2019. "Mapping Militants Project." Accessed February 28, 2022. https://cisac.fsi.stanford.edu/mappingmilitants/mapping militants

The Mapping Militants Project is a web-accessible data resource that charts the relationships that 121 militant groups have with one another, as well as the evolution of these groups over time. The data includes traditional variables about terrorist groups, such as their leadership, ideology, strategic aims, geographic area of operation, and relative size. The dataset's major contributions are outlining the connections that groups have with one another as well as connections between these nonstate groups and government sponsors and their communities. This relational network data is not common but is instrumental for those seeking a systemic approach to the study of terrorism. The resource is especially useful for those conducting background research on the evolution of groups. Some groups adopt regular name changes or undergo splits as they evolve, and these changes can be confusing for new researchers without access to detailed profiles chronicling the changes.

Federation of American Scientists. 2022. "Congressional Research Service Reports on Terrorism." Accessed March 14, 2022. https://sgp.fas.org/crs/terror/index.html

The Federation of American Scientists provide a directory of Congressional Research Service (CRS) reports on terrorism topics. The CRS is the research arm of the U.S. Congress that is housed in the Library of Congress. Researchers with the CRS are tasked with providing summaries of important issues and legislation related to them. Reports are written for members of Congress who are largely nonspecialists in the subject matter yet will vote on legislation and matters related to it. Since the efforts are publicly funded, the reports are widely available. Compared to other resources on terrorism, these reports are free to access and span a variety of topics including legal disputes, legislation, profiles of groups, tradecraft, and other such related issues. Moreover, the reports are updated regularly as situations change or new developments arise. Because of the wide coverage and up-to-date nature, these reports are an invaluable first step in one's own research. The website can be thought of as a type of portal offering gateways to research topics within the umbrella of terrorism.

National Consortium for the Study of Terrorism and Responses to Terrorism (START). 2022. "Global Terrorism Database." Accessed February 28, 2022. https://www.start .umd.edu/gtd

The National Consortium for the Study of Terrorism and Responses to Terrorism (START) housed at the University of Maryland offers the Global Terrorism Database (GTD). The database ranges from 1970 through 2019 and accounts for over 201,000 documented attacks with filters for variables such as the country the attack took place in, the type of attacks, what type of target was hit, what weapon was used, the group that is credited with the attack, as well as data on casualties. One caution in using the data is to be precise with the filters as a fair number of the cases tabulated involve attacks against military and national police forces. By most definitions attacks on those targets are examples of insurgency and not terrorism. An additional warning is that there are a number of cases of duplicate entries regarding attacks. Despite these points the GTD remains the most comprehensive data related to the subject given its wide scope of coverage. Moreover, access to the data is free for research purposes.

National Counterterrorism Center. 2016. "Counterterrorism Guide: The Methods and Tactics of Global Terrorism." https://www.dni.gov/nctc/index.html

The National Counterterrorism Center (NCTC) is an element within the Office of the Director of National Intelligence, and it serves as an interagency body to help coordinate the U.S. government's response to international terrorism. NCTC's website features this International Terrorism Guide with interactive sections on the methods and tactics used by groups. These guides are useful for first responders and other citizens who seek to better understand and prepare for possible attacks. Information includes reference material on different types of conventional explosives and the appropriate evacuation distances for various types of devices, indicators of chemical weapons attacks, the effects of chemical and biological weapons on the human body, and doctored travel documents. The website also features profiles of groups designated as foreign terrorist organizations by the U.S. government. Relatedly, it lists individuals who are wanted by the U.S. government for their involvement in prior attacks and consequently are part of the Rewards for Justice program.

Rand Corporation. 2022. "Terrorism." Accessed February 28, 2022. https://www.rand.org/topics/terrorism.html

The Rand Corporation is a nonprofit think-tank that is commissioned by government, corporate and academic institutions, and private endowments to conduct policy research on matters of relevance. At its creation in 1948 the think-tank focused on defense issues but has since branched out to include many other public policy topics including health and education. Rand maintains a strong national defense portfolio and one subset includes research on terrorism. The website details commentaries from researchers and offers links to its latest reports on various terrorism subjects. The menu on the webpage also allows a user to drill down for resources on specific subsets of terrorism, such as financings, domestic, or that related to different weapons of mass destruction. Since the bulk of this research is commissioned by public agencies access to these resources is free.

United States Department of State. 2022. "Foreign Terrorist Organizations." Bureau of Counterterrorism. Accessed February 28, 2022. https://www.state.gov/foreign-terrorist -organizations

> The State Department has the portfolio in the U.S. government for foreign relations. As part of these duties the department maintains the list of designated foreign terrorist organizations, of which there are presently 73. Individuals in the United States who engage with, finance, or otherwise support groups on this list are engaging in criminal activity as a matter of law. The resource details the process for how a group gets designated within the executive branch, subject to congressional approval. Note that the U.S. government requires that an organization be foreign in nature but that there is no specific requirement that it be a non-state actor. For instance, the U.S. list includes the Iranian Revolutionary Guard Corps of the Islamic Republic of Iran. The website also lists the 15 groups who have been delisted for those conducting historical research of groups or who wish to specifically study the politics surrounding listing and delisting.

7 Chronology

Terrorism is a longstanding form of political conflict even if the contemporary word to describe it was derived from the more recent French Revolution. The following chronology demonstrates how acts of terrorism since the late 1800s were largely perpetrated by small secular groups targeting political leaders for the purposes of launching a wider revolution. Starting in the late 1990s, attacks by terrorists generally shifted to mass casualty attacks based on religious ideologies.

c. 54 The *Sicarii* (dagger-wielders) Jewish zealots first conduct attacks with daggers against fellow Jews who were complicit with Rome's occupation of Judea.

1092 The Ismaili assassins conduct their first political assassination on behalf of the Naziri sultan by killing rival Seljuk statesman Nizam al-Mulk.

June 1793 to July 1794 The French Revolution enters a period called "the Reign of Terror" where Jacobin revolutionaries commit mass executions of aristocrats and monarchists in gruesome public spectacles.

February 17, 1880 *Narodnaya Volya* member Stephan Khalturin uses dynamite to bomb the Winter Palace in St. Petersburg, Russia in a failed attempt to kill Tsar Alexander II.

Many recent terror attacks have been carried out by those adhering to either Salafi-Jihadist or white supremacist ideologies. Here New Zealand citizens lay flowers at a mosque as a show of support after Muslims were targeted and killed by a white supremacist in the 2019 attacks in the city of Christchurch. (Michael Williams/Dreamstime.com)

March 13, 1881   *Narodnaya Volya* member Ignacy Hryniew-iecki assassinates Tsar Alexander II of Russia in St. Petersburg with a bomb.

January 2 and 24, 1885   Irish Fenians conduct a series of bombings in London targeting an Underground station, the House of Commons, and the Tower of London.

May 4, 1886   The Haymarket Riot by American labor work-ers in Chicago ends in a bombing of police by anarchists and a trial that leads to the execution of four, galvanizing the anar-chist worker's movement.

June 24, 1894   Anarchist Sante Geronimo Caserio assassi-nates French President Sadi Carnot in Lyon.

August 8, 1897   Anarchist Michele Angiolillo assassinates Spanish Prime Minister Antonio Cánovas del Castillo in Mondragón, Spain.

September 10, 1898   Anarchist Luigi Lucheni assassinates Empress Elisabeth of Austria in Geneva, Switzerland.

July 29, 1900   Anarchist Gaetano Bresci assassinates King Umberto I of Italy in Monza, Italy.

September 6, 1901   Inspired by the assassination of Umberto I of Italy, anarchist Leon Czolgosz assassinates American Presi-dent William McKinley in Buffalo, New York.

February 1, 1908   Anarchists Manuel Buica and Alfredo Costa assassinate Portuguese King Carlos I and Crown Prince Luis Filipe in Lisbon.

September 14, 1911   Anarchist Dmitri Bogorov assassinates Russian Prime Minister Peter Stolpyin in Kiev, Ukraine.

November 12, 1912   Anarchist Manuel Pardiñas assassinates Spanish Prime Minister José Canalejas.

March 8, 1913   Anarchist Alexandros Schinas assassinates Greek King George I in Thessalonica.

October 13, 1914   Anarchist followers of Luigi Galleani in New York city set off the first of many bombs that target politi-cal figures across the United States over the next six years.

November 1919 to January 1920   In response to the Galleanist bombings, Attorney General A. Mitchell Palmer directs law enforcement authorities around the United States to arrest over 10,000 individuals in a series of raids targeting anarchists and leftist labor activists.

September 16, 1920   Anarchists kill 40 and wound over 100 individuals in a bombing attack on Wall Street's financial district using a device delivered via horse-drawn wagon.

March 8, 1921   Anarchists assassinate Spanish Prime Minister Eduardo Dato Iradier in Madrid.

November 6, 1944   The Jewish militant group LeHi assassinates British Minister for the Middle East Lord Moyne.

July 22, 1946   The Jewish militant group Irgun bombs the British headquarters at the King David Hotel in Jerusalem, killing 91.

September 30, 1956   Women militants of the Algerian National Liberation Front plant two bombs targeting restaurants in the *pieds-noirs* section of the city of Algiers. The French government responds to the terror campaign by deploying its paratroopers to the conflict who use heavy-handed measures.

February 22, 1972   Terrorists from the Popular Front for the Liberation of Palestine (PFLP) hijack Lufthansa flight 649. They direct the crew to fly to Aden, South Yemen, and demand $5 million from the company for the release of the hostages and the aircraft. The West German government pays the ransom.

September 5, 1972   Terrorists from the Palestinian group Black September kidnap and kill 11 Israeli athletes during the Summer Olympics in Munich, Germany. This becomes one of the first globally televised cases of terrorism.

November 21, 1974   The Provisional Irish Republican Army bombs two pubs in the English city of Birmingham, killing 21 and injuring 182.

December 21, 1975   Terrorists from the Popular Front for the Liberation of Palestine kidnap hostages at the meeting of the Organization of Petroleum Exporting Countries (OPEC) in Vienna, Austria.

June 27, 1976   Terrorists from the Popular Front for the Liberation of Palestine and the Revolutionary Cells hijack Air France flight 139 and direct the aircrew to land at Benghazi, Libya, to take on fuel and then on to Entebbe, Uganda, where they are welcomed by Dictator Idi Amin. There the hostages are moved to buildings. Israeli commandos conduct a nighttime rescue operation by landing at the airport, saving the hostages, and flying out. All but four hostages are saved, and one commando dies in the action.

November 19, 1977   The military unit Delta Force is created by the United States government in order to have a dedicated unit to specialize in counterterrorism actions.

October 25, 1978   The Foreign Intelligence Surveillance Act (FISA) enters into effect. The law stipulates the process by which the federal government can surveil those suspected of engaging in espionage. The law is later amended to include those suspected of terrorism.

August 2, 1980   Terrorists from the fascist Armed Revolutionary Nuclei group bomb the Bologna railway station and kill 85. Another 200 are wounded in the attack.

October 23, 1983   Hezbollah suicide bombers attack the U.S. Marine Corps and French paratrooper barracks in Beirut, Lebanon. They kill 241 U.S. Marines and 58 French paratroopers, and the remaining forces from both the United States and France later withdraw from the country.

June 23, 1985   Terrorists from the Babbar Khalsa International affix a bomb to Air India flight 182. The bomb detonates over the Atlantic Ocean, destroying the 747 aircraft and killing all 329 passengers and crew. Most passengers are Hindu, and Babbar Khalsa's aims are to create a separate Sikh state of Khalistan out of the territory of India.

June 19, 1987 Separatist group Euskadi Ta Askatasuna (ETA; Basque Homeland and Liberty) bombs a Hipercor store in Barcelona. The blast kills 21 and wounds 45.

December 21, 1988 Pan American Airlines Flight 103 is destroyed by a prepositioned bomb while flying over Lockerbie, Scotland. The bombing kills all 259 on board, and the falling debris kills 11 on the ground. The government of Libya later takes credit for the attack.

March 17, 1992 A truck-born Hezbollah suicide bomber attacks the Israeli Embassy in Buenos Aires, Argentina, killing 29 and injuring over 200.

July 16, 1992 The Shining Path terrorist group targets a bank in Lima, Peru. The bomb kills 25 and injures 250.

February 26, 1993 Pakistani national Ramzi Yousef and others carry out a truck bombing attack against the World Trade Center that kills six and injures over 1,000.

July 18, 1994 A van-born Hezbollah suicide bomber attacks the Argentine Israelite Mutual Association in Buenos Aires, killing 84 and injuring over 300.

December 24, 1994 Islamic Armed Group (GIA) terrorists hijack Air France flight 8969 while still on the ground in Algiers. The aircraft's intended destination is Paris where the terrorists had planned to crash the aircraft in the city. After multiple days on the tarmac the aircraft is given clearance to depart Algeria but must stop in Marseilles to take on fuel. There French commandos raid the aircraft and engage in a shootout that kills the four terrorists and saves hundreds of passengers with the loss of three hostages.

March 20, 1995 Terrorists from the Japanese group Aum Shinrikyo attack the Tokyo subway using sarin nerve gas, killing 14 and injuring over 1,000. The group hopes the attack will cause a nuclear world war that will bring about the apocalypse.

April 19, 1995   Timothy McVeigh uses a truck bomb to attack the federal building in Oklahoma City, killing 168 and wounding almost 700. The attack remains the deadliest act of domestic terrorism in U.S. history.

July 25, 1995   The Islamic Armed Group (GIA) initiates the first in a series of bombings against the French metro systems in Paris and Lyon for the French government's support of the government of Algeria during the Algerian Civil War. The various attacks wound 190 and kill 8.

November 24, 1995   Chechen rebels place a package filled with the radioactive element cesium in the Ismailovsky Park in Moscow, Russia. The rebels communicate the location of the materials to a Russian television network to demonstrate that they can create a "dirty" bomb that mates the cesium with a conventional explosive to disperse the materials.

December 17, 1996   Terrorists of the Túpac Amaru Revolutionary Movement take the Japanese ambassador to Peru hostage at his residence along with other dignitaries. After months of captivity, Peruvian commandos initiate a successful hostage rescue operation in April that frees most hostages and kills all terrorists.

November 17, 1997   Members of the Islamic Group terrorist organization kill 58 tourists and four Egyptian nationals in a mass shooting and slashing attack at the popular Temple of Hatshepsut in Luxor, Egypt. The attacks serve to discredit the organization by turning public opinion against it.

August 7, 1998   Al Qaeda bombs the U.S. embassies in Dar es Salaam, Tanzania, and Nairobi, Kenya. The attacks kill 224 and injure over 4,000; the vast majority of the victims are Africans. The attacks are revenge for the U.S. government's role in helping the government of Egypt arrest and extradite four members of Egyptian Islamic Jihad from Albania to Egypt.

August 15, 1998   The Real Irish Republican Army faction targets the Northern Irish town of Omagh with a car bomb that kills 29 and injure 220. The bombing causes the governments of the United Kingdom and the Republic of Ireland to pass new anti-terrorism laws and helps mobilize support for the peace process.

September 4 to September 16, 1999   Four large apartment buildings across Russia are bombed, killing over 300 and wounding over 1,000. The government claims that Chechen separatists are responsible, but many suspect the involvement of Russian security services. The attacks help catapult Vladimir Putin into the presidency in 2000 to lead Russia through the Second Chechen War.

May 23, 2001   The United Nations International Convention for the Suppression of Terrorist Bombings enters into effect and is ultimately ratified by 170 countries. The treaty outlaws terrorist bombings.

September 11, 2001   Al Qaeda operatives kill nearly 3,000 and injure tens of thousands more in a set of complex coordinated suicide attacks against targets in New York and Washington, D.C., using hijacked airliners as missiles. The attacks are the most lethal terrorist acts in history.

September 18 to October 12, 2001   Seven letters containing weaponized anthrax spores are mailed to media personalities and senators in the weeks after 9/11. The spores kill five individuals, most working in mailrooms after some of the materials leak from the envelopes.

October 26, 2001   President George W. Bush signs the Patriot Act into law, giving increased surveillance and arrest powers to federal law enforcement.

December 13, 2001   Five terrorists from Lashkar-e-Taiba assault the Indian Parliament in New Delhi with automatic and explosive infantry weapons. The perpetrators die in the attack attempting to kill Indian politicians but kill nine Indian security members. Some speculate the attack was directed by Pakistan's Inter-Services Intelligence (ISI) to help Osama bin

Laden escape from Afghanistan into Pakistan by redirecting Pakistani security forces away from the Afghan border.

April 10, 2002   The United Nations International Convention for the Suppression of the Financing of Terrorism enters into effect and is ultimately ratified by 188 countries. The treaty outlaws the financing of terrorist acts.

May 8, 2002   Jose Padilla is arrested in Chicago and charged with being part of an al Qaeda plot to use a radiological weapon against the United States. Padilla had extensively traveled in the Middle East and Central Asia in the company of al Qaeda members. One month later he is designated an enemy combatant and remains in detention until standing trial in May 2007. The case is controversial given he is an American citizen but was not granted *habeas corpus* due to President Bush's designation of him as an enemy combatant. He later was indicted and went to trial but for charges different than those originally levied against him.

October 2, 2002   Over the course of three weeks John Allen Muhammad and Lee Boyd Malvo begin randomly targeting people in the Washington, D.C., area with sniper attacks. They kill 10 and wound three before being arrested at a rest stop in Virginia.

October 12, 2002   Two operatives from the al Qaeda-linked terrorist Islamic Group (Jemaah Islamiyah) target two nightclubs in Bali, Indonesia killing 202 and wounding over 200 more. The terrorists use a suicide bomber wearing a backpack bomb in one strike and a parked car bomb in the other.

October 23, 2002   Chechen terrorists of the Special Purpose Islamic Regiment take hundreds hostage at the Dubrovka Theater in Moscow. Russian security forces pump chemical agents into the air ducts and storm the theater in a rescue attempt that kills 130 hostages and injures over 700.

November 25, 2002   The Department of Homeland Security is created after President Bush signs the Homeland Security

Act into law. It reorganizes the federal government and absorbs Customs and Border Protection, Citizenship and Immigration Services, the Federal Emergency Management Agency, the U.S. Coast Guard, and the Secret Service, and it creates the Transportation Security Administration. The department officially begins operations on March 1, 2003.

September 1, 2004 Terrorists from the Chechen group Riyad us-Saliheen take hundreds of school children hostage at Beslan in the Caucasus. Russian forces storm the school in a military assault that leads to the deaths of 333 and the wounding of another 783.

March 11, 2004 Al Qaeda terrorists conduct a coordinated bombing of Madrid's commuter rail services. The explosions kill 193 and injure over 2,000 just three days before the general election. The conservative government that participated in the war in Iraq falls in the election to the Socialist party that removes Spanish forces from participating.

July 7, 2005 British jihadi terrorists attack London's bus and rail transportation network with a series of coordinated bombings that kill 52 and wound 784. Al Qaeda later claims credit for the strike.

July 23, 2005 Members of the Abdullah Azzam Brigades carry out a coordinated attack using three suicide bombers against markets and hotels in Sharm El Sheikh, Egypt. The locations were filled with tourists, and the bombers killed 88 while wounding another 150.

February 22, 2006 al Qaeda in Iraq terrorists execute a complex coordinated bombing of the al-Askari Shrine in Samarra, Iraq. The shrine is one of the holiest in Shi'a Islam, and the explosions enflame tensions between Iraqi Sunni and Shi'a such that hundreds more die in reprisal killings in the following days.

August 14, 2007 Terrorists use four vehicle-born suicide bombs to attack Yazidis in Iraq's Nineveh governorate. The coordinated strike involved a fuel tanker with the resulting explosions killing close to 800 and wounded over 1,500 more.

November 26, 2008 A group of 10 militants from the Pakistani group Lashkar-e-Taiba carry out a multiday terror attack against various targets in Mumbai, India, using assault rifles, grenades, and other explosives. The terrorists are aided by Pakistan's Inter-Services Intelligence (ISI) with tactical intelligence during the attack.

July 22, 2011 Terrorist Anders Breivik attacks Norwegian government buildings in Oslo, Norway, with a vehicle-born bomb before moving to Utøya Island to engage in a mass shooting of youth at the Norwegian Labor Party's summer camp. Breivik kills 77 and wounds more than 300 in the attacks.

September 11, 2012 Terrorists from Ansar al-Sharia kill four Americans and seven Libyans, including U.S. Ambassador Christopher Stevens, in an attack on the American consulate in Benghazi, Libya.

April 15, 2013 Brothers Tamerlan and Dzhokhar Tsarnaev bomb the finish line of the Boston Marathon, killing three and injuring 264.

September 21, 2013 Al Shabaab terrorists attack the Israeli-owned Westgate mall in Nairobi, Kenya, using automatic rifles and grenades. The operatives kill 67 and injure 175 in the mall over the course of the next two days.

May 5, 2014 Boko Haram militants kill over 300 Nigerians in the towns of Gamboru and Ngala using machine guns and automatic rifles. The militants baited Nigerian security forces away from the village to commit the attack.

January 7 and 9, 2015 Al Qaeda in the Arabian Peninsula terrorists attack the *Charlie Hebdo* publication's offices, and an Islamic State terrorist later attacks the Hypercacher kosher market in Paris. The terrorists target the publication for having drawn the Prophet Muhammad in earlier magazine issues.

June 2, 2015   The USA Freedom Act is signed into law to continue with certain provisions of the Patriot Act but to partially curtail government surveillance of internet metadata by requiring that telecommunications companies store the data.

June 26, 2015   An Islamic State terrorist carries out an attack at a beachside resort in Sousse, Tunisia. The gunmen kill 38 European tourists and injures another 39 persons.

October 31, 2015   Islamic State terrorists from the Egyptian Wilayat Sinai affiliate plant a bomb on Russian Metrojet flight 9268 containing tourists returning to their home countries in Russia and Eastern Europe. The bomb detonates approximately 23 minutes into the flight, killing all 224 on board.

November 13, 2015   Terrorists from the Islamic State carry out a series of highly coordinated attacks on various targets in Paris, including the Bataclan theater. They use assault rifles and suicide belts to kill 130 and injure 416.

December 2, 2015   A San Bernardino County employee and his wife kill 14 of his coworkers in a mass shooting at their workplace and claim to be motivated to die as martyrs for jihad. The terrorists are later intercepted by law enforcement in the city of Redlands and are killed in a shootout. After the attack the Islamic State claims the two as belonging to the organization.

March 22, 2016   An Islamic State cell conducts a complex coordinated suicide bomb attack against the airport and two metro stations in Brussels, Belgium. The five terrorists kill 32 individuals and wound over 300 others in the bombings.

June 12, 2016   Terrorist Omar Mateen carries out a mass shooting at the Pulse Nightclub in Orlando, Florida. The club was frequented by members of the gay community. Mateen kills 49 and injures another 58 over the course of the shooting and calls 9-1-1 during the attack to pledge loyalty to the Islamic State.

July 3, 2016　The Islamic State carries out a coordinated suicide bomb attack in the Karrada district of Baghdad, Iraq, targeting Shi'a shoppers. Over 340 die with nearly 250 more injured. The attack takes place days following the recapture of Fallujah by the government of Iraq from the Islamic State.

July 14, 2016　An Islamic State terrorist driving a large cargo truck intentionally drives into crowds celebrating Bastille Day in Nice, France. The terrorist kills 87 and wounds over 450 members of the public.

December 19, 2016　An Islamic State terrorist intentionally drives a large delivery truck into crowds at the Christmas Market in Berlin, Germany. The terrorist first shot and killed the truck's driver before killing 12 and wounding 55 others in the vehicle attack.

June 7, 2017　Islamic State terrorists attack the Iranian Parliament and the Tomb of Ruhollah Khomeini in Tehran using assault rifles and suicide bombs. The terrorists kill 18 and injure 52 over the course of the attacks in retaliation for the Iranian government's efforts against the Islamic State in Iraq and Syria.

October 14, 2017　Al Shabaab terrorists kill nearly 600 and injure over 300 when a truck bomb packed with over two tons of explosives detonates at one of Mogadishu's busiest intersections. Officials believe that the target was international forces at the airport nearby, and that the moment of detonation was unplanned.

November 24, 2017　Islamic State terrorists from the Egyptian Wilayat Sinai affiliate target Sufi Muslims at the Al-Rawda Mosque in Sinai, Egypt, using small arms and explosives. The gunmen kill 311 and wound 128 in the attack.

July 25, 2018　Islamic State terrorists attack ethnic Druze at As-Suwayda, Syria, in a coordinated assault involving firearms and suicide explosive vests. The terrorists killed 258 and injured another 180.

March 15, 2019   Terrorist Brenton Tarrant targets a mosque and Islamic center in Christchurch, New Zealand, where he shoots 51 Muslims dead and wounds another 40. In a manifesto Tarrant cites the Oslo attack in 2011 as an inspiration and his desire to halt non-white immigration.

April 21, 2019   Terrorists with ties to the Islamic State kill 269 and injure over 500 in complex coordinated bombing attacks against churches and hotels in Sri Lanka on Easter Sunday.

August 3, 2019   Terrorist Patrick Crusius kills 23 and wounds another 23 in a shooting at a Walmart in El Paso, Texas. Crusius specifically targets Hispanics in the attack and in an online manifesto cites inspiration from the Christchurch attack along with opposition to corporate environmental destruction and use of immigrant Hispanic labor.

October 15, 2021   The Islamic State Khorasan Province group kills 65 Afghans in a coordinated suicide bomb attack at the Fatima Mosque in Kandahar, Afghanistan. The group used four bombers and wounded over 70 in the attacks.

August 26, 2021   The Islamic State Khorasan Province group kills 170 Afghans and 13 American military troops in a suicide bomb attack at the Kabul International Airport during the fall of Kabul to the Taliban.

March 4, 2022   An operative of the Islamic State Khorasan Province group kills 62 and injures 196 in a combined shooting and suicide bomb attack at a Shia mosque in Peshawar, Pakistan.

March 23, 2022   Members of al Shabaab carry out coordinated terror attacks in Beledweyne, Somalia, in the run-up to parliamentary elections. The attackers first kill a female Member of Parliament with a suicide bomb before attacking the hospital with a suicide car bomb where the injured had been taken. The terrorists kill 48 and wound 108 in the blasts. On the same day in Beledweyne terrorists also kill a retired politician in a restaurant in a shooting attack.

October 29, 2022   Al Shabaab terrosists attack a busy inter-section in Mogadishu with two sequential car bombs. The first bombing hits the Education Ministry and the second hits emergency responders after they arrived at the site. The blasts kill over 121 and wound over 350.

Glossary

This glossary provides a list of key terms commonly used in the context of discussing terrorism and counterterrorism, both at the national and global levels.

Anarchism an ideology calling for the elimination of societal order and governmental authority, to be replaced by voluntary forms of organization by individuals.

Asymmetry the condition between two political organizations or actors where there is a dramatic imbalance between them regarding power and/or the ability to use force.

Caliphate an Islamic empire whose leader, the caliph, is a political ruler over a society based around Islamic law (*sharia*); first created with Muhammad's opening conquests in the Arabian peninsula c. 630.

Censorship the prohibition of speech, art, or written works when governing authorities deem it to be politically dangerous or threatening to the security of their rule.

Christian Identity Movement a radical white-supremacist belief system adhering to the idea that God's chosen people are only of European-white origin and that all non-European whites, including Jews, are associated with Satan; not associated with mainline Christian theology.

Counterterrorism the set of policies implemented by a government to stop or hinder a terrorist or terrorist group's ability to carry out attacks.

Decapitation strike   the use of force by counterterrorists to specifically eliminate or remove the senior or mid-level leadership of a terrorist group; often lethal, but in some cases operations involve capturing rather than killing the leader.

Deterrence   a credible threat of force to prevent an actor from taking an action that they would take if the threat was not made.

Domestic terrorism   terrorism carried out by groups or individuals within a specific country against civilians within that same country, with the main criteria being the shared national citizenship of both perpetrator and victim.

Extraordinary rendition   the transfer of an individual from the custody of one nation to another in order to skirt the former's laws that restrict enhanced interrogation or torture.

Fascism   a collectivist and ultranationalist authoritarian ideology that promotes dictatorial rule, strong security policies by the state, and repressive policies against domestic regime opponents; features a strong presence of the government in the economic management of the state and the personal lives of citizens.

Forensic theology   an academic discipline where scholars of religion apply their knowledge to help law enforcement prevent or address crime; scholars share their understanding of how religious beliefs motivate the behavior of groups and individuals who adhere to the belief system.

Habeas Corpus   Latin for "you shall have the body"; legal principle that those accused of a crime must appear in court to determine the legality of their detention, to hear charges against them, and to begin the process of a trial if their detention is deemed legal.

Homeland security   a nation's effort to prevent terrorist attacks, respond to hazards, and secure its national borders.

Identity   that which addresses who an individual is and how they see themselves.

Ideology   a system of ideas and ideals that prescribe how a society is to be ordered and how power is to be used within it to advance or protect those ideas and ideals.

Islamist   an orientation held by Muslims who want Islamic law (*sharia*) to be applied to society and enforced by an Islamic government; the term is general and not restricted to adherents of any one sect of Islam and does not apply to all Muslims.

Jihadism   based on the Arabic word *jihad* (holy war), an orientation of Islamists who believe that the use of violence against non-Muslims is religiously justified in order to defend or expand the territory directly governed by Muslims.

Leftwing ideology   broad political beliefs that are generally socially liberal while also calling for a heavy governmental role in redistributing tax income by expanding the welfare state through the provision of education, housing, healthcare, food, and income.

Marxism   a form of leftwing ideology that views the world in terms of a global class struggle between workers and owners who exploit them; predicts that the workers' class will unite to overthrow the owners and calls for a new communist society to be created that eliminates private ownership of property in favor of public ownership.

Nationalism   an ideology that promotes the legitimacy and self-determination of an identity within a state-based framework; nationalism based on an ethnic identity is ethnonationalism.

National security   the ability of a national government to prevent foreign adversaries from using force to harm citizens or the interests of that government.

Outcome goal   a policy aim that defines the reason for a militant group's existence and to justify its use of violence to achieve that aim; most groups have more than one declared outcome goal that are interconnected, but often a group will have less than four such goals, and these goals tend to be long-term in nature.

Politics   the process of determining who governs, how they do so, and ultimately how scarce resources are distributed in a society.

Process goal   an objective that serves to increase the ability of a group to survive and continue its efforts toward pursuing its long-term outcome goals; these goals tend to be more immediate and short-term in nature and can be at odds with a group's progress toward securing its outcome goals.

Rational choice theory   an approach in the social sciences where the subject of study is assumed to make decisions based upon ranked and ordered preferences, their access to information, the probability of success with available choices, and their expected costs and benefits.

Relative deprivation   a collective psychological dynamic where a group perceives a difference in the goods and conditions it presently has and the goods and conditions it feels it is due given its current status.

Religion   a specific set of beliefs and behaviors based on the organized worship of a god or gods.

Rightwing ideology   broad political beliefs calling for social conservatism and a reduced governmental role in the management of economic affairs while encouraging private sector activity and free market approaches.

Salafism   a fundamentalist theological orientation in Sunni Islam derived from the word *salaf* ("ancestor") as a reference to the original companions of Muhammad; compared to other Islamic theological belief Salafists see the development in the practices of the faith after the first three generations of Muslims as illegitimate and look to the *Quran* (Islam's holy text seen as God's word given to Muhammad) and the *Sunnah* (collection of Muhammad's practices) for guidance while discounting the contributions of generations of successive Islamic scholars.

State   a governmental authority that is widely recognized by other governments and its own population, has clearly defined territorial boundaries, and whose use of physical force is seen as legitimate in the execution of its orders and laws.

State-sponsored terrorism   when a national government funds, trains, equips, provides safe haven, or otherwise aids terrorist operatives in carrying out attacks against another country.

Strategy   a program of identifying end goals and mobilizing the means available to attain them.

Suicide attacks   an attack by a terrorist or insurgent who intentionally kills themselves in the course of the attack, commonly although not exclusively performed with an explosive device.

Terrorism   the threat of or use of violence by a non-state actor against civilians or noncombatants in order to advance a political agenda.

Transnational/foreign terrorism   when a terrorist group crosses a defined international boundary in order to prepare, plan, or attack its civilian or noncombatant target; includes attacks against a country's individuals and interests located in a foreign country.

Index

About the Author

Steven J. Childs is an associate professor in the Department of Political Science at California State University, San Bernardino, where he teaches in the National Security Studies program. He received his Ph.D. in political science from Claremont Graduate University in 2011 in the fields of world and comparative politics. During his graduate studies he interned with the U.S. State Department's Security Assistance Team within the Bureau of Political-Military Affairs. His research interests focus on national security policy, conventional arms proliferation, nuclear deterrence, the security politics of the Middle East and Asia regions, and unconventional conflict. His scholarship has appeared in various academic publications including *Comparative Strategy, Defense & Security Analysis, Journal of Advanced Military Studies, Journal of the Middle East and Africa,* and *Studies in Conflict & Terrorism*. He is also coeditor of the book *The Middle East in a Global Era*. Outside of his research and teaching he loves spending time with his wife Lauren and their two children, Ethan and Elizabeth. His hobbies and interests include foreign travel, hiking, plane-spotting, and home brewing.